Jennifer Higdon

JENNIFER HIGDON
Composing in Color

Christina L. Reitz
Foreword by Marin Alsop

McFarland & Company, Inc., Publishers
Jefferson, North Carolina

All musical notations have been provided courtesy of Lawdon Press.

Library of Congress Cataloguing-in-Publication Data

Names: Reitz, Christina L. author. | Alsop, Marin, writer of foreword.
Title: Jennifer Higdon : composing in color / Christina L. Reitz ; foreword by Marin Alsop.
Description: Jefferson, North Carolina : McFarland & Company, 2018. | Includes bibliographical references and index.
Identifiers: LCCN 2018023998 | ISBN 9781476664064 (softcover : acid free paper) ∞
Subjects: LCSH: Higdon, Jennifer, 1962– | Composers—United States—Biography.
Classification: LCC ML410.H613 R45 2018 | DDC 780.92 [B] —dc23
LC record available at https://lccn.loc.gov/2018023998

British Library cataloguing data are available

ISBN (print) 978-1-4766-6406-4
ISBN (ebook) 978-1-4766-3314-5

© 2018 Christina L. Reitz. All rights reserved

No part of this book may be reproduced or transmitted in any form or by any means, electronic or mechanical, including photocopying or recording, or by any information storage and retrieval system, without permission in writing from the publisher.

Front cover: Jennifer Higdon (photograph by J Henry Fair); background photograph by King Ho Yim (iStock)

Printed in the United States of America

McFarland & Company, Inc., Publishers
 Box 611, Jefferson, North Carolina 28640
 www.mcfarlandpub.com

To the memory of my father, Scott L. Reitz (1946–2013),
and in honor of my mother, Linda Marie Reitz

Acknowledgments

The author wishes to gratefully acknowledge the following:

Dr. Jennifer Higdon and Ms. Cheryl Lawson, vice president of Lawdon Press, for their kindness, thoughtfulness, generosity, excitement about this project, and for their copyright permission to this wonderful music.

Maestra Marin Alsop for her eloquent and touching foreword that captured the professional and personal spirit of Higdon.

Mr. Gene Scheer for his permission to use his beautifully crafted libretto to *Cold Mountain*.

Mr. Samuel Simmons for his assistance with the images.

A truncated version of Chapter Seven was published as the article "*Cold Mountain:* A Journey from Frazier's Magnum Opus to Higdon's Magnum Opera" in the *North Carolina Literary Review*, number 26, 2017.

Table of Contents

Acknowledgments	vi
Foreword by Marin Alsop	1
Preface	3
One. Biography and Orchestral Compositional Traits	7
Two. *blue cathedral*	24
Three. *Concerto for Orchestra*	39
Four. *City Scape*	80
Five. *Concerto 4–3*	107
Six. *Violin Concerto*	133
Seven. *Cold Mountain*	168
Eight. *Cold Mountain*: The Music	184
Codetta	225
Chapter Notes	229
Bibliography	244
Index	251

Foreword
by Marin Alsop

I can't remember the first time I met Jennifer Higdon because it feels as though we've known each other forever.

There are only a handful of people in life that I feel as though I've known forever and Jennifer is one of them. I know that our first encounter must have been the result of me programming a piece of hers, but that fact quickly became secondary to the fact that she is pure and simply a wonderful human being. Honest, loyal, compassionate, funny, and willing to show her flaws—these are the qualities that I so admire in Jennifer and in most of the people I adore.

Jennifer's musical milestones are numerous and varied. But what I so admire is her willingness to consider every project, regardless of its origins or "stature." She brings the same commitment to a piece for marching band or children as she does to a piece for the Philadelphia Orchestra.

Her music is inclusive, accessible and embracing. That is exactly who she is, and that authenticity is extremely appealing.

I have had the great pleasure of working with Jennifer on numerous projects but my favorite was performing and recording her Percussion Concerto with percussionist Colin Currie and the London Philharmonic. The concerto holds a special place in my heart because it was written as a result of my introducing Jennifer and Colin. (This must be how people feel when their matchmaking works out! Speaking of that, officiating at Jennifer and Cheryl's wedding ceremony was one of my life's greatest privileges.)

Jennifer is always herself, through and through. She is politely yet doggedly committed to the advancement of women in our field, both as composers and as conductors. She is a devoted teacher and wonderful role model because she lives by one ruling principle: follow your heart and you can create your own destiny. This is the Jennifer Higdon I know, love and admire.

Marin Alsop is the music director for the Baltimore Symphony Orchestra.

Preface

Jennifer Higdon: Composing in Color examines the musical style of one of the United States' most frequently performed composers, Jennifer Higdon (b. 1962). This study begins with a brief biography and overview of her stylistic traits followed by subsequent chapters that provide compositional history, detailed analysis, and critical reception. The selected symphonic works, along with Higdon's first opera, are arranged in chronological order: *blue cathedral, Concerto for Orchestra, City Scape, Concerto 4–3, Violin Concerto,* and *Cold Mountain*. One of the most frequently cited elements of Higdon's orchestration is her attention to tone color resulting in an array of fascinating sounds that appeal to critics, audiences, and musicians. Because this distinguishing trait has undoubtedly contributed extensively to her popularity, it likewise influenced the title of this book.

While the composer has been the subject of numerous articles in journals and magazines, a book dedicated exclusively to her orchestral compositions has never been published. She and her music have been included in earlier works that have not focused solely on Higdon but on several composers grouped through a minority status. She identifies as a woman and a lesbian; however, her music need not and should not be relegated as the voice of a marginalized people. It stands alone on its fine quality as demonstrated by the countless performances her compositions receive annually. Higdon does not believe her gender or sexual orientation have had much, if any, impact on her music or career and thus outside of the biographical chapter, any references to her as a minority are excluded.

Several theses and dissertations examine selected works of Higdon, seemingly chosen based on the researchers' instrumental backgrounds. With the exception of my own dissertation, none of these has studied her orchestral works, and an academic monograph dedicated to this topic is long overdue. This addition to the literature will prove beneficial to conductors and musicians performing Higdon's works, music researchers at any level, and even the aficionado.

My initial interest in the music of Higdon stems from graduate studies at the University of Florida. One of my external cognates was women's studies and as such, research projects focused nearly exclusively on female composers and musicians. Contemporary music was also a passion and while a member of the New Music Ensemble, I pursued additional collaborations with a saxophonist and percussionist. The latter introduced me to Higdon's music and thereafter, I chose several of her flute works for the topic of an independent study. It became painfully obvious and grossly inconvenient when I immediately realized there were very limited academic sources on her music. Knowing of this scholarly void and the popularity of Higdon's orchestral compositions, I chose three of her symphonic works for the topic of my dissertation, a perfect consolidation of my research and applied interests. I interviewed Higdon in her hotel suite in Atlanta, Georgia, in September of 2006 and was surprised, and initially dismayed, to learn that in her opinion, neither being a woman nor a lesbian had influenced her works or critical reception. I turned my focus solely to the music, an approach which proved more liberating. Instead of writing, "This is fine music by a woman composer," one can simply declare without apology, "This is fine music." I do not mean to discount the very real discrimination and biases that remain in art music but that is a topic outside the scope of this research.

Since finishing the dissertation, Higdon's music has continued to be of great interest to me and I have been fortunate to attend several world premieres including *Concerto 4–3*, *On a Wire*, the *Piano Concerto*, *The Singing Rooms*, and most recently, *Cold Mountain*. Her works have maintained a significant role in my research agenda through article publications and conference presentations but always lurking in the back of my mind was the need for an expanded and detailed scholarly monograph.

The scope of this study has expanded over the years. The choice to include *blue cathedral*, *Concerto for Orchestra*, and *City Scape* was made early, because of my familiarity with the works; however, those chapters were entirely rewritten and improved, I hope, by years of teaching and study. Additional compositions were chosen based on several factors. First, having presented and published previously on *Concerto 4–3* made that work a logical choice. It is a concerto for three string soloists that utilizes bluegrass techniques inspired in part by the composer's adolescence in Eastern Tennessee. Because Higdon's chamber writing often contains more elements of the avant-garde (extended techniques, unorthodox notation, and so forth) than her orchestral works, including *Concerto 4–3* was an ideal way to incorporate that aspect of her style. Secondly, the *Violin Concerto*, as winner of the 2010 Pulitzer Prize in Music, was an essential inclusion that served as an example of a Higdon solo instrumental concerto while simultaneously contrasting the string writing of *Concerto 4–3*. Finally, McFarland recommended *Cold Mountain*, which at the time of the proposal was two years away from the world premiere. The opera is not a purely orchestral work, of course, yet it was highly publicized due to the fame of the composer and as her first opera, significant to include. Its Appalachian setting and use of vernacular elements, albeit sparingly, conveniently complemented *Concerto 4–3*.

The research methodology consisted of correspondences with Higdon and Cheryl Lawson, extensive score study, and examinations of primary sources. A review of the literature, as mentioned previously, reveals surprisingly few scholarly publications. Because the subject is a living composer, the references include newspapers which frequently feature interviews with Higdon about her music. For each of the selected works, the research happened well after their premieres with the exception of *Cold Mountain*. Lawson graciously mailed the score to me the previous spring and consequently, I was able to familiarize myself with the music prior to the initial performances. Due to the generosity of Lawson and Higdon, I attended the closed dress rehearsal followed by the premiere which allowed me to see the work fully performed twice in close proximity.

I truly believe that Higdon represents the future of both American and Western art music. Her personality and music relate to diverse demographics and her compositional philosophy of communicating effectively has been clearly well received. In the 21st century, it is most unusual for an art music composer to support oneself solely through composition but Higdon proves it remains a viable possibility and her success should appease the naysayers who believe the genre is in grave trouble. Indeed, Jennifer Higdon provides an exemplary model of navigating a fulfilling and successful compositional career in the contemporary world.

CHAPTER ONE

Biography and Orchestral Compositional Traits

Biography

Jennifer Elaine Higdon was born in Brooklyn, New York, on December 31, 1962, but six months later, the family moved to Atlanta, Georgia. Reared by artistic parents, she explored creative literary outlets in her youth such as writing short stories and poetry. At the age of 10, Higdon's parents relocated to a bucolic farm in Seymour, Tennessee, to be closer to extended family[1] as well as to distance Higdon and her younger brother, Andrew, from urban violence. Her mother did not work outside of the home; her father, a freelance graphic artist, worked in a studio on their property for art agencies in Atlanta communicating with them through the early fax machine and using Delta Dash to transfer materials.[2]

Higdon was not introduced to art music as a child and her earliest musical influences stem from her counterculture parents who encouraged expression. The family regularly supported the arts and attended experimental films and art exhibits. Her early exposure to the avant-garde led her to question experimentation for its own sake; these experiences have shaped her compositional philosophy that communication to an audience of varying backgrounds is critical. Although her father, who passed away in 2014, was not a musician, his influence as an artist remains prominent in her life. She recalled fondly:

> And as I'm moving in to writing new pieces, I can also still feel his presence. I think a lot about what he speaks to in terms of art. What is the art? What does it mean? What's art supposed to do? That question is different for every artist and the answer is also different but my dad kind of gave me a lot of different ways of thinking about it so I'm finding myself thinking a lot about my own childhood, where my art experiences came from, what he exposed me to, what kinds of things we built as kids; we used to build these giant forts with boxes. I mean *huge* fortresses that were incredible, he used to have me do Claymation, animation with an 8mm camera, so before I ever got to music, I was making different kinds

of visual arts and that stuff really left an impression on me [...] because it comes up so vividly in my head now and so I think about what is art. He and I used to have this ongoing conversation about John Cage because when I was in high school, I used to say, "John Cage isn't music" and he would say, "John Cage is certainly music" so we were in fact arguing the opposite of what you would expect with the adult arguing one way and the kid arguing the other way except we were arguing in the opposite directions. But when I think about my studies with George Crumb and the extended techniques I sometimes use in my piece [sic] [...] I don't think I would have used those had my dad not talked about Cage and how any kind of sound can be music and I don't think I would have thought it had I not studied with George Crumb who uses unusual sounds in his pieces so I could kind of see the path of my composition from my dad to where I am now, there's actually like direct links that I can see.[3]

An absence of traditional musical training contributes extensively to Higdon's creative personality. The composer stated:

> My background is completely different than most classical musicians' backgrounds ... my background is much more similar to most people who grow up in this country ... very, very little Classical, and a lot more of everything else. But because I listened to the Beatles so much, as well as Simon & Garfunkel, reggae, [the] Rolling Stones, Peter, Paul, and Mary, bluegrass, and country, I believe that I have to have been influenced by that music.[4]

The most significant album to Higdon was the Beatles' *Sgt. Pepper's Lonely Hearts Club Band*, introduced to her by her father who found the cover appealing. She and Andrew played the album daily and as she recalled:

> It influenced the way I think about orchestration now. I'm always aware of sudden changes in sound and that's the hallmark of that album. There are times when I try to make those changes in sound. You wouldn't think that I would still be having a reaction to it, but there's so much color on the album.[5]

Her lack of early training provided freedom from compositional systems. It undoubtedly has also contributed to her success amongst many contemporary art musicians and audiences with similar backgrounds.

The peaceful nature and mountains that decorate the countryside of Tennessee continue to provide Higdon with inspiration as she explained, "I often think a lot of the mountains in all my pieces."[6] Although not always evident to the audience, this presence can be clearly seen in the bluegrass style of *Concerto 4–3* as well as in the vernacular elements of *Cold Mountain*.

Her adolescent literary interest endures through the use of poetic titles and the writing of her program notes. Additionally, she stated, "Writing poetry and stories taught me about rhythm and pacing. For me, musical themes are like the characters in a play."[7] Although few of her compositions are explicitly programmatic, her compositional method is directly informed by her past literary experiences.

Higdon's earliest encounter with applied music occurred at age fourteen as a percussionist in the Heritage High School marching band. Rhythmic emphasis remains crucial in her compositions that originate from this initial experience. Soon afterwards, Higdon discovered in the attic an inexpensive flute her mother had bought at a pawn shop[8] and taught herself using the *First Division Band Method, Part I: C Flute* manual. After completing the first book in the series, her mother purchased the next three levels.[9] Following her sophomore year, Higdon auditioned and became first chair; in the flute section, she met her future wife, Cheryl Lawson.[10] The flute became her primary focus and she has recorded her own solo and chamber works for the instrument. While in high school, she began listening to art music from the library and because she had not been exposed to it previously, found it captivating.[11] One of the earliest works she vividly recalls encountering was Aaron Copland's *Appalachian Spring*.[12]

Higdon studied formally only a few months with a flute instructor in Maryville, Tennessee, Jan Vinci, a former student of Bowling Green State University's (BGSU) applied flute teacher, Judith Bentley. Higdon also attended a summer flute camp at BGSU with Bentley on the faculty and quickly realized Bentley's outstanding gifts as a teacher.[13] The future composer subsequently enrolled at BGSU for her undergraduate studies in 1981 as a flute performance major.

Although excelling in lessons, Higdon felt insecure in the core musical knowledge because of her background. She remarked, "I had to take theory for dummies and learn what an interval is [...] I didn't grow up around classical music and I'm sure that has influenced my choices in musical language and also my love for melody."[14]

Higdon's first exposure to composition originated from Bentley who proposed she write a work for a masterclass with flutist/composer Harvey Sollberger. Bentley explained the twelve tone method limited to six tones that resulted in Higdon's first piece, *Night Creatures,* a two-minute work for flute and piano.[15] She remarked, "I found it fascinating to put sound together. I don't know why that hadn't occurred to me before. I could tell that was something I was going to be doing down the road."[16] Bentley then asked her to write for the flute ensemble and also encouraged her to pursue a work for horn and saxophone for another studio.[17]

BGSU replaced the quarter system with semesters late in Higdon's studies which prevented her from graduating in the standard four years. With the extra year, she considered registering for composition lessons but these were restricted to majors only.[18] Before finishing at BGSU, however, she did study composition minimally with Marilyn Shrude and Wallace DePue.[19]

Robert Spano was a newly hired conductor at BGSU during Higdon's final year and with his consent, she enrolled in his graduate conducting course. She continued composing, compiling a modest collection to be used for graduate applications; acceptance letters followed from prestigious institutions including Juilliard, the Curtis Institute of Music, and the University of Michigan. As a Curtis alumnus, Spano encouraged her to pursue the Artist Diploma there and "he locked Higdon in his office until she agreed."[20]

One of the lasting lessons she received at BGSU was from composer Philip Glass, a guest at the university's New Music Festival. At the close of the festival, students socialized with Glass and while discussing professional compositional careers, he advised them to always maintain copyright ownership. Higdon reflected, "And now that I'm working in the field running my own publishing company, and observing his smart business practices, I can see how things work clearly in relation to that conversation. I'm grateful that he was willing to stand around and talk with the students in casual conversation in a kitchen."[21]

At Curtis, Higdon's primary teacher was David Loeb but she also studied with Ned Rorem, who she credits with teaching her about writing for the voice.[22] Her continued emphasis on melody serves as a lasting tribute to his influence. Today, Higdon is not particularly known for song writing, but the genre is the only one she composes in for fun rather than on commission.[23] On the different pedagogical styles between Rorem and Loeb, Higdon commented:

> Ned provided a perspective different from Loeb. Loeb is a very intelligent man, and he gave me a lot of historical background on just about everything related to music. Ned made me think about the voice a lot. And also I think he was a good example of a professional musician, which is always nice for young students.[24]

Higdon encountered numerous obstacles in graduate school. After earning an Artist Diploma in Composition from Curtis,[25] she was turned down twice from the University of Pennsylvania but studied free of charge with Jay Reise. Reise continued to encourage her[26] and with the third attempt, she was accepted and subsequently completed a Master of Arts Degree in composition. Higdon's lack of early training created a significant hurdle during her doctoral qualifying exams. She remarked, "Since I grew up on rock and roll, I just didn't know this stuff. Getting through the doctoral exams for me was a nightmare. I took them a lot."[27] Two submissions by Higdon were not approved by the committee for her doctoral thesis[28]; Higdon recalled, "There were members of my doctoral committee who claimed that I was having too much success. I didn't fit the box of what they were expecting."[29] Her third effort, "Blitz" the opening movement of her *Voices* string quartet (1993) commissioned by the Philadelphia Chamber Music Society, resulted in the Doctor of Philosophy degree the following year.[30]

Her principal composition instructor at the University of Pennsylvania was George Crumb. Student and professor shared a similar rural American background and like Crumb, who was reared in West Virginia, Higdon continually finds her inspiration from the natural environment. His influence on her works is evident in her exploration of sound and colors in orchestral settings, particularly through less traditional orchestral techniques. She recalled, "Where I really learned was listening to him talk about all kinds of music, and watching him play even simple things on the piano, such as a chord progression. And of course, looking at his scores and marveling at the extraordinary world of color that he would get from instruments."[31] In her lessons, she had the freedom to bring any music she was currently composing; however, more traditional works did not result in lengthy feedback because they differed so much from Crumb's own sounds. Compositions, such as *rapid.fire* for solo flute, produced much discussion due to the unorthodox notation and extended techniques required.[32] Crumb and Higdon do not actively remain in contact due to her traveling schedule but they regularly see each other at Philadelphia music events.

Higdon's first orchestral work, *Shine* (1995) was composed for the Oregon Symphony, at the time led by James DePreist, and originated from an ASCAP grant for budding composers.[33] This work was subsequently submitted to the Philadelphia Orchestra as a representative example of her compositions that led to the *Concerto for Orchestra* commission propelling her to international fame.

Mystical is an applicable description of some of the moods in her orchestral works which is primarily achieved through unorthodox instrumentation such as the water gong, Chinese health reflex bells, and crystal glasses. Although not raised with organized religion, Higdon describes herself as a spiritual person. As a child, her parents had resources ranging from Eastern religions to the *Holy Bible*[34] and although her paternal and maternal grandparents were practicing Baptists and Presbyterians, respectively, her immediate family did not participate. The children were educated to respect religions and to learn from varying spiritual beliefs. She commented on her spirituality as an adult:

> For me music speaks to a part of each person that is hard to define with words. The truth is, there is not a way to anticipate or even explain this. And while the reason for composing is different for each person who creates music, for me it's about communicating with something undefinable within musicians and audience members. That's spiritual communication and a true inspiration for composing.[35]

Higdon currently spends between four to six hours composing daily, a schedule that she has maintained for years with the exception of *Cold Moun-*

tain, when she wrote eight hours a day, seven days a week. Her career since the year 2000 has required significant travel and she frequently composed in hotel rooms, libraries, and wherever necessary; however, more recently, she spends less time composing outside of her studio. She has also accepted fewer invitations into residency programs because it's more difficult for her to compose away from home and the trips' schedules leave her exhausted.[36]

She has been a member of the Curtis faculty since 1994,[37] and her teaching assignments have included courses in theory, counterpoint, solfege, and serving as a private tutor. Her commissions steadily increased so that in 2002, she reduced her responsibilities at the Institute.[38] At the present time, she teaches only private composition lessons and holds the Milton L. Rock Chair in Composition Studies. She works with two students for an academic year to maintain Curtis's rotation policy amongst the faculty. On site lessons are more beneficial in her opinion, but when she is away, the students send scores electronically, often with a specific question followed by a lesson over the telephone. The number of performances, residencies, and commissions Higdon receives means that she does not need to teach to supplement her income, but she enjoys it and learns from her students. She wrote, "Good teaching means being willing to learn from your students. Nothing clarifies your process like trying to communicate it to another individual."[39]

Higdon remains one of the few self-supporting composers; her publishing company, Lawdon Press, began in 1994. The name originates from the amalgamation of the names of herself and Cheryl Lawson. Lawson, a former event planner for medical associations, left her career to manage the company in 2005[40] and is currently Vice President of Lawdon Press. Nearly all of Higdon's works are published and distributed by Lawdon Press with a few exceptions. A work for flute choir, *Andante Cantabile*, from the composer's undergraduate studies at BGSU, is published by Alry. Additionally, Hal Leonard has published two works (along with supplementary materials), *Rhythm Stand* and *Hear My Voice*, as part of an agreement from a commission with the American Composers Forum. Band Quest and Choral Quest, programs within the ACF, commission well-known composers to write for young musicians in middle school ensembles. Lastly, *Gilmore Variation* is published by Peters as part of a project commissioned by the Irving S. Gilmore International Keyboard Festival, "13 Ways of Looking at the Goldberg."[41]

Higdon has always identified as a lesbian but does not believe discrimination has been an obstacle in her career. She and Lawson were high school sweethearts and after American laws changed, the couple married on August 3, 2014. The date is the anniversary of private vows exchanged by the couple in 1990 but was also chosen to accommodate the schedule of Marin Alsop, the officiator, during a break from the Cabrillo Festival of Contemporary Music in California; curiously, Alsop also presided over the 2008 nuptials of Mark Adamo and John Corigliano. Higdon and Lawson have resided in Pennsylvania for years but by the time same sex marriage became legal there, the California wedding planning had already begun. Previously they considered marrying in a neighboring state but as Lawson explained, the licensing guidelines in Maryland, New York, and Washington, D.C., were a formidable challenge as was trying to find a suitable date to allow their families to attend. California law does not require a waiting period for a marriage license and Higdon and Lawson obtained theirs on breaks between rehearsals. Some of the couple's family were already on the West Coast while others traveled for the event; Key, Higdon's half-brother, served as the best man. The intimate ceremony was attended by sixteen guests with no live musicians performing.[42]

Higdon believes gay musicians do not experience discrimination because so many composers in preceding generations were (or are thought to be) gay. She stated, "It's not a big deal in the classical music world. History is littered with composers who were gay. It's such a non-issue. In classical music, nobody even talks about it. My guess is that music is probably the most obviously gay of all the art forms."[43]

Higdon along with Christopher Theofanidis, Osvaldo Golijov, Michael Gandolfi, and Adam Schoenberg comprise what is known as the Atlanta School of Composers. The group works frequently with the Atlanta Symphony and its music director, Robert Spano; although Higdon's relationship with Spano initially stems from BGSU, they had not remained in contact until he conducted the premiere of *blue cathedral* at Curtis in 2000, the same year as his Atlanta appointment. During his first years with the Atlanta Symphony, he worked with several composers in live performances and recorded their works. At a retreat with the Board of Directors, Spano spoke about this group of composers and in subsequent meetings, the name, "Atlanta School of Composers," emerged. To Spano, the group is cohesive through their ages, use of "tonality tunes and an interest in World music, popular culture, or both."[44] He also believes the group is united through their use of writing music to evoke an emotional response and their philosophy of placing the music before the theory.[45] Another significant professional relationship Higdon maintains is with conductor, Marin Alsop, who frequently champions new music at both the Cabrillo Festival and with the Baltimore Symphony. Higdon is a returning composer at Cabrillo where the two initially met in the early 2000s.[46]

Higdon listens to a variety of genres; outside of art music, she listens to country, rock, and rap music, particularly Eminem. The latter may seem surprising considering the criticism he has received for homophobic, misogynistic lyrics. Higdon explained that prior to writing her opera, she focused on the musical elements rather than the lyrics in her listening. She wrote, "His shaping of phrasing, rhythm, and pulse, [...] I have always found engaging. Now that I've gone through the process of writing the opera, my brain seems to have rewired, and I hear words differently than I used to."[47]

Since Higdon's beginnings in composition, she has received commissions from the most prestigious ensembles and performers to grace the symphony halls and concert stages, including nearly all the major orchestras in the United States. In addition, Higdon has received numerous awards and grants; 2010 was a particularly remarkable year for the composer. She received the Grammy Award for Best Contemporary Composition for her *Percussion Concerto* and the Pulitzer Prize in Music for the *Violin Concerto* composed for Hilary Hahn.

Compositional Method and Philosophy

Audience appeal remains a significant aspect of Higdon's compositional philosophy and she believes accountability to her audience is justified. She stated, "I feel a responsibility to be articulate in the music and not waste their time."[48] As an avid listener to the Beatles in her youth, she relates with audiences from that generation and as such, is intimately familiar with music such listeners are likely to enjoy. She remarked on the similarities between the music of her childhood and her own compositions:

> What do the [...] types of music have in common? Melody, Rhythm, Harmony. What they don't have in common ... there isn't an exclusivity between either genre, but usually musical events (and the speed in which they unfold) run at different speeds. In terms of writing for a broader audience ... I don't think I have more understanding than any other composer. Music is communication. Otherwise, I don't see the point.[49]

Although she strives to communicate to audiences of varying musical backgrounds, this does not impact the quality of the music. She explained, "I believe wholeheartedly in melody, I believe in clear rhythm, I love to be able to hear the harmonic movement."[50] As expected, this philosophy and Higdon's great success resulted in much discussion regarding accessibility and the future of art music.

Higdon's self-described method of composition is defined as intuitive; yet to infer that her music emerges without calculated purpose would be erroneous since she spends much time in thought before beginning a work.

Higdon believes that the extensive years of theory, composition, conducting, and score study work subconsciously as part of her intuitive style. To the composer, the process retains a bit of mystery and it is indeed remarkable that she usually begins composing a melody in the middle of the work but the final product can be related in some way to a traditional form.

Higdon is capable of composition at a rapid speed that suggests musical ideas are occurring almost immediately. She stated, "I'll spend more hours [writing] than an average composer but because it's happening at a faster and a shorter time frame, it means a lot of these things have to happen instinctively. I think things are happening at a subconscious level."[51] She remarked, "I think actually what happens is [when] I start working on a piece, I'll do a lot of sketching, my brain will put these elements together and I don't know they're there. I don't realize it even, it just comes out."[52] This would in fact seem to be the case; detailed analysis of her compositions has produced results that surprised even Higdon, but upon reflection, she believed such findings were examples of her intuitive style.

Since 1992, Higdon composes only on commission; the information given in the preliminary negotiations includes approximate length, orchestration, and for large ensembles, the number of rehearsals allotted before the premiere. She usually inquires if the commission is in response to a special event, such as a celebration or commemoration, and will sometimes consider the remaining repertoire of the program to complement the style and mood of the planned concert.[53] When writing for a particular soloist, she researches the type of music that person has programmed in the past as well as their musical preferences. Lastly, Higdon considers what kinds of colors and sounds she wants to include.[54]

When writing a work featuring a specific instrument, Higdon conducts research on its literature through extensive listening and score study unless the soloist is the flute or another instrument with which she is intimately familiar. This method was particularly significant for her *Piano Concerto* and *Violin Concerto* where the genre is incredibly extensive. Higdon also studies the performer themselves through their recordings to find their strengths and the styles of music they enjoy performing. Her research occurs before a single note is penned allowing the musical ideas to present themselves rapidly once the writing begins. The end result is an original piece truly about the performer/ensemble while maintaining her own distinctive voice.

Usually, Higdon begins a work with the first forthcoming melodic idea[55] which never occurs in the opening measures. In the multi-movement works, the interior movements are composed initially and similarly, in the tone poem *blue cathedral*, the process originated with the soli in the central sections.

The method for composing *Cold Mountain* differed considerably due to the sheer size of the opera and is explored more fully in Chapter Seven.

Although musical themes are frequently the starting point, on occasion, a particular sound itself may ignite the creative spark. Higdon attributes her curiosity of sound possibilities to Crumb[56] and her early experiences in orchestra.[57] Today, as a mature composer, she continues to refer to the joy of sound as a source of inspiration.

Because of her background as a flutist, she hears music as a single line, and thus during the compositional process, she works with individual voices contrapuntally rather than harmonically. This is combined with her background in percussion that creates a rhythmic vivacity present in all of her fast works.

Although she composes daily, the speed in which she produces music depends on the time allocated by the commission. *Concerto for Orchestra* was written over several years while in contrast, the first movement of *City Scape* emerged in only five days. In the latter, the music appeared to her so quickly she first wrote it in short score (approximately 6 notated lines) before returning to the orchestration.[58] This exceedingly rapid pace of composition is more often the exception rather than the rule.

Since her graduate studies when composers were writing by hand, technology has evolved significantly. Higdon utilizes all elements at her disposal: hand sketching musical ideas and notes to herself in her sketchbook, notating on paper, taking ideas to the piano, and even improvising. Then she begins handwriting the score before putting the work in Finale, the program she uses exclusively. For larger ensemble pieces, she composes in short score and later re-orchestrates the work. The only playback option she utilizes is MIDI to sound like a piano, regardless of the ensemble for which she is composing. In her view, computers are ineffective in reproducing the color she is imagining or the rhythmic freedom of a live performer, so during the compositional process, she envisions the sounds and uses playback solely for timing purposes and to review harmonies.[59] After the piece enters the editing or adjustment phase, the work is completed electronically.

Higdon revises her compositions numerous times. The underlying concern at all times is if the music can be made more interesting to the listener which frequently leads her to experiment with instrumental timbre, combining sounds, and adding nontraditional instrumentation or techniques. Although Higdon's method is intuitive for devising the initial melodic ideas, after they are notated, considerable effort follows to rework the musical elements.[60]

Higdon's focus is singular and she only works on one composition at a time. Immediately after finishing one work, she begins the next one and to date, has not felt the need to take an extended break from composing to restore creativity.

Higdon's previously limited exposure to Western art music may have been problematic during her schooling but has proved beneficial to her career. Because of her self-admitted lack of experience with the standard canon, quotations and references to other composers and their music are nonexistent. A complete avoidance of systems remains absent in Higdon's oeuvre; indeed, nearly all of her works emerge from an exploration of sound which contributes to her unique compositional voice.

Perhaps the most fascinating aspect of her style is the subtle, yet consistent, appearance of unifying devices. Higdon stated that such occurrences are not intentional and in several examples, she was not aware of these connections. Yet, separate rhythmic and melodic motives permeate individual movements. That such connections were not purposely included demonstrates Higdon's internalization of years of intense study that informs her intuition.

Stylistic Traits

Because she thinks linearly, Higdon does not compose with key centers or harmonies in mind. When a tonality clearly emerges, she explains it as a manifestation of her subconscious.[61] Particularly noteworthy is the continuous appearance of D major, a key associated with great rejoicing and triumph. In the early orchestral works, *blue cathedral*, *Concerto for Orchestra*, and *City Scape*, this tonality is prominent; similarly, the more recent works, *Concerto 4–3* and the *Violin Concerto* also conclude on D major chords. Higdon did not consciously choose that tonality but after reviewing the numerous examples, she realized it does occur frequently but, emphasized that it was not a conscious decision.[62] This author suggests that passages in D major in Higdon's music reflect her optimistic and sunny personality, qualities remarked on by those fortunate enough to have come in contact with her.

Higdon does not utilize functional harmony, but rather incorporates aspects from the Common Practice Period to create her own harmonic idiom. The most prominent feature of her musical language is the use of perfect fifths that, according to the composer, evolved from major chords in her earlier works; exploring the sounds, she simply removed the thirds. *blue cathedral* was the first composition to consistently use perfect fifths,[63] but the intervals appear frequently in her subsequent orchestral works. Higdon occasionally varies the intervals by expanding the sounds to both major and minor sonorities that result in an ambiguous modal mixture.

Higdon's parallel fifths generally appear as accompanimental material orchestrated for the lower strings to present either sustained harmonies or a progression moving in stepwise motion. Perfect fourths, an inversion of fifths, occur less prominently, but several sections are comprised of these quartal harmonies. Passages utilizing such sounds are fleeting but without question, are directly related to Higdon's use of the perfect fifth.

As Higdon remarked, major chords also maintain a significant role in her harmonic language. Like the fifths, the sonorities may be static or move in stepwise motion. When utilizing slow, sustained harmonies, the chords generally appear in root position. To orchestrate these sections, Higdon divides an instrument's parts into three lines supplying each with a note of the chord. This scoring most frequently occurs in the lower strings to create a warm and lush sound.

Major chords do not only serve as accompanimental material in Higdon's music. Numerous examples abound with melodic scoring for three trumpets utilizing these sonorities that provide a stark contrast from their use in the lower strings. When the composer employs these chords for melodic purposes, the tempo is quite rapid. Additionally, Higdon explores juxtapositions of major chords to produce brief, bitonal passages. Two major chords whose roots are separated by an interval of a major second are sounded simultaneously to create harmonic tension that counters the consonant sections of perfect fifths.

Although Higdon's harmonic idiom places great emphasis on fifths and major chords, major and minor seconds comprise an integral aspect of her musical language as well. *Ostinato* patterns frequently alternate rapidly between these intervals and similar to the bitonal sections, this tension is released upon the return to the open fifths.

Melody

Higdon incorporates several melodic devices that may be labeled compositional traits. Most prevalent is the abundant lyrical soli for various instruments that produce the colorful orchestration for which she is known. In these passages, less orthodox instruments, such as the English horn and the bass clarinet, are featured. The length of these soli spans the gamut from expansive, lyrical melodies to greatly truncated, concise moments. Many of the solo sections present motivic material featured subsequently throughout the remainder of the composition, an essential element to unifying her works.

Ascending melodies are complemented by a gradual *crescendo* that culminates in a *fortissimo* marking to create musical climaxes that are subsequently relaxed by the melodic descents and *decrescendi* that follow. Higdon's melodies are generally consonant and thus tension and release is achieved through contour and dynamics.

Although Higdon composes contrapuntally, only one theme is prominent at a time and is clearly audible above the ensemble. Exceptions that present a countermelody do not interfere with the principal theme; even less common are imitative or fugato passages.

Rhythm

Higdon places significant emphasis on rhythmic motives that frequently function as a unifying device. Their appearances are subtle and not always audible in full ensemble passages. Although the patterns appear consistently in the same instrumentation, their return may be truncated or otherwise manipulated. Consistent repetition and rapid overlapping of these motives create intensity in the music and complexity in the texture. It is important to note that these motives may also be imbedded within the melodic line to permeate the theme with a vibrant rhythmic aspect. Less common are syncopations and accents but the former may occur in accompanimental material to provide an understated urgency beneath the prominent melody.

In full ensemble passages, rapid sixteenth notes combine with a gradual crescendo to fortissimo for powerful musical climaxes. The tension is subsequently released through a decrescendo and substantially slower note values. Highly rhythmic passages occur most frequently with the entire ensemble and rarely accompany chamber-like sections where the instrumental color remains the prominent feature.

Meter changes in Higdon's music are generally utilized to separate large formal sections within a movement or work; they may also herald significant musical passages. Alternating meters appear infrequently and the composer's use of metrical flux contributes to a sense of unpredictability and excitement.

Texture

Varying musical texture to maintain listener interest has been employed by many composers and Higdon is no exception. Her rare polyphonic passages may exhibit fugal qualities with imitative entries occurring rapidly. These sections are frequently complemented by a crescendo to further the intensity of the passage. During the loudest dynamic marking, Higdon exchanges polyphony for homorhythmic texture that releases the earlier tension. An essential aspect of her texture is the *basso ostinati* that function as unifying devices. These motives are used primarily in polyphonic passages that may become a catalyst for imitation.

Prominent solo passages are accompanied by a sparse texture for the practical reason that the soloist needs to be clearly heard above the ensemble. When the section nears its conclusion, the instrumentation slowly increases; as the density of the texture increases, the volume naturally does as well.

The composer invented a phrase to define a phenomenon in *blue cathedral* that recurs in her subsequent works. "Counterpoint of textures" refers to two independent musical lines or sections progressing simultaneously at seemingly different tempi.[64] Although not present in all of her works, the technique resurfaces infrequently.

Orchestration

An appealing factor of Higdon's music lies in her colorful orchestration. Typically, her orchestral works contain an instrumentation that resembles a late nineteenth-century ensemble with the exception of the greatly expanded percussion section which receives both significant rhythmic and melodic material.

Some of the unusual sounds in Higdon's orchestral scores arrive through experimentation, particularly in the percussion. Sometimes, she will speak to percussionists explaining the sound she wants and they will offer suggestions of how to realize it. Other times, she will simply go to the percussion studio at Curtis and experiment; she has even visited hardware stores in search of a desired sound.[65]

Soli and duets in Higdon's orchestral works feature a variety of timbres. In the composer's exploration of sound, melodic lines are doubled by instruments with contrasting colors, such as piccolo and trumpet or oboe and trombone. Ensemble passages also utilize expansive doublings to balance the chamber-like sound accompanying the soli. Melodic material performed by a single soloist utilizes less orthodox performers, not just the principal players. One particularly noteworthy aspect of Higdon's orchestration is the unusual scoring of string soli. Rather than notating a solo for the concertmaster, she may provide parts for the assistant concertmaster, the first desk of a section, or even soli for the second violins. The result is a string sound that emerges out of the depths of the ensemble. In doing so, Higdon increases significantly the opportunities for musicians who play these instruments to be featured soloists while simultaneously experimenting with sound possibilities. Such unique orchestrations are essential to her style.

Previous musical material is frequently recalled and although the returning passage is instantly recognizable to provide form and structure, the orchestral color is varied. The composer's penchant for changing the timbre remains one of her most intriguing qualities and the subsequent instrumentation utilized is never predictable.

Forms

During the compositional process, Higdon considers all of the elements of music with the exception of form. She explicitly stated, "I don't ever think about the form. A lot of my male colleagues do. That's the first step for them. My method of writing is instinctive, trying to find those sounds that are interesting to combine."[66] Higdon rarely adheres to strict formal structures; her works are best described as sectional. New sections in the form usually contrast the previous material in texture and dynamics and are frequently introduced by *accelerandi* and *ritardando* to allow for seamless transitions.

Codas play a significant role in Higdon's compositions. For example, in *blue cathedral*, Higdon concludes the work with numerical references to herself and her late brother that provide a deeply personal aspect. In doing so, this ending contains great meaning rather than functioning solely as a cadential extension; the significance of this coda is explored in greater detail in the subsequent chapter.

The multi-movement works adhere to various structures and forms. The five movement *Concerto for Orchestra* is in arch form. Although the first movement of this work retains elements of sonata allegro form, it is best described as sectional, a form also used in the third movement. Both are scored for the entire ensemble and alternate passages between the full orchestra and individual soli or sections. As expected in an arch form, the second and fourth movements relate to one another, a connection Higdon achieves through an exclusive instrumentation, the second is scored for strings and the fourth for percussion. In the liner notes to the recording, Nick Jones described the second movement as a scherzo,[67] and although Higdon did not originally conceive the movement as such, she purposely included a contrasting middle section that does in fact adhere to ternary form. This string movement provides the singular example in this work of a traditional structure inherited from the Viennese Classicists. To further enhance the connection to the second movement, the fourth begins with the percussionists playing their instruments with a string bow. Higdon did not intentionally compose these movements to balance the arch form but suggested her subconscious was responsible.[68] The finale, performed *attacca*, serves as a coda to the entire work with previous musical material recalled to provide cyclical coherence. As mentioned earlier, codas in Higdon's works are extremely significant and in the *Concerto for Orchestra*, the finale functions as a grand summation of the work's essential musical content.

One exception to the sectional forms of her orchestral works is the final movement of *City Scape*; however, the decision was dictated by the commissioning ensemble. The Atlanta Symphony Orchestra stipulated that the third movement, "Peachtree Street," serve as an example of form for school children. Higdon opted for a rondo, yet she strays somewhat from formal parameters by not stating the theme identically to its original statement. This entire work is discussed in greater detail in Chapter Four.

Similarly, the *Violin Concerto* utilizes recognizable forms in the second and third movements. The former is entitled "Chaconni," the plural of chaconne, a variation form stemming from the late Renaissance. Higdon's title alone indicates that she is straying from the traditional form by using two chaconnes and rather than focusing on a basso ostinato, her chaconni are comprised of chord progressions. A traditional chaconne is nearly always found in triple meter, which Higdon maintains only in the second chaconne. This movement is an excellent example of how Higdon's style is informed by traditional structures that serve only as a point of departure. The third movement, "Fly Forward," could also be viewed as a rondo since the opening theme returns numerous times; however, the reprisal does not occur in the traditional places. Precisely for these reasons, sectional is far more appropriate. The *Violin Concerto* is explored further in Chapter Six.

Program vs. Absolute Music

Titles such as *blue cathedral* and *City Scape* suggest a programmatic element that may be misleading since neither of the works contains a descriptive storyline. While composing *blue cathedral*, Higdon imagined a scenario with characters, but initially, performances of the work did not always include explanation in the program. Since the synopsis became public, however, it is always shared with the audience. Previous research has attempted to locate these specific events in the score, but the composer has not divulged details leaving much to the interpretation of the listener. *City Scape*, *Concerto 4-3*, and the *Violin Concerto* portray no explicitly programmatic content despite the poetic titles found in all three movements. The works are simply Higdon's musical portrait of places and ideas.

Concerto for Orchestra is purely absolute music. Commissioned by the Philadelphia Orchestra, the work contains solo passages inspired by specific members of the ensemble whose faces Higdon imagined while composing.[69] The result is not program music but rather an homage to these musicians' personalities and musical styles. All of her concerti, conceived with specific soloists in mind, fall strictly into the genre of absolute music.

Chapter Two

blue cathedral

Higdon's tone poem, *blue cathedral*, was commissioned for the Curtis Institute of Music's 75th Anniversary and premiered by Robert Spano with the Curtis Symphony Orchestra in Philadelphia, Pennsylvania, on May 1, 2000.[1] Since then, it has been performed countless times by both professional and collegiate ensembles and remains one of the most contemporary orchestral works programmed; in a short time the work has already entered the canon and is even included in the Eleventh Complete Edition of *The Enjoyment of Music* by Kristine Forney and Joseph Machlis, a music appreciation textbook published by W.W. Norton and Company.

Although commissioned originally for a celebration, the death of Higdon's younger brother from melanoma greatly informed the compositional process and the programmatic content. She recalled, "He died very fast. We called my mother and said he may die in the next hour."[2] The score is dedicated "in loving memory of Andrew Blue Higdon."[3]

The composition in its entirety represents to Higdon, "a story that commemorates living and passing through places of knowledge and of sharing and of that song called life."[4] The descriptive title of the work derives, in part, from her brother; "Blue" was Andy's middle name but the color also refers to the sky in this context. In the liner notes to the recording, Higdon expands, "Blue—like the sky. Where all possibilities soar. Cathedrals—a place of thought, growth, spiritual expression, serving as a symbolic doorway into and out of this world. Blue represents all potential and the progression of journeys. Cathedrals represent a place of beginnings, endings, solitude, fellowship, contemplation, knowledge, and growth."[5] To some, the use of the word cathedral may suggest a reference to Christianity (and primarily Catholicism) due to the prominence of well-known cathedrals as places of worship. Higdon interprets the term more generally and as explored in the previous chapter, while spiritual, she subscribes to no organized religion. She recalled during the compositional process, however, that because the work was commissioned by Curtis, an institution of higher learning, cathedral seemed fitting. The composer stated:

> I didn't want to say *blue Curtis* that makes no sense, but cathedral—the idea of the fact that so many things happen in a lifetime. So cathedral was just a general picture. I was originally going to call it *blue* but one of my friends said, "That's not very interesting." I don't know where cathedral came from though sometimes words will come in my mind when I'm writing and I'll write them on the margins of my sketches and then I'll go back and something looks like it's supposed to be the title.[6]

Curiously, Andy lived on Cathedral Street in Baltimore. This coincidence was brought to the composer's attention by a friend and Higdon stated, "This shows how I work on a subconscious level ... there are connections there that are interlaced that are subconscious."[7] Throughout this work, Higdon did not consciously create many of the analytical results; however, she regards these findings as valid and believes that many of these elements were instinctual during the compositional process.[8]

The intentional small case letters in the title signifies the work is about humanity rather than the music. In various publicized materials, *blue cathedral* may erroneously appear capitalized. According to Higdon, either is adequate,[9] but in the score, the letters are purposely set in lower case, as is the composer's name. She stated, "I'm too bashful to put my name in caps if I'm not putting the title [in capital letters]."[10]

Higdon struggled emotionally while simultaneously grieving and composing. She stated:

> I cried as I wrote the last two-thirds of the piece. I couldn't sleep, and I worried that I might have written something incoherent. It wasn't until the first rehearsal that I realized that I had a piece. Writing it was a cathartic and therapeutic experience. I thought about my brother but also about my students. What makes a life? I lost my brother—what can you take from an experience like that?[11]

Because of this situation, *blue cathedral* retains a highly personal element that makes the composition unique amongst her oeuvre.

The orchestration is standard for Higdon's symphonic works and resembles a large Romantic ensemble that includes lesser traditional instruments such as English horn, bass trombone, harp, and piano/celesta. The percussionists are comprised of three musicians and a timpanist performing a vast array of instruments; at the close of the work, crystal glasses and Chinese bells are performed by select musicians in the ensemble. The eight crystal glasses are played by the four hornists, three trombonists, and the tubist who tune the crystal glasses to definite pitches indicated in the score by adding water. The sound results from the musicians running a wet finger around the rim of the glass. In the performance notes, the composer recommends fine lead crystal.[12] The Chinese bells, sometimes referred to as Chinese health reflex balls, are performed by the second clarinetist, the principal oboe, the bassoonists, the trumpets, the harpist, the piccolo player, the timpanist, and strings. Chinese bells are small, chrome spheres twirled in the palms of the hands that produce a bright bell-like timbre. The performance notes suggest that approximately 50 Chinese bells are needed and may be ordered directly through Lawdon Press.[13] Nearly all of the orchestras that perform this piece request these instruments from the publisher who orders them in large quantities from numerous outlets.[14] Higdon discovered the sound accidentally after Lawson had given her a box of the bells as a present and she bumped into them only to realize they could produce an ethereal ambience in the work.[15] The piano is altered in the final bars through the application of two screws. As is typical of prepared piano, the exact preparations are specifically designated by the composer in the score. In this instance, they represent "that of a clock, chiming in the distance."[16]

blue cathedral is in paratactic form, meaning the work is sectional without significant repetition of material. Although this work is not programmatic in the traditional sense, a fairly detailed imagery was applied during the composition. The piece is included on the Atlanta Symphony Orchestra's album *Rainbow Body* and in the liner notes, Higdon explained that while composing, she was

> imagining a journey through a glass cathedral in the sky. Because the walls would be transparent, I saw the image of clouds and blueness permeating from the outside of this church. In my mind's eye the listener would enter from the back of the sanctuary, floating along the corridor amongst giant crystal pillars, moving in a contemplative stance. The stained glass windows' figures would start moving with song, singing a heavenly music. The listener would float down the aisle, slowly moving upward at first and then progressing at a quicker pace, rising towards an immense ceiling which would open to the sky. As this journey progressed, the speed of the traveler would increase, rushing forward and upward. I wanted to create the sensation of contemplation and quiet peace at the beginning, moving towards the feeling of celebration and ecstatic expansion of the soul, all the while singing along with that heavenly music.[17]

This was the imagery that Higdon used during composition but cannot necessarily be seen in the resulting score. Although not mentioned above, one specific musical association occurs with the flute and clarinet. These instruments represent the composer and her late brother, respectively, because those are the instruments each played.

Originally, the composer did not intend to share the program with the audience since she believed it was unnecessary to understanding the music. The work has been performed without program notes and Higdon remarked that audience reaction is similar. She received letters following performances that describe the piece's strength in communicating and audience members have asked if she had lost someone close to her. Higdon believes *blue cathedral* "will speak without any kind of programmatic"[18] explanation. She debated whether or not to include the program in the liner notes to *Rainbow Body* because she was concerned about being accused of playing on the audience's emotions. She voiced her concern to Spano but he told her, "People can decide for themselves."[19] The composer recognized that once a reporter published the programmatic material, it would become well-known and nearly impossible to omit from that point. Indeed, nearly all orchestras that perform the work today incorporate the composer's program for the audience.[20] As author of the liner notes in the recording, Higdon declares those words to be the definitive source regarding the issue.[21]

The composition initially was inspired by Andy, Higdon's grieving process, and the questioning of life's purpose. While writing, the composer reflected on the meaning of life. In the liner notes, she stated that she asked herself "the question of what makes a life" and the experience allowed her to "reflect on the amazing journeys that we all make in our lives, crossing paths with so many individuals singularly and collectively, learning and growing each step of the way."[22] The people one encounters in a lifetime are represented through various instrumental soli; yet unlike the flute and clarinet, no portrayals of specific individuals are depicted.

The sectional form is informed by the programmatic content and thus can be analyzed as following:

Measure Numbers	Programmatic Content	Musical Content	Letter
1–7	Ethereal Introduction	Pitched percussion and solo lower strings *con sordini*	Introduction
8–55	Higdon and Andy introduced	Flute (Higdon), clarinet (Andy), and violin soli	A
56–70	Various soli representing the people each person comes in contact with through their life; slowly moving upward at first and gradually increasing in speed	English horn solo, rising contours in smaller soli	B
70–84	(Unidentified in program notes but clearly a new section; a previous researcher refers to this as "Questioning" but this interpretation is not endorsed by Higdon)	Harmonic tension	C
84–130	Celebration and ecstatic expansion of the soul; flying theme (horns)	Brass fanfare	D
130–147	Characters of Higdon and Andy return, Andy continues his journey	Return of flute and clarinet soli	A

Measure Numbers	Programmatic Content	Musical Content	Letter
147–153	Higdon siblings' birthdates	Unorthodox instrumentation: prepared piano, Chinese bells, and crystal glasses	Coda

blue cathedral opens unassumingly with only the soft pitched percussion and celesta to set the mystical tone of the composition. These instruments are joined in measure three by two soloists from both the viola and the cello sections presenting descending major chords that simultaneously demonstrate Higdon's unique solo scoring and her penchant for parallel fifths. The warmth emanating from the lower strings contrasts the bright timbre of the percussion.

Following the introduction in measure eight, the composer introduces the characters of herself and her brother through the flute and clarinet joined by the entire string section in extensive divisions. The celli and the bass are each divided into two parts while the violas and violins are subdivided into three to present G major and A minor chords simultaneously. The flute solo in measure eight is presented initially because "going first is the privilege of being the older sibling."[23] Immediately following in measure 12, the clarinet solo commences. Although the general mood of this passage is peaceful, meter changes occur nearly every measure to produce an underlying unpredictability in the pulse; when the meter eventually stabilizes, it is 5/4 as in the introduction.

Higdon has made it known that the birthdates of her and her brother were purposely included in the coda but these numbers also appear elsewhere throughout the work. Higdon's birthdate is December 31 (12–31) while Andy was born on July 13 (7–13). The flute ceases in measure 12 (her birth month) and the clarinet begins in the pickup to measure 13 (his birthdate); the composer believes this to be more than coincidental and attributes it to her subconscious and intuitive style. Higdon commented on this author's discovery, "That was amazing. I was thinking after you mentioned that. I had some distant recollection of the 13 because his birthday was on the 13th [...] but because it was the first year after his death, my brain was so foggy. I just can't remember certain things but that felt familiar but I have just not been able to put my finger on it."[24] Subsequently, the flute and clarinet then join in a duet.

Distinct soli were composed to demonstrate the virtuosity and musicianship of the Curtis Symphony Orchestra. In measure 24, the woodwind duet is complemented by an extended violin solo that provides stark contrast from the remaining con sordino strings. The violin melody holds no particular significance in relation to the programmatic content; the composer included it because she felt it was necessary.[25] The violin solo ascends gradually and in step-wise motion. In the context of the imagery Higdon used while composing, one could associate this solo with celestial or heavenly places. It may also be interpreted as a figure in the stained glass but the meaning remains open to interpretation. The three trombones and three trumpets, all muted, exchange sustained major chords that are doubled by the piano and the celli which present parallel fifths outlining the same chords. The upper strings present separate sustained chords and intervals that enhance the reverent mood beneath the soaring soli.

Beginning in measure 29, a transition begins with the *poco a poco accel.* complemented by a gradual *crescendo* that peaks in measure 39. The solo violin ceases in measure 40 and all the strings, with mutes removed, sound *fortissimo* to change the mood from the mystical opening. The violins and upper woodwinds are separated by the interval of a second also characteristic of this composer. The dissonance occurs between the upper strings and the doubled instruments of the flute, piccolo, and keyboard; the violas are a major seventh below the second violins which in turn are a minor seventh below the violins. In the accompaniment, the lower strings, lower woodwinds, and brass present sustained perfect fifths. The persistent use of these consonant intervals provides relaxation from the tension produced by the dissonant upper orchestral parts. This passage also features a miniature fanfare beginning at measure 40 played by the horns and subsequently the trombones alternating major and minor sonorities. Questioned about this modal change, Higdon stated, "I was going back and forth"[26] (Figure 2-1).

Figure 2-1. *blue cathedral*; mm. 40-44, modal ambiguity between horns and trombones.

Between measures 46–50, the meter alternates between 3/4 and 5/4, the latter stabilizing in measure 50 to begin the transition to the subsequent section. At measure 50, the marimba and bassoons sound repeating fifth intervals that are the same pitch class as the prepared piano at the close of the work, purely coincidental according to the composer.[27] In a syncopated rhythm, the vibraphone and later, the chimes present different perfect fifths. Higdon stated that "these fifths are like church bells ringing in the distance, expressing an empty quality since there is no third in the chord."[28] As is her style, the transition is facilitated through a *decrescendo*, a *poco rit.*, and thinning texture. The strings are limited to only violas and celli in measure 54 complemented by a solo line for the principals of these two sections. Parallel fifths continue in the subsequent section making the transition seamless.

Higdon began writing the composition with the English horn solo beginning in measure 56. The choice of this timbre bears no specific significance other than the composer's preference for a melancholic sound[29] and her admiration for the talented players at Curtis. Higdon stated:

> Part of that grew out of the fact that the English horn, or oboe teacher at Curtis is so good. Richard Woodhams is the principal oboist of the Philadelphia Orchestra. I noticed when I would hear them [Woodhams's students] play the English horn, it was so gorgeous [that] I made up my mind early on that I wanted an English horn solo. It wasn't connected to anything it just fit. So I don't know what that solo represents. I can remember my initial thought was, "I got to have an English horn solo in here."[30]

The etymology of the English horn derives from the Middle German "engellisch," which curiously, translates to both angelic and English[31] and although Higdon did not consciously associate the English horn with its celestial history, it seems not only fitting but appropriate that this instrument serves a vital role in *blue cathedral*.

This section, with its numerous instrumental soli, signifies the separate lives a single person touches, an idea which stemmed from the time of her brother's illness. The composer stated to Brenda Rossow Phillips:

> When Andy was sick, we were at a house in Virginia Beach and there were a lot of his friends from Baltimore who would drive down to see him and I was very struck. One of the couples was getting ready to have a baby and they decided to name the baby Blue because Andy's middle name was Blue [...] I thought, "Wow, Andy has crossed the path of a lot of other people and a lot of people have crossed his path in his lifetime and people come and go but in some way they all touch you." And it is hard to draw a musical portrait of that. You almost have to make little tiny solos but they have to be little. I think the English horn solo is probably longer because that was the first thing I thought of.[32]

Brief soli appear in the piccolo, oboe, viola, cello, and bassoon. The variety of timbres represents "all of the individuals that one crosses paths with in a lifetime"[33] and although this is not included in the program notes, there can be no doubt, based on Higdon's own words, that this is the meaning of the soli. The length of the soli varies but the opening English horn and the smaller soli have similarities to one another. For instance, all but the piccolo present an ascending contour with syncopated rhythms related to the opening English horn solo. The upward motion also reflects the imagery Higdon utilized during the composition specifically the "slowly moving upward at first and then progressing at a quicker pace"[34] that coincides with the first tempo increase at measure 70.

The soli passage ceases in measure 70 and as is characteristic of this composer, the new section is introduced through a crescendo and a change of tempo, albeit a subtle one to quarter note=72. Many of Higdon's compositional traits are included: the harmonies present perfect fifths transposed to various degrees and both major and minor second intervals in the upper strings. The persistent employment of the fifth interval in the preceding and current sections connects two otherwise quite contrasting passages. While the harmonies presented are consistent with the previous section, the mood has clearly changed through the quickly alternating dynamic contrasts, the removal of the string mutes, and most importantly, the direction of "forceful-expressive."[35] Here, the music consists of a contrapuntal duet between the violas and violins that become subsequently more agitated and the sextuplet rhythm sprinkled throughout the strings connect this passage with the material that follows. Previous interpretations suggest a composer frustratingly demanding answers,[36] although this is not endorsed by Higdon.[37] The harmonic movement continues the parallel fifths in the accompanying instruments of horns, clarinets, and lower strings. Only the trumpets present fully realized descending major chords, another significant compositional trait.

"My counterpoint teacher would be having a cow"[38] was Higdon's initial response on her extensive use of fifths. Upon further reflection, however, the composer traces the influence to her earlier fascination with major chords. "But in *blue cathedral*, they [fifths] really made a statement for the first time just as fifths and I was thinking about bells."[39] When questioned specifically about the potential connection to the title of the work and the Notre Dame organum style, Higdon replied, "It's not that logical. Someone else brought that up but no, it was much simpler than that I'm afraid."[40] The instrumentation of the fifths in this work represent bells as stated above by the composer; however, *blue cathedral* marks the beginning of this interval as distinctive of her orchestral style.

During the increasingly complex soli of the viola and violin, the orchestration expands paired with a crescendo directly into the next section (measure 84), evidenced clearly by a double bar with an even faster tempo (quarter note=98–104). This passage, although beginning *forte*, clears the orchestral texture with central focus relegated to the strings, percussion, and trombones. The strings and the bass trombone alternate brief rhythmic motives within a narrow range often no larger than a perfect fifth, while the woodwinds present persistent *sforzando* chords in syncopation to enhance the intensity. The percussionists playing the glockenspiel, crotales, chimes, and timpani (with the instructions "with cover or piece of cardboard on head to deaden sound"[41]) present their respective parts in sextuplets that rhythmically unify this passage with the preceding one.

Higdon explores orchestral color with the bass trombone solo at measure 84 comprised of a brief recurring rhythmic motive of two sixteenth notes that is subsequently manipulated and extended. Complementing this solo, trombones one and two perform in unison in the sparse texture. For centuries, trombones have aided in musical depictions of the Underworld in operas with Greek subjects and death and divine retribution in sacred, Christian works. One may erroneously conjecture myriad of subconscious possibilities for such a scoring here; however, the instruments' use in *blue cathedral* bears no correlation to the symbolic association of its history. Higdon chose this instrument simply because she needed more sound and power.[42]

Beneath the bass trombone solo, the timpani and low tom-tom present repeated notes in a forte dynamic marking. This full orchestration is complemented by a crescendo that erupts in measure 95 where the meter alternates between 5/4 and 2/4 to obscure the downbeat. An omission of a strong metrical pulse and the beautiful, lush orchestration serves to project the protagonist rushing upward as the glass cathedral ceiling opens towards the sky. Beginning at measure 95, the lower strings present major chords joined subsequently by the horns, piano, and the violins separated into multiple parts.

In measure 100, E and Eb major chords are juxtaposed in the divided strings, piano, and horns for a bitonal sound in a passage full of chord planing that aids significantly in the floating scenario. This leads to a brass fanfare in measure 102 that undoubtedly marks the "feeling of celebration and ecstatic expansion of the soul."[43] While composing the fanfare, Higdon recalled, "That's actually a moment where I really had this revelation where maybe life is going to be about living.[44] That fanfare felt like a liberating moment for me."[45] The opening four measures present only the trumpets and trombones in unyielding sixteenth notes that provide the driving rhythm that defines Higdon's style. The passage is then repeated with the addition of the tuba and the bass trombone, the latter stemming from one of Higdon's students. She recalled, "[He] was studying solfege with me at the time and I was torturing him a lot about counting. So I said I'm going to put in a counting part for you so that's how that got in there."[46]

While the fanfare lasts only eight measure and the trumpets and trombone immediately drop out, the musical material is repeated in the high woodwinds, bassoons, harp, piano, and strings for four measures. Subsequently, in measure 114, the flute, piccolo, and strings expand on the material while the remaining woodwind instruments, joined by the trumpets and

Figure 2-2. *blue cathedral*; mm. 114-117, Higdon's "counterpoint of textures."

trombones, present chords of both major and minor sonorities. These supporting harmonies are in a decidedly slower harmonic rhythm to transition to the next significant section. Higdon refers to the contrasting harmonic rhythms between the lively sixteenth notes of the upper woodwinds and strings and the slow note values of the remaining winds as a "counterpoint of textures,"[47] a phrase explained in the previous chapter (Figure 2–2). Within these slower rhythms, the horns present a prominent rising, lyrical solo beginning in measure 115 that according to the composer represents the "ultimate flying theme."[48] This entire passage represents the peak of the work as the music soars in a fortissimo dynamic; the transition to the final solo section begins in measure 126 with the *molto ritardando*.

A new section begins promptly in measure 130, complete with meter and slowing of the tempo to the original quarter note=60. Regarding this passage, Higdon stated:

> I often think about drawing the audience in, they are in on this and by the time they get to that loud part [measures 100–128], they are with you; no one is sleeping at all. But if you can bring it down to a more intimate setting really fast you actually pull the audience more with you. They are caught off guard by the flute and the clarinet coming in [measure 131] but because they have heard that material before and it sounds familiar, they are okay with it.[49]

This passage evokes the ethereal environment of the opening; the *pianissimo* chimes presented by the three percussionists each sounds three different notated pitches in "any quick rhythm, without synchronizing with [the] other players."[50] This imagery according to Phillips represents "bells in the distance."[51] The nebulous rhythm is further enhanced by the divided second violins' alternation between D and E: one section alternates the pitches in eighth notes while the other is in triplets that tie the third triplet to the first. To add to the otherworldly effect, the composer introduces the crystal glasses and Chinese bells starting with the back of the orchestra performing softly. The strings enter with the Chinese bells beginning with the last stand, then the next stand in the subsequent measure, and the pattern continues through the remainder of the work.

Above these accompanying lines, the flute and clarinet soli representing the Higdon siblings return in measure 131. The flute solo is similar to its predecessor in bar eight, although scored an octave lower. The composer provided a practical rationale for this change:

> I can see an orchestration reason for putting that an octave lower [...] if you look at the flute line in the measures leading up to it is high and when I'm writing I try to make sure I vary the high and low to keep it interesting for the listener [...] I'd be willing to bet this came about because [...] it was something that practical.[52]

The clarinet solo enters in the same measure but unlike the flute, the range is unchanged from its initial appearance and here, represents Andy continuing his journey upward. As the woodwind dialogue progresses, two violas and two celli present descending chords. Although not an exact replication, the lower strings recall the opening measures of the composition. Higdon stated:

> I knew that Andy's journey was going on. When I was writing the chords, I was thinking I had to get the music to settle down [...] it's got to feel like it's coming to an end and the descending chords felt like the best way to do that to move toward a resolution. Now the flute cuts out because the clarinet is actually continuing on its journey. This is the part where I said, "Oh no, I can't really end this." This piece is not appropriate to end that way. I've got to find a way to bring it down and calm it.[53]

Reappearing at measure 134 is the English horn solo whose meaning remains open to interpretation according to the composer, who stated, "Could be God, could be the universe. Could be anything. It was there and it seemed logical and it is still as much a mystery to me today as it was when I wrote it."[54] Similar to its initial solo in measure 56, the range remains quite narrow but expands chromatically from its previous presentation.

The English horn ceases in measure 140 quickly followed by the flute in 142. In the liner notes, Higdon writes, "At the end of the work, the two instruments continue their dialogue, but it is the flute that drops out and the clarinet that continues on in the upward progressing journey."[55] The clarinet solo diminishes with the beginning of the coda in measure 147. Here, Higdon purposefully included the birthdates of herself and her brother although she has not stated precisely where they occur. As mentioned previously, Andy's birthday was July 13 (7-13) while Higdon was born on December 31 (12-31). Curiously, the days are palindromes of one another.

These significant numbers appear elsewhere throughout the work as a result of Higdon's subconscious, intuitive style. For instance, the final duet between the flute and clarinet commences in measure 131 (a hybridization of Andy and Higdon's days of birth). When questioned about this, the composer replied, "In terms of measure 131 [...] I don't think it was intentional.... I hadn't noticed that ... although it is a little amazing."[56] Although Higdon did not explicitly compose this measure to be numerically meaningful, she has not dismissed the possibility of a subconscious reference.[57] She stated, "I think there's probably something to that. I actually have no doubt. I don't think that was coincidence. It's a little too much our two birthdays [...] it makes sense."[58]

Again, Higdon has not specifically outlined the appearance of the two birthdates in the coda. Phillips's analysis proves noteworthy but does not include the composer's birthdate, and Higdon has publicly declared, "I put in my birth date and Andy's birth date (mine: 12–31; his 7–13) in the piece in a very exposed location."[59] As Phillips's research demonstrates, the lower crotales presents the third of a D major chord seven times to represent the month of July, while the glockenspiel strikes 13 times to represent the day.[60] Working with Phillips, Higdon explained:

> This is hysterical. Brenda [Phillips] asked me about this and she couldn't figure it out, then I was trying to figure it out. I actually did it and I was trying to figure it out! It was tricky [...] I did have trouble when Brenda started asking me about it. When I went back to look at the sketches, I couldn't find where I had written it down [...] but that had more to do with the fact that I have so many sketches of so many different things. It could have been written on a napkin and I may have lost the napkin.[61]

Additional locations not mentioned in Phillips include the 13 strikes of the vibraphone, the 13 strikes of the low and high triangle combined, and the 13 pitches with the stems facing downward in the crotales.

Because Andy died at the age of 33, the composer also assigns significance to this number.[62] Following the final clarinet solo, a prepared piano enters in measure 147 to chime a perfect fifth interval 33 times. The Higdons originally believed Andy's birthday was July 14 (7–14, rearranged in the measure number). The composer stated, "We must have celebrated his birthday on the 14th for 6, 7 or 8 years before my mom found his birth certificate and went, 'Oh, it's the 13th.'"[63]

In measure 149, the percussionists present a visual realization of the number three through the notated triplets, a connection to Andy's age at the time of his death that Higdon did not consciously employ. She stated, "I always pick up on the auditory sensation of an attack. I don't think of it as a visual element. In fact, I think when I wrote this, I was surprised at how it came out."[64] Finally, the three strokes of the lower triangle appear in measure 149, a pattern that repeats following four beats of rests (Figure 2–3). Although Higdon declared openly the significance of the 33 piano chimes, all other numerical appearances were discovered by Phillips and this author. These findings should not be dismissed as coincidental; the composer validates such discoveries as examples of her instinctual compositional method.

The opening and concluding measures of the work utilize a similar instrumentation but no numerical significance is present in the introduction. Higdon explained:

> There's nothing there, I was trying to figure out how to start the piece. I wrote that before the ending but this wasn't connected to anything because I hadn't thought about using the numerology at that point. I wrote this first, I didn't get the organization sense until I got to the end [...] and then I knew I wanted to bring back this material.[65]

Figure 2-3. *blue cathedral*; mm. 149-153.

In fact, the decision to incorporate the birthdates occurred as the composition was nearing completion.[66]

Although composed in the wake of Andy's death, the composition is neither mournful nor a lament and in fact, featured at times is the tonality of D major, a key associated with vibrancy, triumph, and rejoicing. While initially uncertain about her perspective of life, Higdon stated, "I was surprised it turned out so positively."[67] Notating passages in the key of D major may suggest that, subconsciously, Higdon harbored positive assumptions, a theory that leaves the composer skeptical. She explained, "That wasn't conscious because when I was writing *blue cathedral*, I was literally trying to figure out whether life was going to be about living or whether it was going to be about death. I was agonizing. When I started that piece, I did not feel like things were going to be ok."[68]

blue cathedral remains one of Higdon's most well-known and loved works; its reception by critics and audiences alike has been overwhelmingly positive since the world premiere. Music critic David Patrick Stearns reviewed the initial performance and described the composition as "full of beguiling timbres and thematic ideas employed with a poised emotional presence."[69] The *San Francisco Classical Voice*'s Jeff Dunn called it "magical" and stated, "Higdon is expert at varying soloistic opportunities among instruments."[70] Bob Keyes of the *Portland Press Herald* (Maine) proclaimed *blue cathedral* as "among the most daring and inventive new compositions to surface in years."[71] Finally, while reviewing the Annapolis Symphony Orchestra's performance of the work, David Lindauer opined, "This is a remarkable piece of music, not only beautifully crafted and full of special effects, but communicating intensely personal feeling as well."[72]

As noted previously, this work was recorded by Robert Spano and the Atlanta Symphony Orchestra on the Telarc label on a disc entitled *Rainbow Body*, the name of the opening work by Christopher Theofanidis. This CD also features Samuel Barber's *Symphony No. 1* and Copland's *Suite from Appa-*

lachian Spring. Released in 2003, the recording was reviewed by Gilbert French in the *American Record Guide* who wrote of *blue cathedral*:

> The result, with its light, distant wind chimes, evokes a feeling of sky, space, sacredness, floating, peace, and ascension. While the harmonies are traditional, the subtle textures and weaving lines [...] lead to two big climaxes [...] they occur with a naturalness and unobtrusiveness, conveying finally an exultant feeling [...] the Higdon is a truly lovely work.[73]

Undoubtedly, *blue cathedral* has attained an elevated status among modern symphonic compositions and its countless performances indicates the work's ability to communicate successfully to both audiences and performers. Several explanations account for its continuing popularity. Firstly, the programmatic content relates easily to the human condition. Secondly, while the piece contains dissonant passages, the composition is aurally pleasing and accessible which facilitates audience acceptance. Of course, popular approval alone has not historically guaranteed posterity but *blue cathedral* is also held in great esteem by highly trained musicians that confirms a level of sophistication beneath the audible pleasantry. Musicians, conductors, and critics are drawn to the unique timbres and artistry required in the individual soli that permeate the composition. Finally, this work, while technically challenging in certain passages, is not nearly as difficult as many of Higdon's compositions and thus is also played frequently by collegiate ensembles. The immediate and resounding success of *blue cathedral* was compounded even further by the 2002 premiere of *Concerto for Orchestra* explored in the next chapter.

CHAPTER THREE

Concerto for Orchestra

Similar to *blue cathedral*, *Concerto for Orchestra* materialized from a celebratory occasion; the Philadelphia Orchestra had substantial plans to inaugurate its centennial year that included several commissions from different composers.[1] Higdon's *Concerto for Orchestra*, the largest work she had yet written, was a result and has since appeared frequently on orchestral programs throughout the United States.

Because Higdon believes that quality compositions will spread by word-of-mouth, her works themselves are the primary method she uses to promote her music which indeed was how this opportunity with the Philadelphia Orchestra emerged. A musician[2] in that ensemble had performed her music, heard a recording of her orchestral composition *Shine* (1996), and suggested Higdon as a composer worthy of commission. Subsequently, she received a telephone call from Simon Woods, the then Vice President for artistic planning and operations, requesting a score and recording. She recalled, "I didn't know why he was asking. I actually had a couple [of] pieces but they weren't very good but I had this one piece called *Shine* and I took that to him."[3]

Of the composers selected, Higdon stated, "I know that they were going to have to commission a Philadelphia composer in this mix because they would get a lot of flak. They looked at a lot of people but somehow they came up with me [...] that was a shock to all of us."[4] Lawson recounted that several members of the established composition community in Philadelphia were upset that a less familiar composer at the time was chosen.[5] Higdon humorously related how she discovered she was selected:

> I forgot about it, and about one month later I was walking down the street [...] and the first flute player, Jeffrey Khaner was running down the street, jumping up and down motioning to me. He goes tearing across three lanes of traffic, almost getting hit, and he said, "The Philadelphia Orchestra is going to commission you."[6]

The composer also recalled her initial uncertainty:

> As soon as I was out of grad school, suddenly I got this commission, I was completely horrified. In fact, really for the next two or three days I just wasn't sure I heard him correctly.

> It took a while for that to sink in. And then panic set in, literally for about a year. What have I gotten myself into because all my teachers, all these people were pointing at me saying, "She's the one with the Philadelphia Orchestra commission." You could hear the whispering.[7]

Higdon commented on the potential gossip within the Philadelphian musical circle:

> I'm sure there was [sic] probably mumblings and grumblings. There had to be [...] I'm in a city with [...] some amazing composers and I had literally just come out of graduate school. I had only graduated four years before. Thank goodness there was a gap from the time they asked me to write it than when the premiere [occurred] because I needed that time to adjust my thinking. It was too much pressure. I would have been in trouble if I had to turn out that piece within a year. I'm glad there was time for me to think about it.[8]

Due to the prestige of the commissioning ensemble and its surrounding circumstances, the composer allowed herself a wide time frame to write. Higdon began the work fairly soon after receiving the commission and vividly remembers her hesitation. She remarked, "What the hell am I going to write for the Philadelphia Orchestra? It was scary."[9] The commission, originally granted in 1998, was not scheduled to premiere until 2002.

Early in the composition process, Higdon identified her piece as a *Concerto for Orchestra* following a distinguished list of works with the same title from composers such as Zoltán Kodály, Roger Sessions, Witold Lutosławski, Joan Tower, and the most well-known, Béla Bartók. While composing, she was conscious to preserve originality and distance herself from these significant predecessors; she recalled:

> I stopped listening to [...] those [Lutosławski and the Bartók] works. I would never be able to make my own kind of *Concerto for Orchestra*; I was afraid that my head would be replaying their music. So I intentionally stayed away from those pieces for four years. I was aware of them, but, boy, I tried not to think about it.[10]

Because of the extensive popularity of the Bartók, parallels between his work and Higdon are frequently drawn regardless of the fact that over twenty compositions bear this title. Similarities between the Bartók and Higdon are limited to the number of movements and the overall arch form. Higdon commented, "Because I stopped [listening to Bartók during the compositional process] and I let that out of my system, I forgot about the fact that the Bartók's in five movements. I honestly didn't realize."[11] It is worth noting that outside of the large formal structure, little similarity exists between the two compositions. The continuous parallels drawn between the two stem more from a lack of knowledge of existing works with the same name rather than any actual likenesses. Many journalists make comparisons with her music; she recalled, "One reporter said this piece reminds me of Lutosławski and

Schoenberg and Mozart and Stravinsky. They went on with the whole list and all the composers [were] completely contradictory and I [thought], 'What the hell are they saying? I don't understand what this means.'"[12]

In some of her earlier works, Higdon chose descriptive titles but in this case, she abandoned this idea because from its inception, it was a concerto composed specifically for the musicians of the Philadelphia Orchestra. She expanded:

> That's a very unusual thing for me. It's so absolute that I couldn't come up with a more original title. They [people] actually said, "What the hell's wrong with you?" They're [the compositions] often about the ensemble I'm writing for and I'm thinking about the ensemble. My brain [...] doesn't come up with any kind of imagery.[13]

As an active member of Philadelphian musical life since her graduate school years, Higdon has established personal relationships with many of the orchestral members. Intimate knowledge of the differing personalities of the musicians in addition to the familiarity with the style of music the principal players prefer enhanced the uniqueness of the composition. During the compositional process, she explained, "I've worked with a lot of the Orchestra's musicians in new-music concerts. I went to school with some at Curtis, or they are former students of mine. I'm tailoring the Concerto to the individual players and to the Orchestra as a whole."[14] This awareness informed much of the work, particularly the solo sections. Today, personal relationships between members of a premiering ensemble and contemporary composers are infrequent; however, similar circumstances were much more common in preceding eras, for example in the operas of Mozart. In a similar way, Higdon crafted soli for specific instrumentalists in *Concerto for Orchestra* based on the musicians' talents and personal preferences.[15]

Concerto for Orchestra was composed in various U.S. cities due to Higdon and Lawson's frenzied schedules. For example, the second movement alone was written in Pensacola, Florida, Los Angeles, and Chicago. Because of these locations' close proximity to oceans and lakes, this movement reminds Higdon of wind blowing on the water and even the hotel rooms remain vivid in her memory. The association with water, however, is the composer's alone; it does not transfer to the listener nor was it intended to do so. Higdon unequivocally stated, "There's no literal reference to water."[16] The entire five movements, unlike *blue cathedral*, fall strictly within the genre of absolute music.

As is typical of Higdon, the work was composed in order of ideas, rather than chronologically. She began with the third movement and recalled how instrumental soli became the primary feature:

> So many of the players were asking me for solos or wanting things specifically so [...] I decided [that movement] was just going to be solos featuring the principal players. This piece was so big I knew that I had to go with whichever felt instinctively like the first movement to write [and] because I had the most ideas for the solos, I just started there [...] otherwise I never would have started, I was too nervous about it.[17]

The string movement (II) came next followed by the percussion movement (IV), followed by the finale and finally, the first movement.[18]

Concerto for Orchestra is in a symmetrical arch form that places the climax of the work in the third movement. The last movement, performed *attacca*, functions as a large coda by returning musical ideas from earlier movements. Higdon remarked that she did not initially conceive the composition as an arch but did strive to make the third movement the heart of the work. In the composer's words, "It does kind of have an arch. It makes perfect sense. It's tutti orchestra in I, III, and V. The faster music's in I and V."[19] Movements II and IV, scored for strings and percussion respectively enhance the arch form. The inspiration for the fourth movement emerged from a request by timpanist Don Liuzzi, who asked to play percussion, a non-traditional role for a timpanist.[20]

The scoring for *Concerto for Orchestra* is extensive and requires nearly all of the instruments in a percussionist's arsenal. The woodwinds and brass utilize three players per instrument (with the exceptions of four F horns and a single tuba). A fully scored string section, harp, and piano/celesta complete the orchestration.

After the work was completed, Higdon was invited to attend the Philadelphia Orchestra's rehearsals. She recalled her mixed emotions:

> We went into the Kimmel Center, it's a brand new hall in Philadelphia and they [...] put me in the middle of the audience which is [...] basically empty, it's just a lot of seats and suddenly you hear these notes that you've labored over for quite some time coming out of the orchestra but what's interesting is for a composer [...] when it's first done, when there's first rehearsals, it never sounds like you think it's going to, there's no way that it can because the musicians are learning the music [...] it sounded to me at first like kind of a cacophony of sound coming from the stage. It was amazing because it was the Philadelphia Orchestra and [...] you can't live in Philadelphia without being aware of the legacy of that symphony [...] I could not comprehend that the sounds were going to kind of mesh into what I had written on the page [...] my first rehearsal was only 45 minutes, it's a 35 minute piece. They didn't rehearse the whole thing but I wasn't even sure when we came out of the first rehearsal, if it worked and I don't know if that was from the amount of adrenaline in my system or was it the orchestra learning the music since it's brand new [...] so as the days went on as we got closer and closer to the premiere, it started to sound closer to what I thought it probably would sound like.[21]

The composer continued to recount her initial feelings hearing the ensemble rehearse, "I was shocked [...] I was completely terrified. My friend[22] who went with me to the rehearsal [said], 'Holy cow, do you realize what you've done?' I [responded with], 'No, what happened?' A totally goofy reaction."[23]

The world premiere of Higdon's *Concerto for Orchestra* occurred on June 12, 2002, with Wolfgang Sawallisch leading the Philadelphia Orchestra at the newly opened Kimmel Center for the Performing Arts.[24] Last of all the commissioned compositions to be performed, the work was followed on the program by Richard Strauss's tone poem, *Ein Heldenleben*. In attendance were members of the American Symphony Orchestra League who were holding their annual conference in Philadelphia at the time and thus, the impact from such an influential audience was significant. Higdon recalled, "There were 3,000 orchestra managers out there. If it worked, things were going to go great for the rest of my life, if not it was going to be bad."[25] The premiere opened the program while Higdon listened backstage. She vividly recalled:

> I was so nervous that I didn't sit out in the audience. So the orchestra allowed me to sit backstage [...] I realized everything was kind of riding on these 35 minutes. But the other thing was I was completely unknown, so I was thinking to myself [...] "perhaps people are [...] having coffee, staying longer at their dinner." Are they going to want to hear this piece? But I didn't know because I was actually sitting backstage. What happens backstage at an orchestra concert is, there are a lot of people standing back there as soon as the music starts, once the conductor walked out on the stage, everybody disperses, they go off, they've got stopwatches, they know when to come back, when the end of the piece is. So then I was alone backstage and [...] my entire life was passing in front of my eyes. I thought, "Well, it was a good run, you know." And I actually was sitting there pondering to myself, I thought, "Well, geez [...] it was like twenty years ago that I actually had [...] that first basic theory class, [...] and maybe I could have done better" [...] I'm sure time was moving pretty quickly for me and I could hear the audience applauding and people re-gathered backstage because the conductor was coming off. Someone came back there with a towel for the conductor and someone had some water and he came off the stage and [...] he motioned to me like, "You're going to walk out with me" [...] I don't know why I didn't think of this but he took me out onto the stage and the entire audience got up on its feet.[26]

Following the premiere, Higdon's life was completely altered and people referred to her as a celebrity. With her customary laid-back personality, she stated, "What? Are you kidding me? Oh my God, [John] Corigliano's famous, I'm not [...] I never think of myself that way."[27] Regardless, this composition in combination with *blue cathedral* put her name on hundreds of orchestral programs where it remains. Since its premiere, *Concerto for Orchestra* has been performed by the nation's most prestigious orchestras such as the Atlanta Symphony Orchestra, the Dallas Symphony, the Houston Symphony Orchestra, the National Symphony, the Pittsburgh Symphony, and the BBC Orchestra. The work has also been featured by prominent university orchestral ensembles including the Cleveland Institute of Music and the Oberlin Conservatory of Music. *Concerto for Orchestra*, paired with *City Scape*, was recorded by Robert Spano and the Atlanta Symphony Orchestra on the Telarc

Label. The composition continues to be programmed by major American orchestras more than ten years after its premiere.

Movement One

The opening caused Higdon much anxiety as she recalled, "It was the most terrifying moment. I thought, 'I'm going to mess up all these other movements.'"[28] The movement utilizes the full ensemble separated by passages that feature orchestral sections with her purpose to recognize "the fact that it takes many individuals to make the whole of the orchestra."[29] At first glance, the form may erroneously be viewed as sonata allegro based on the order of returning material from sections A and B (where A and B represent themes one and two, respectively). Upon closer analysis, however, it becomes evident that even under the most lenient of definitions, this is not the case. Unifying motives are present that link the sections rather than exploring contrasts and these sections share musical elements that continue to build upon one another. The form can be broken down into the following:

Measure Numbers	Music	Letter
1–28	Introduces significant elements of entire work: ascending contour, perfect fourth followed by augmented fourth, exploration of octatonic scale, $OCT_{2,3}$; 4/4 meter established in measure 2	Introduction
29–50	Full orchestra remains in 4/4; exploration of fourths and ascending contour in horns, demonstration of specific Higdon style traits of major chords in root position separated by an interval of a major second	A
51–81	Opens with solo dialogue between bass clarinet and piccolo, fourth intervals explored throughout ensemble, $OCT_{2,3}$	B
82–152	Exploration of orchestral sections in following order: strings, woodwinds, brass, and return of strings	C
153–168	Full orchestra in 5/4; greatly truncated from A	A'

Measure Numbers	Music	Letter
187–251	Material from B section followed by exploration of orchestral sections in following order: woodwinds, percussion, and brass	D (functioning as a combination of material from B and C to conclude the movement)

Typical of both Higdon's compositions and multi-movement works in general, the first movement is endowed with a spirited tempo, quarter note=122–132, that remains consistent until the closing *ritardando*. This is significant because Higdon usually incorporates tempo changes, although sometimes only minimally, to delineate the beginning of a new section. Because of the length of this work, tempo changes are unnecessary since various moods and tempi are explored in subsequent movements.

Introduction to *Concerto for Orchestra*

The opening is of the utmost importance because it introduces the primary motives that connect all five movements. Higdon begins with only the timpani, chimes, strings, and horns and it bears mentioning the prominence bestowed upon the percussion in the first measure. Instructed to play *fortissimo*, these instruments sound the pitches of F and Bb that expand to F, Bb, and E melodically (Figure 3–1). Thus the opening is comprised of a perfect fourth followed by an augmented fourth, intervals that continue to be featured until measure 23. On the importance of these intervals, Higdon stated:

> I'm glad you see [the intervals] [...] you're the only one. When I was writing, I was literally just thinking about the intervals. I want[ed] the intervals to unfold and I thought [they were] more interesting sounding. Instead of going perfect fourth, perfect fifth, I put perfect fourth and a tritone. I can't tell you how many people who prefer atonal music have gotten ticked because they thought it had tonal implications [...] people usually look at that in tonal[ity] and I wasn't thinking that way at all. It was literally intervals.[30]

These intervals, as well as the pitches themselves, play a prominent role in the subsequent movements. On the opening measures, the composer continued, "I thought the sound was fascinating.... I knew I needed something that sounded like it was revving up.... I thought, 'How am I going to write something ... and make it lead logically into all the rest of the stuff?'"[31]

The strings begin in measure two displaying fast, imitative sixteenth notes that support Higdon's statement that the piece is "revving up." The melodic material derives from the octatonic scale, a scale that alternates half steps and whole steps. There are three possible octatonic scales that subsequently will be referred to as $OCT_{0,1}$, $OCT_{1,2}$, and $OCT_{2,3}$.[32] Higdon utilizes the $OCT_{2,3}$ scale beginning on B; thus, the octatonic scale used in the opening string

Figure 3-1. *Concerto for Orchestra*; I, mm. 1-4.

passage is spelled B-C#-D-E-F-G-Ab-Bb (Figure 3-1). She recalled how her teaching informed this choice, "I remember we were doing Stravinsky and Bartók in my classes during that time. I had a lot of kids in those classes, so we were looking theoretically. I think that's actually what happened: 'These are cool scales! Let's see how this sounds!'"[33] The strings' imitation ceases in measure 11 and although the texture changes to homorhythmic, the persistent rushing sixteenth notes reinforce the momentum initiated in the opening.

The horns are the only additional instrument found in the introduction and their importance is reinforced by the *forte* dynamic marking and accents. The material is significant for two reasons: their first notes are the concert pitches of F, Bb, and B natural and the line features the ascending contour that defines the entire work. The introduction closes at measure 28 with ascending lines and a *crescendo* in the strings that culminate with the opening of the A section.

A Section

The A section unmistakably arrives at measure 29 with a fortissimo and the first full presentation of the *tutti* orchestra. The oboes, clarinets, bassoons, and piano continue the rushing sixteenth notes and octatonic passage from the introduction. The octatonic scale, however, is not strictly observed as in its opening appearance.

The strings (still doubled by several woodwinds) demonstrate a significant Higdon compositional trait, two major chords separated by a second interval. The first and second violins present one progression, scored as minor sixths and perfect fifths respectively, while the violas and celli present identical material a major second below. Moving in homorhythmic texture, this bitonal passage provides contrast from the polyphony of the introduction. Also at the start of the A section and independent from the strings, one of the most defining traits of this composer's orchestral works is present: root position major chords for three trumpets. Finally, a link between the introduction and the A section is immediately apparent here: all four horns, marked fortissimo, sound ascending perfect fourths that recall both the opening percussion interval and rising contour (Figure 3–2).

Figure 3–2. *Concerto for Orchestra*; I, mm. 29–33.

After this brief demonstration by the entire ensemble, the orchestration is minimized by the omission of the trumpets and piano in measure 46 in preparation for the B section. The now tacet trumpets have been replaced by the clarinets with the descending major chords in similar rhythms.

The chimes melodically present the opening intervals in measure 46 as transitional material to the B section. As the dynamic softens, fifths are sustained in the trombones and basses. The upper strings, doubled by woodwinds, continue to present major chords separated by a second but the harmonic rhythm is considerably slower to only one chord per measure to contribute to the transition to the B section.

B Section

Measure 51 begins the second section. The texture thins considerably with only the vibraphone (doubled by flutes) and horns. Higdon uses these instruments as accompanimental material to soli featured throughout this section. The bass clarinet presents the first solo in the work, beginning with an ascending $OCT_{2,3}$ scale. This instrument is paired with the piccolo creating a striking contrast in ranges. The piccolo line balances the bass clarinet through a descending melodic line while utilizing the same scale to create a question-answer dialogue. At the close of this duet, the instrumentation increases gradually to include the strings and the full woodwind section.

Throughout this passage, the perfect and augmented fourth intervals become increasingly prominent beginning in measure 58 where the oboes sound the F, Bb, and E identical to the opening percussion. Exploration of the tritone, and several measures later perfect fourths, continues in the bass and contrabassoon in measure 68. Ascending perfect fourths also appear in the horn lines in measure 76 comparable to the earlier appearance in 29 of Section A with changes only in the articulation resulting in a unification between this section and the two previous ones.

C Section

Typical of Higdon, a new section commences with a meter change in measure 82 that examines soli for many of the musicians in the ensemble. A dream-like quality is presented initially through the scoring of celesta, harp, glockenspiel, and marimba. Although this wistful excursion does not involve the full orchestra, the texture contains enough density to provide contrast before a lengthy exploration of instrumental soli ensues. This passage features ostinato patterns in the flute, piccolo, glockenspiel, marimba, and harp complemented by an ascending scalar passage in the celesta similar in content to the strings' material in the introduction.

Higdon turns her attention to the strings in measure 86 with soli for the four principal players from the first violin, viola, cello, and bass. The range of the bass is significantly high and in several instances, is comparable to that of the first violin. The texture of the string soli is homorhythmic and combined with the like timbres and ranges, the four soli sound as one instrument although Higdon did not originally conceive it in this way. She commented:

> Once the strings got going I did think of that, I find it fascinating. I thought, "What would it sound like to get all the strings moving together?" And I did something really unusual. They had to play *detache* in places where they normally wouldn't. They might be doing three bows or three notes per bow and I [thought], "Let's see what it sounds like. How much power would there be with the Philadelphia string section?" [...] it was just me wanting to hear what the sound was like.[34]

The strings complete their soli in measure 93 followed by a curious circumstance. A solo rhythmic dialogue ensues in the second violins, the instrument omitted from the previous quartet. This dialogue is scored for divided first desk meaning that not only is the principal second violinist a soloist but also the assistant principal. The parts, however, do not constitute a melodic line but rather a continual, highly rhythmic sounding of the same pitch. This solo emerged from Higdon's personal connections to the orchestral personnel; she recalled:

I did know Kim[berly] Fisher. I know her very well. Kim [...] is still the principal second violin of the Philadelphia Orchestra and I had gone to school with her at Curtis. At one point when I was a student and I had a piece performed by the Curtis Orchestra,[35] she was the concertmaster. I couldn't leave her out. Kim would have been very upset with me.[36]

Higdon reiterated and expanded upon her belief that second violinists are equally strong players as the firsts. She explained:

In my head, the second violinists are so good today that they're just as good as the firsts [...] some of the second violinists, often [comment], "My part's higher than the first violin." [To which I respond,] "Why not? [You have] all this training." I look at them as equal [...] but in this particular piece it's because I knew the principal player.[37]

Although Higdon may view all violinists as equal, she jokingly recalled that not all the principal second violinists who perform this solo enjoy the limelight:

Of course there have been a lot of principal second violinists that have not been too happy with me since then. "What are you doing to me?" [they ask] [...] another comment [I heard], "I could throw you off a roof."[38]

The soli for the first desk of the second violins accompanies an exploration of soli for all four woodwind instruments. Unlike the preceding homorhythmic texture of the strings, Higdon utilizes independent lines. The previous ostinati for woodwinds cease here to leave only the soloists. Because of this scoring and the staggered entrances, the unique timbre of each instrument is clearly demonstrated until measure 98 when the texture shifts to homorhythmic. This change presents the unique colors of the woodwind timbres as opposed to the previous homogenous string sound. As this brief passage comes to a close, the harmonic rhythm slows considerably.

The brass features subsequently in measure 105 with the disappearance of the woodwinds and the second violin ostinato soli. To fully demonstrate the contrast of color between the woodwinds and brass, the latter's entrance maintains both the homorhythmic texture and slower harmonic rhythm previously established. As with the other featured sections, there are four soloists: the tuba and the principal horn, trumpet, and trombone.

Following the exploration of the brass, the composer expands the orchestration to combine soloists from various sections of the ensemble. The solo string quartet (violin, viola, cello, and bass) returns in measure 116 with descending major chords that are nearly identical to the trumpets in measure 29. Between these solo string statements, the woodwinds sound homorhythmic figures to create a dialog between the orchestral sections. While these winds are no longer soloists, Higdon scores only one musician from each section that complements the material of the strings.

There are two moments of great significance at the close of the C section.

In measure 133, the second trumpet forcefully sounds the F, Bb, and E of the chimes' opening. A few measures later, at bar 138, the horns recall their opening motive in transposition from measure two. To enhance this recognizance, the texture is drastically reduced only for this measure.

A' Section

The return of familiar material is easily recognizable at measure 153, which is a reiteration of the A section greatly truncated from its initial appearance. As typical of Higdon, the section commences with a meter change and a crescendo to fortissimo. In measure 153, the ensemble section initially found in measure 29 returns with only slight variations, for example, this passage utilizes the meter of 5/4 rather than the 4/4 used previously. As with the earlier section, there are numerous meter changes but their occurrences here are not identical to the earlier passage; however, all of the significant material found previously, although transposed, is also present: the ascending fourths in the horn, the major chords in root position in the trumpets, and the major chords separated by a major second interval in the strings.

D Section

The final section serves as a summation to the movement and incorporates material from both B and C. Beginning in measure 168, Higdon incorporates the closing measures of the B section (corresponding to measure 76) distinct through the fortissimo trills in the violins and the woodwind flourishes. This passage is greatly expanded from its earlier occurrence to allow a gradual entrance of the entire ensemble; frequent meter changes provide the rhythmic vitality associated with Higdon's music. Of particular interest are the pitches F, Bb, and E first presented in measure 173 in the violas, celli, bass, and contrabassoon. By measure 178, the timpani, and of great importance, the chimes reiterate these pitches repeatedly: first in eighth notes and then gradually slowing down to transition to the opening of the B section.

Measure 187 corresponds with the opening of the B section (measure 51); however, the bassoon and oboe replace the earlier bass clarinet and piccolo as soloists. As with the earlier section, the strings are tacet and will remain so for the rest of the movement. By omitting this timbre from the close of the first movement, an abrupt change in color is automatically evident at the start of movement two, scored exclusively for strings.

Higdon uses the remainder of the movement to feature soli in the orchestra that summarizes the significant passages from the C section. Because of the omission of the strings, there is, of course, no solo quartet here. In measure 197, four woodwinds present soli that differ substantially from their earlier presentation in measure 93. First, the instrumentation does not include the principals of each woodwind but rather two flutes, clarinet, and bass clarinet. Additionally, the texture is homorhythmic, decidedly different than the polyphony that introduced the earlier passage. A few of the rhythmic figures in this passage recall elements of the string quartet solo found earlier but not enough similarity exists to support comparison.

Immediately following the woodwind soli, the percussion, thus far not explored present a solo passage in measure 205. The harp and piano are soloists complemented by an array of instruments that include the small triangle, crotales, glockenspiel, and vibraphone. Thematic material from this section derives from the polyphonic woodwind soli in measure 94 and in fact, is identical except now appearing in homorhythmic texture rather than the staggered entries found previously. This exploration of earlier musical content in new instrumental colors and appearances remains an essential element of Higdon's compositional style.

As the movement nears its close, the orchestration gradually increases and two significant sections of music return. In measure 216, the brass soli echo its earlier occurrence in measure 105 while in bar 239, the oboes recall the trumpets' descending major chords from measure 29. Such chords scored for trumpet are a stylistic trait of Higdon; however, the change in timbre here complements this unassuming ending.

With a composition bearing the title *Concerto for Orchestra*, the full ensemble may be expected to close a movement that featured various solo episodes amidst tutti statements but again, Higdon eschews predictability. As mentioned previously, the strings remain tacet in preparation of a stark timbral contrast to the second movement. Gone from the ending measures is the highly intensive polyphonic texture abounding with rhythmic verve; the movement ends discreetly with a decrease in tempo and dynamics.

Movement Two

The composer's many years in Philadelphia afforded her a familiarity with the "traditionally lush string sound of the Philadelphia Orchestra."[39] About the second movement, Higdon stated, "The entire movement came from that saying 'the Philadelphia string sound.'"[40] With a string section famous for its luxuriance, one would anticipate a slower tempo with harmonic richness. Higdon commented on her original conception of the movement:

> I wanted that to be a slow movement. I fought that for the longest time [...] but the only music coming to me was fast and finally [...] I caved into it. But the entire time I wasn't convinced it was going to work until we got through the first night's performance. I thought I'd write something lush and slow. It wasn't happening probably because I wrote slow music in the third movement.[41]

While the opening movement showcased the full ensemble, the second movement examines the capabilities within the string section exclusively. The composer explained, "I was thinking about *pizz* versus *arco*, thin versus thick, the solo strings. I was debating sound."[42] Because of the homogeneity in timbre, Higdon utilizes different techniques to enhance contrasts. The alternation from pizzicato to arco in addition to string soli and frequent textural changes provides this diversity. Pizzicato scoring is scarcely novel, of course, but due to its absence in the first movement, its sudden use in the opening of the second movement alters the sound considerably.

During the eighteenth century when symphonies and concerti were becoming standard, the tempo of the second movement was frequently slow to contrast with the preceding allegro. This pattern became more flexible throughout the nineteenth century and thus Higdon's employment of two consecutive fast movements is not unorthodox. The tempo is marked dotted quarter note=112–120.

As mentioned in Chapter One, this movement is described in Jones's liner notes as a scherzo,[43] a term derived from the verb "to joke." A scherzo traditionally is cast in a ternary form, triple meter, and in a very fast tempo, all of which are present here; however, Higdon did not conceptualize the movement as a scherzo during the compositional process.[44] She commented on Jones's liner notes, "I wasn't thinking of it that way [as a scherzo] [be]cause my brain was still wanting slow music but it wasn't coming out that way [...] it is kind of scherzo-like [...] it's kind of [a] romping along sort of feeling. It really is a dance for strings."[45]

Initially, a different B section was used, but Higdon composed an alternative to replace the original. She stated:

> I'm glad I threw out the right one [be]cause the one I ended up with was more appropriate. I can't even remember the texture but I listened to it [...] [and thought], "It doesn't work, it doesn't work." And I wrote another one, the one that's currently there and I thought, "I don't know if I like this as much," but it fits better so I left that one.[46]

The form of this movement is the least complex of the entire work:

Measure Numbers	Music	Letter
1–63	Pizzicato, transition to arco, soli for principals	A
64–91	Slower note values, B minor established	B
92–114	Arco, soli from A returns in tutti	A'
115–129	B minor re-established, dominance of fourth and fifth intervals	Coda

Three. Concerto for Orchestra 53

The movement, set in a compound meter, begins with pizzicato and immediately the pitch content stipulates comparison with the first movement. In the composition's opening, the first violins presented an imitative passage based on an octatonic scale, B-C#-D-E-F. In the second movement, the unison violins pluck B-C-D-E, subsequently repeated and expanded to include an F# making the two movements' openings remarkably similar. Higdon did not consciously compose this link but this provides an example of her subconscious compositional method. She stated, "I didn't realize the connection between the first and the second movement. I learned something today. Probably on a subconscious level [...] my brain did make that connection."[47] The five pitches are the basis for much of the second movement and like the opening movement, these pitches are quickly treated imitatively in the lower strings.

The violins, the only instruments sounding in the first measure, play in unison while stating the opening motive, making the link to the first movement abundantly clear. Immediately following in measure two, the texture becomes imitative between the violins and viola accompanied by a continuous B pedal pizzicato in the celli and bass. The motives that pass through the strings are very concise because, as the composer explained:

> I wanted to write longer lines for the strings. I went into Curtis [...] and I asked the kids in my class [...] "How long can you do these [pizzicato] at this speed without hurting yourself?" They said, "Well you better only do it a beat or two because that's actually pretty fast." It was a practical consideration to keep from hurting the players. It looks like a dance because it's getting handed off and I didn't realize that because I stayed backstage in most of the performances. The people who were in the balcony could actually see the trade-offs, but it's just a practical consideration of what would be dangerous for the players because they could hurt themselves easily at that speed. This is [be]cause the kids at Curtis said, "Dr. Higdon, don't do more than this." I [thought], "All right, I'll figure out a way to write it." So that's how we got the motive the way it is[48] (Figure 3–3).

In measure ten, the pedal pizzicato in the celli and bass is lowered by a half step to Bb and similarly, much of the opening motive is also transposed down a minor second. The consistent presentation of the motive combined with the pedal pizzicato continues through bar 17 where the motive is moved to the bass, cello, and viola.

A different character is achieved at measure 17 through dynamic contrast, the motive beginning on the original B natural, and as noted above, the low strings' presentation of the motive. Additionally, the composer provides the musical indication *ala guitara* above the violins as they sound a rhythmic ostinato pattern in double stops. The result is a restatement of the opening in a completely varied context.

In measure 21, the lower strings maintain a separate homorhythmic

Figure 3-3. *Concerto for Orchestra*; II, mm. 1-2.

texture from the violins that provides a brief moment of relaxation from the preceding polyphonic activity. This measure serves as transitional material to the new musical idea in the subsequent bar. The tutti strings converge in measure 22 to commence a new ostinato beneath the five soloists.

Higdon's trademark perfect fifth interval appears in various guises during this solo passage. The ostinato pizzicati of the violins are separated by this interval while the viola and celli are separated by a perfect fourth, the inversion of the fifth. In addition, the first violin solo's opening pitches sound an ascending perfect fifth. As mentioned earlier, rising sounds are prevalent throughout this entire composition and hence, it is significant that the initial solo here begins with this distinguishing feature.

The principal soli are performed arco, the first appearance of the style in this movement. The soli are neither imitative in pitch content nor rhythm and act solely as independent melodic lines albeit with staggered entrances. Due to the pizzicato of the string tutti section, the arco soloists are clearly heard. It is worth noting that the viola, cello, and bass soli begin with an ascending contour.

The pizzicato ostinato pattern in the tutti strings gradually diminishes before becoming tacet in measure 29 when the homorhythmic texture of the ostinato is transferred to the soloists. Here, the violins are separated by the interval of a perfect fourth, as are the celli and the basses, simply an inversion of the Higdon perfect fifth.

In measure 31, the soloists rejoin the ensemble sections to present a unified arco sound with a forte dynamic to create tension further enhanced by the same staggered entrances of the preceding solo section. The order of entrances and pitch content mirrors the earlier musical material with the five parts transposed.[49]

Measure 44 concludes the tutti restatement and the music returns to the polyphonic activity found in the movement's opening but performed arco. Although the pitches are almost exact replications of measure ten, the change from pizzicato presents a stark distinction. In addition, Higdon notates accents in the upper strings' melodic lines that were absent from the corresponding preceding passage. The accents are neither rhythmically consistent nor do they appear to conform to any specific pattern which greatly increases the unpredictability, urgency, and momentum of the movement.

Measure 51 corresponds to earlier material from measure 17 with several adjustments. The homorhythmic ostinato double stop chords previously sounded by the violins now appear in the celli and bass. The intervals of the celli are comprised of minor thirds, simply inversions of the previously heard second violins' major sixths.[50] The "ala guitara" indication is omitted in measure 51 and the ostinato chords are no longer arpeggiated but performed arco in an innovative polyrhythmic pattern: the celli play consecutive eighth notes in the compound meter while the basses present duplets. Above this altered ostinato pattern, the violins employ imitation at the octave. Although neither the structure of the melody nor the pacing of the imitation corresponds to measure 17, the ostinato pattern and polyphonic texture provide the connecting link while allowing the violins and the viola to explore new material.

New melodic motives appear in measure 59 in the upper strings while the celli and bass continue the ostinato. As in measure 22, the ostinato gradually occurs less frequently before becoming altogether tacet. The violins and viola return to an imitative polyphonic texture in which the descending fourth interval in the viola line is echoed and expanded to a fifth by the second violins and later the firsts betraying once again the significance of this interval.

The B section begins in measure 64 and although not immediately apparent, the key is B minor as demonstrated through the priority given to the tonic and the appearance of appropriate accidentals. The first violins begin this passage, distinct through its much slower rhythmic values that contrast considerably the flurry of activity prevalent in the A sections. A previously unseen motive appears in the cello in measure 68. Because this motive is the only material in the lower strings, its sudden appearance is quite conspicuous. The new motive, with an ascending contour, is featured several times in the celli before being imitated in the bass and eventually the viola.

These sightings appear more frequently and ultimately overlap at a rapid pace.

Returning musical material appears in a new guise to unify the movement in measure 81. The second violins sound repeated major sixth intervals (along with minor thirds in the first violins) that briefly recall a similar scoring in measures 17 and 51. The scoring and consistent repetitions unite this B section with the surrounding A sections.

The returning A section begins at measure 92 complete with the Higdon trait of a meter change. By truncating the original motive to only three notes, the music is intensified naturally. The melodic interest retains the initial scoring of violins and viola with the Bb ostinato scored separately for cello and bass. As the movement nears its close, Higdon returns to several musical ideas heard previously in a varied order from their initial presentations. Measure 99 corresponds to measure 51 while in measure 107, Higdon recalls the solo section from measure 22 that is nearly identical but without designated soli.

The coda begins in measure 115 with emphasis in the first violins and celli on the interval favored by Higdon: perfect fifths (or their inversions). Ostinato patterns, so characteristic of this composer, appear in all five string parts and outline the key of B minor. This ostinato varies after several statements and by measure 119, only ten measures from the close, the basses regularly sound the pitches of B and F#, leaving little doubt to the tonal center.

The final pitch of the movement is a unison B scored as a snap pizzicato thus bringing the movement full circle to its pizzicato opening. Higdon stated her purpose in scoring a snap pizzicato, "I thought, 'I'd love to hear the Philadelphia Orchestra do a snap pizz together.' All right, let's put it in, that's actually how it happened. Like a kid in a candy shop to be quite honest. Someone had given me the biggest box of crayons around and I was going to have fun with it [...] joy in sound."[51]

Movement Three, "Mystical"

The third movement features not only individual sections of the orchestra but soli for principal players as well. The result is a more extensive exploration between the full ensemble, sections, and soloists than the first movement and displays the orchestral capabilities under the hands of a master craftsperson. Higdon recalled the process of writing this movement:

> It's a concerto for orchestra, and individuals make up an orchestra. So I actually drew out a little map for myself. Because the second movement was going to be just strings, I knew

I couldn't start the third movement with string solos—the color contrast wouldn't be enough. So I decided right off the bat to start with the winds. I knew the brass would be the best to push the emotion up in a piece. So I thought I should do the winds first, then the string solos, and then I'll put the brass after. Just simply thinking about color made me design the piece the way that I did. I wasn't sure it was going to work, because that's a lot of different music compacted into small segments. But they seem to flow into each other.[52]

Unlike the opening two movements, the third carries a descriptive adjective rather than a sole metronome marking. The tempo is placed at quarter note=92–108 accompanied by the term "mystical" which Higdon does not specifically define. Many of the instrumental soli are presented in groups of three; however, Higdon stated:

> The number three doesn't have to do with anything [such as a reference to the Holy Trinity]; it was a coincidence just because that was the size of orchestra. The winds were in threes because [...] it's too expensive to play a piece if winds [are] in four. It was a practical consideration.[53]

The movement begins with a soft dynamic marking to enhance the mystical character. Similar to the second movement's opening link to the first, connections are immediately apparent between the second movement and the beginning of the third. The lower strings alternate between pizzicato and arco while the opening pitches in the strings, harp, and piano consistently sound the pitches of F and Bb, notes that figured prominently in the preceding movement and of course, were the opening interval of the entire work.

When asked about the unifying elements between movements two and three, Higdon stated this was not initially intended:

> I hadn't thought about it [the similar alternation of pizzicato and arco styles in movements two and three] because I was trying to create mysterious sounds and I knew it was like when you whisper, you draw them in. I knew if I did that in the strings it would [increase the attention of] the audience [...] I saw a movie around that time [with] a sound effect [...] I remember thinking, "That's an interesting sound," but [it] is so different that it make[s] you stop in that movement. So, even though I was writing that movement first I thought, "Let's create some magic to set up the solos." What would create solo magic? I always find string harmonics interesting.[54]

Although this technique was not consciously utilized as a link, it is undoubtedly the fruition of Higdon's intuitive style.

As with the preceding movement, the third movement can be broken down into a large ternary form as follows:

Measure Number	Music	Letter
1–35	Introduction of significant material: string harmonics, major chord accompaniment, chimes outline perfect fourth, flute soli	Introduction

Measure Number	Music	Letter
35–127	Opens with harmonic strings from Introduction, features all woodwinds followed by tutti statement	A
127–171	Features strings	B
172–233	Opens with harmonic strings from Introduction, features brass with melodies borrowed from A followed by tutti statement	A'
234–251	Returns all significant material from Introduction: string harmonics, major chord accompaniment, chimes outline perfect fourth, now with only one flute solo	Coda

Introduction

The introduction provides all significant material explored in this movement (Figure 3–4). As mentioned previously, the opening string harmonics emphasize F and Bb drawing prominence to the tonality of the preceding movement; these string harmonics recur several times as transitional material. One of the most important unifying elements of this opening is the descending perfect fourth found in the chimes in measure eight, echoed in the piano that unquestionably relates to the opening of the entire *Concerto*. Finally, in measure ten, the violas are divided into three to present major chords that play a substantial role in nearly all of the following accompanimental material. This orchestration was chosen for contrast in range and timbre to the opening flute solo[55]; it is worth noting, however, that such scoring is stylistic of Higdon.

As noted above, the composition of *Concerto for Orchestra* began with this movement because Higdon already had soli for specific musicians in mind. Atypical of Higdon, she composed this movement from the beginning rather than the middle. The opening features the principal flute and it is not surprising that when Higdon embarked on this elaborate work, she began with the instrument of her youth. She recalled, "The choice for flute was connected with my background … there was a certain comfort there in knowing the instrument, but it also just felt appropriate, since I came to composing through flute."[56] The principal flute in measure 12 derives from $OCT_{1,2}$ accompanied by the continuous major chords in the viola and the descending perfect fourth in the chimes. The solo flute is joined at measure 25 by the second and third flutes in homorhythmic texture. Simultaneously, the major chord

Three. Concerto for Orchestra

Figure 3-4. *Concerto for Orchestra*; III, mm. 1-6.

progression in the violas expands to include the celli enhancing the warm luxuriance of the music.

A Section

A brief transition that recalls the movement's opening leads into the A section which features the remaining woodwinds. The major chord accompaniment scored initially for the violas appears re-orchestrated for three trombones beneath the principal oboe solo in measure 42, based largely on the OCT $_{0,1}$ scale (Figure 3-5). Similar to the flutes' material in the introduction, the principal oboist presents a brief melody before being joined by the others in the section; in bar 56, upon the entrance of the second oboe, the trombones are replaced by the returning violas. Here, a change in texture provides a stark contrast between the presentation of the flutes and oboes. While the flutes exhibited homorhythmic texture, the oboes present polyphonic lines initially as a duet before branching into a trio. As the number of oboes increases so too do the accompanimental lower strings with the celli and basses joining the violas.

Figure 3-5. *Concerto for Orchestra*; III, mm. 42–47.

The clarinets follow as soloists in measure 78 entering in reverse order from the flutes and oboes. They present the material in homorhythmic texture before the principal clarinet is given the solo while the major chord accompanimental pattern is re-orchestrated for the trumpets with added syncopations. As evidenced previously, major chords for three trumpets are stylistic of this composer, but here, the scoring is used to vary earlier material; furthermore, throughout this section, second violins alternate major seconds later switching to minor sevenths in *divisi*. The composer remarked on the change of intervals:

> I did invert that. I do remember doing that intentionally there [be]cause I wanted the same sound but I needed something different. It had to be different enough to clear out for the clarinet to be heard along with the trumpets. And I did look at the second violin and thought, "If I do a minor 7th, I'm going to have a problem here because that's a wide leap, so I [have] to divide the strings to thin the sound enough that the clarinet can break though." It's a problem; that leap really makes the sound pop out much more than I wanted. I wasn't thinking theoretically in terms of the harmonic movement but I was thinking [of] the inversion of the major 2nd. I remember thinking, "Yeah the 7th would work well" [...] [I had] to change the sound [to] be interesting.[57]

The principal clarinet solo ceases abruptly in measure 95 followed immediately by the bassoons' featured section and again, Higdon varies the manner in which the soloists are presented. The principal bassoon provides the melodic line, a variation of the oboe solo from measure 42. Beneath the solo, the second bassoon and the contrabassoon move in thirds before all three combine to form a homorhythmic texture. The second bassoon and the contrabassoon, previously marked *mezzo piano*, join the principal in a forceful final statement that creates a spirited transition to the full ensemble. Throughout this section, additional soli are found in both violin sections. This unusual orchestration remains typical of Higdon although here, it was a practical consideration due to the soft timbre of the bassoon.

Beginning in measure 108, the remainder of the orchestra gradually re-enters beginning with the flutes and first violins presenting the composer's signature major chords. The intensity rises slowly with increased scoring of these chords and the inclusion of the full orchestra to close the A section. In measure 121, the bass, celli, timpani, tuba, contrabassoon, harp, and the left hand of the piano consistently present the intervals F-B and B-E, an augmented fourth and perfect fourth, respectively, the intervallic link appearing throughout the entire composition. Because these intervals occur in the lowest instruments, the sound is unmistakable.

B Section

As a brief transition to the B section begins, the orchestration thins to only the woodwinds complemented by the chimes' descending perfect fourth motive from the introduction. In measure 129, the strings return as soloists while the woodwinds gradually diminish in number and volume. Unlike the polyphony previously utilized to feature the woodwinds, the strings begin immediately with a homorhythmic texture that recalls a similar instrumentation in the opening movement. Throughout this solo section there is a noticeable omission of the major chord accompaniment that figured substantially in the A section. This pattern is replaced by the alternating major seconds in the woodwinds, borrowed material from the second violins in measure 78.

The first string instrument to be featured is the bass with a melodic line scored in a relatively high range followed by a concise homorhythmic phrase by all five soloists. As the string section progresses, each individual instrument receives a smaller solo. The second violin solo enters in measure 139 and similar to the bass, is scored in a high range. Particularly noteworthy in measure 146 is the pairing of the cello solo with a descending fourth in the vibraphone, initially outlining identical pitches as those in the chimes in this movement's introduction. The lengthiest string solo in the section is presented by the concertmaster in measure 159, an ascending passage that returns in the coda. This significant solo closes the B section. In comparison to the woodwinds, the strings' soli are greatly truncated because of the attention this section received in the preceding movement. Of importance, all five of the string soli begin with an ascending contour, one of the central features of *Concerto for Orchestra*.

A' Section

In measure 172, Higdon turns again to the alternation of pizzicato and arco from the introduction as a transition to the next section. Although this appearance is rhythmically varied from its original statement, the musical material remains quite recognizable and continues a sense of unity within the movement. The brass is prominently featured in the A' section but in contrast to the woodwinds, Higdon does not present each section individually. The horns herald the opening of this section with the composer's signature major chords in measure 175 while the strings complete the transition passage.

In measure 177, the tuba presents the first solo, quickly followed by the first trombone and bass trombone; the melodic material is an exact replica of the opening of the principal oboe solo in the A section in bar 42. In this appearance, however, the theme is produced polyphonically. Previously, the principal oboe was the sole purveyor of melody, while here Higdon alternates the line between separate brass instruments. The horns also allude to the aforementioned oboe solo in their duplication of the opening interval of a minor sixth in measure 180 while the accompaniment provides an additional commonality: the major chords, scored for three trombones in the earlier passage, return in the low strings. While introducing familiar material, Higdon has imbued it with a sparkle of originality and freshness (Figure 3–6).

In measure 191, Higdon combines the material from the oboe duet and trio. The third trumpet and the second trombone present the duet of measure 56 while simultaneously, the tuba varies the third oboe line from measure 63. As above, Higdon has produced contrast and repetition simultaneously through a mixture of timbres and varying the placement of musical statements. This complex musical activity increases until the orchestra returns to its full grandeur in measure 210 when Higdon partially references the orches-

Figure 3–6. *Concerto for Orchestra*; III, mm. 177–182.

tral section that closed the A section. This varied restatement progresses until measure 231, followed by an immediate thinning of the texture in preparation for the coda.

Coda

The coda of this movement recalls all significant previous material and begins unassumingly in measure 234 with the entrance of a solo for the first two stands of celli. In measure 238, the strings sound a truncated version of the harmonics from the introduction and transitional material. The melodic material is presented by the principal flute in measure 239 in a much abbreviated account of its solo in the introduction. The remaining principal woodwinds present sustained major and minor chords, related to the accompanying material present throughout the movement. In measure 244, the celli recall the violas in the introduction at measure ten through the *con sordino* marking and the division of the section into three that present major chords in a similar rhythm and range. Simultaneously, this passage recalls all of the accompanying material found in both the A and A' sections. In the concluding measures, the chimes sound a descending perfect fourth, transposed up a minor second from the introduction, but clearly connecting the coda with the movement's opening. Finally, and as mentioned previously, the concertmaster's solo, paired with the chimes, echoes similar material from measure 159. These numerous references to the introduction bring this central, significant movement full circle.

Movement Four

Movement four exclusively features the percussion section expanded to include the harp, piano, and celesta. Unlike other sections of the ensemble, the percussion was not highlighted in the previous movement. In fact, the work up to this point has provided little solo attention to this section; thus, an enormous contrast is immediately present. As mentioned previously, the scoring for strings in the second movement and percussion here strengthen the arch-form structure. The two movements also occupy similar durations that balance the elaborate and lengthier full orchestral movements.

On the Pittsburgh Symphony's website, Higdon explained her motivation for the unorthodox percussion scoring:

> I did this because the percussion section is the one section of the orchestra that has developed the most in the twentieth century. It's the one section that has added instruments, and the

skill of the players has probably developed more than in any other section. I decided to make a movement which would have the quietest sounds in this entire piece in the percussion.[58]

An additional rationale for the movement was simply "because Don Liuzzi the timpanist wanted to play percussion."[59] Higdon recalled her compositional process:

> I also realized that everyone would assume that the percussion movement would of course be loud because it's drums. That's kind of an automatic assumption. So I made the decision early on that the percussion movement should be the quietest point, the beginning of the percussion movement should be the very quietest moment in the entire piece [...] I was determined to use as many different sounds as possible. And I only picked instruments that I thought an orchestra would have in house so they wouldn't have to rent a lot of instruments.[60]

The fourth movement bears the slowest tempo of the entire composition, quarter note=42, providing an opportunity to savor the timbres still unfamiliar to many an ear. The movement begins with pitched instruments played by a bow. By using a technique commonly associated with strings, there is another connection between movements two and four that further enhances the arch-form. The composer stated:

> I hadn't thought of that. It could very well be [...] I probably stole that [bowed percussion] from George Crumb. All of us were doing it at Penn when we were studying and I did it in *blue cathedral* in the vibes.[61] It worked so well that I thought, "What would it be like [...] to have a bunch of percussionists doing that?" so it was a curiosity of sound.[62]

Higdon's rationale for the slow tempo combined with a soft dynamic is due in part to Maestro Sawallisch. She stated:

> I wanted him to hear that not all percussion was loud. He just didn't want percussion so I [thought], "If I write really slow at the beginning and it's really quiet maybe he'll be convinced by it." It actually worked. That became one of his more favorite movements. He didn't want to rehearse that movement; in fact, he didn't rehearse it until the dress rehearsal.[63]

The composer remarked on the opening orchestration, "[The goal was] to make it mysterious. It's like the string opening in the third movement [...] I wanted to do the same thing with the percussion to make the audience kind of lean in a little and figure out what the sound was."[64] The instrumentation at the close of the third movement is greatly reduced but includes the chimes and the glockenspiel; however, these higher pitched instruments were not scored to serve as a connecting link to the fourth movement and in fact, the composer initially had concerns about the similarity. She recalled:

> I remember having anxiety about having that high percussion sound at the end of the 3rd movement, because I knew that the color was so similar to what I wanted to do in the 4th movement. I had a serious day of debating whether to change the color at the end of the 3rd, but in the end, I decided just to go with my initial impulse and put it in (knowing that I could change it later if it didn't work).[65]

The composer explained how the rehearsals informed her final edits to the opening:

> When I originally wrote it, I actually had written that they [the percussionists] should let [the sound] vibrate through. But in the dress rehearsal, Sawallisch [said], "We should stop the sound and make it clearer" and that was the right decision. It sounds better [...] so I changed it. It's more work for the percussionists but it clears out the chords enough that you can hear them. When they were ringing through, it was noisy.[66]

Higdon also remembered that

> the percussionists were so proud of having their own movement. I finished that movement a whole year before the premiere so I gave them the music saying, "Tell me, can you do all this?" They passed the parts around [and] said, "It's do-able, it's hard but it's do-able." I was surprised that movement worked better than I thought it would.[67]

So enamored with the music of this movement, the percussionists encouraged Higdon to transcribe the score for percussion ensemble.[68]

The composer features the percussion in a systematic fashion. Beginning with pitched instruments, a small transitional passage leads to scoring for non-pitched instruments which is reminiscent of the second movement's rotation from pizzicato to arco. Higdon found this movement to be particularly difficult to compose because she "had to find a convincing way to go from pitched to non-pitched instruments and that was hard. The wood-blocks were kind of my in-between. Really, it was difficult."[69] Because the movement demonstrates the variety in a percussion section as it switches from pitched to non-pitched instruments, there is no sectionalized form.

Throughout the movement, intensity is gradually increased by an acceleration of the tempo in phases, a comparison she likens to a "victrola being wound up"[70] that erupts into the attacca finale. The composer commented:

> It was kind of dangerous doing just percussion in the fourth movement [be]cause [...] if it's a concerto for orchestra, it's the orchestra. I also was fascinated to see if I could speed the orchestra up [be]cause I didn't know any other piece that did it quite that way so I thought, "This'll probably [be] the last time I'll ever be asked to write an orchestra piece, so let's throw that in. Let me see if I can actually make that happen." Part of it was actually just a compositional challenge.[71]

Higdon also imagined marching bands at times during this movement. She stated, "I played percussion in marching band and I thought, 'Wouldn't it be funny to have a little tribute to marching band in there?'"[72]

The fourth movement's opening texture is homorhythmic; indeed, the composer has instructed "Freely & Together" as a musical direction. The timpanist and the second percussionist play the vibraphones while the first and third percussionists are stationed at the crotales. Immediately with the first pitch, the Higdon perfect fifth is prevalent as it separates the vibraphone lines and the distance between the crotales. Throughout the opening measures, an abundance of dynamics is employed quickly that grow louder from mezzo piano to forte. Such quick and striking contrasts in volume are somewhat atypical of Higdon's orchestral music (Figure 3-7).

Figure 3-7. *Concerto for Orchestra*; IV, mm. 1-5.

The harp enters in measure six arpeggiating different perfect fifth intervals while punctuations of open fifths continue below by the percussionists. Throughout this intervallic activity, a significant motive is introduced initially by the crotales and subsequently echoed by the celesta. The motive is an ascending augmented fourth, the same interval that featured prominently in the opening of the *Concerto*. Its appearance here unifies the work and returns in various guises through measure 22.

Measure ten ends with a rest that clears the texture and sound; the subsequent passage expands the instrumentation to include the small and large triangle and the glockenspiel, performed by the timpanist, sounding an augmented fourth interval. The homorhythmic, sustained parallel fifths of the movement's opening continue to be featured in the vibraphone but also in the celesta and chimes in much faster rhythms. Nowhere else in this work are the Higdon parallel fifths more prominent. These intervals comprise an essential part of the melodic section and only begin to subside with the introduction of non-pitched instruments.

Beneath the parallel fifths in measure 20, Higdon alternates the vibraphone and woodblock in the second percussionist's part that anticipates the eventual substitution of the former by the latter. This exchange is significant and heralds the beginning of the transition to the non-pitched section. Once the second percussionist begins this alternation, the fluctuation occurs at a faster rate and only a few measures later in measure 24, the second percussionist is playing only woodblocks.

Following the path of the second percussionist, the timpanist's part (playing the glockenspiel) undergoes a similar transformation. Beginning in measure 24, the scoring changes to temple blocks which along with the woodblocks, are instructed to play softly for a smoother transition.

As stated previously, the tempo undergoes multiple *accelerandi* throughout this movement. The initial increase occurs in measure 29 with a new tempo in the following bar that places the quarter note at 60. This tempo change announces the beginning of the non-pitched section but the woodblocks and temple blocks remain to facilitate the transition. The passage featuring the non-pitched percussion utilizes an entire measure of rest (although the meter is 1/4 so in actuality only a single beat) twice in the first six bars to clear the sound. The changes in tempo begin to occur more frequently and the next employment of an accelerando transpires at bar 42. With the quarter note now placed at 80, Higdon has nearly doubled the tempo from the opening. The piano, technically a percussive instrument, is instructed by the composer here to "use other hand to dampen strings very close to hammer ... [THE SOUND SHOULD BE VERY DRY]."[73] The piano part comprises consecutive sixteenth notes in its lowest register. The resulting dry sound combined with the low range evokes a more percussive and non-pitched atmosphere. To further increase the intensity, Higdon notates an extremely quick crescendo in the piano that carries the dynamics to its extremes from *pianissimo* to *fortissimo* within a single measure.

In bar 45, the remaining percussionists join in the fortissimo dynamic. The high rhythmic complexity is complemented by a solo for timpani that contains intervals significant to this composer: seconds, fifths, and sevenths. Of particular interest is the cleverly hidden augmented fourth, now heard as an augmented 11th that connects this section to the opening of the movement as well as to the work as a whole (Figure 3–8).

Another accelerando and crescendo appear in measure 50 and the

Figure 3–8. *Concerto for Orchestra*; IV, measure 45–46, timpani solo.

quarter note is increased to 90 in the subsequent bar that is complemented by a change in texture that incorporates brief occurrences of homorhythmic unity. These instances provide a succinct moment of relaxation to the high rhythmic tension created previously and the composer uses this opportunity to alter the instrumentation by introducing the tom-toms in the first and second percussionists and the floor tom-toms for the third. To feature only non-pitched instruments, the piano is omitted from this point and the timpani no longer presents solo material. The composer utilizes frequent dynamic contrasts that span the gamut of sound possibilities similar to the opening of the movement; however, the context could not be more different.

Measure 64 includes unorthodox instructions for the timpanist and the first percussionist (still on tom-toms) by having them "play rim of drum [whichever drum is convenient]."[74] By playing the rim, this non-pitched instrumental passage has reached its peak and when this section ceases at measure 72, the coda begins to segue into the finale.

An introduction of the final set of percussive instruments begins in the coda and includes castanets, maracas, and sandpaper blocks. As previously noted, the fourth movement leads attacca to the full orchestral, final movement. Higdon connects the movements through a transitional passage here of new ostinati that continue into and link the subsequent movement. Each of the percussion lines figures prominently in this transition. The maracas play a consistent eighth-note rhythm while the castanets have a syncopated ostinato (Figure 3–9). These rhythms remain consistent until the final bars of the movement further revealing the composer's penchant for ostinati. The castanets continue their ostinato pattern from measure 72 that repeats in two measure intervals. The rhythm changes to consecutive sixteenth notes in bar 89 accompanied by a *subito* forte dynamic that heightens the anticipation of

Figure 3–9. *Concerto for Orchestra*; IV, mm. 72–74.

the final movement. In the opening measure of the fifth movement, the castanets occur less frequently before becoming tacet altogether by measure three. This instrument's main role is to increase tension and rhythmic drive while the other percussionists provide the primary unification between the two movements.

Similar to the castanets, the second percussionist's maracas continue its own rhythm from measure 72. The final three bars of the fourth movement replace the maraca with the tom-toms and begin a more rhythmically complex pattern. It is the latter instrumentation and new ostinato that function as the transition between movements. The sandpaper blocks, played by the first percussionist, follow a related path that continues a rhythmic ostinato pattern. Beginning in measure 91, the connecting link to the finale is presented through a thirty-second note rhythm that lasts through measure 15 of the fifth movement.

Unlike the three percussionists, the timpanist's part does not employ an ostinato during the transitional passage. Because the timpani are a pitched instrument, the transition combines rhythmic and melodic material; however, neither conforms to a strict pattern. In measure 91, a consistent rhythmic and intervallic content emerges that are also found in the opening of the finale yet the patterns vary considerably. The pitches in the timpani are based on the $OCT_{2,3}$ scale that will also be used in the finale (Figure 3–10).

Forte dynamics close the fourth movement while the attacca finale opens with a more subdued mezzo piano. Regarding this sudden change, Higdon remarked, "I originally had loud dynamics in the percussion [but] that didn't work. I had to have them come down to *piano* to clear out for the strings. That was changed in the rehearsals."[75] The fourth movement erupts immediately into the finale where the other three sections of the orchestra rejoin the percussionists.

Movement Five

Because the musical material that connects the final two movements is similar and played without pause, the beginning of the finale is unassuming. While the tempo remains the same, the meter changes to 4/4. Only after the syncopated entrance of the violins does it become obvious that a new movement has commenced. Like the preceding movement, this work is in paratactic form with no significant sections of contrast and repetition; however, Higdon's orchestral compositions abound in unifying material that establishes brief moments of familiarity to the listener. Here, she incorporates musical

Figure 3-10. *Concerto* for *Orchestra*; IV, mm. 91–95 and V, mm. 1–5.

material from the previous movements. In fact, the finale may be viewed as a coda to the entire composition. Higdon responded to this interpretation:

> It is. It had to be something that wrapped everything up. I also want[ed] some swing in that last movement, too but I knew the conductor who was 82 wouldn't exactly be able to swing so I had to figure out a way to write it so that it would swing on its own [...] I know that everything in my brain was connected from the previous movements though [be]cause that's just the way my brain works.[76]

The opening measures of the finale build the intensity from the previous movement through unison violin scoring marked forte above the percussion ostinati. Beginning in measure four, a reference to an earlier musical technique appears in the cello line through the arco and pizzicato alternation that recalls the second and third movements. The pitch content of the instruments utilizes the OCT$_{2,3}$ scale providing a link to previous sounds heard throughout the work.

The bassoons enter in measure ten with a trill that encompasses vast dynamic contrasts in only two beats, uncharacteristic of this composer. Following the cessation of the bassoon trills and percussion ostinati in measure 16, Higdon supplies a new repeating pattern in the celli and basses that spans two measures. Unrelated to the material in the percussion, this new motive begins, significantly, on the pitches F-B natural-F-Bb that draws attention to the augmented and perfect fourths that are crucial to the *Concerto*. Additionally, the violins present melodic material based solely on the OCT $_{1,2}$ scale. In the opening of the finale, therefore, an accumulation of recurring musical material is presented: the continuation of the ostinato percussion patterns, the alternation of string techniques in the celli, and the octatonic scale.

A section featuring several woodwind soli begins in measure 24. Unlike the preceding movements that incorporated extensive solo material, presentations in the finale are greatly truncated. It is interesting to note that in the three movements that featured the full ensemble, the initial soli are performed by the woodwinds. In this presentation, the scoring utilizes four woodwinds: the principal clarinet, oboe, flute, and third flute with the timbre of the bassoon omitted entirely. Beneath the woodwinds, a significant pattern for marimba and glockenspiel emerges that reappears throughout the finale. In this first appearance, the instruments alternate the pitches of Bb and B complemented by a consistent F in the piano and harp to sound perfect and diminished fifths that recall the significance of these pitches and intervals used throughout the *Concerto*.

Following the brief appearance of woodwinds, the strings reenter in measure 28 with the material from measure 16 of the finale transposed a major second higher (resulting in the OCT $_{0,1}$ scale). This same passage returns in measure 34 transposed up a minor third (but retaining the OCT $_{0,1}$ scale in the violins). The sequencing of earlier musical material at steadily rising pitches increases the momentum. In each of these three recurrences, the timpani present rhythms found earlier in the transition between movements four and five.

As with movements one and three, string soli are featured next in measure 32. Similar to the woodwinds, the length of the soli is greatly truncated and the orchestration does not include the entire section. Four violinists from each section comprise the soloists which present two major chords in homorhythmic texture separated by an interval of a major second, an always significant Higdon trait. An accelerando appears in measure 38, the first to be utilized within the finale that serves as an extension of the tempo increases in the fourth movement. In measure 42, joining the orchestra for the first time since the third movement, the trumpets and trombones also sound major chords separated by the interval of a second. The violin soloists continue their respective chords independent of those in the brass but the pattern is quickly monopolized by the latter when the violins become tacet in measure 44.

Simultaneously, separate ostinato patterns begin in the viola, the vibraphone, and the snare drum. The composer directs the viola section to sound their ostinato "angrily."[77] Such markings are used sparingly by Higdon and when present, must be made note of. Marked fortissimo, the violas are instructed to play *portamento*, a technique used frequently in the third movement; however, here the mood contrasts greatly from the mysterious, earlier setting.

Beginning in measure 52, the left hand of the piano, the viola, and celli alternate quickly between the pitches of B and F to reference the unifying interval of a diminished fifth (augmented fourth) heard throughout the work. Following this brief reminiscence, the pianist, doubled by the strings, presents two major chords separated by a major second in measure 60. Although this bitonality is common with Higdon, the specific orchestration and voicing here recalls Section A of the opening movement through the scoring of the minor sixth intervals in the first violins and violas coupled with the perfect fifths in the second violins and celli (Figure 3–11). In measure 65, an accelerando is employed while the chords in the piano and strings continue to rise in pitch until the new tempo at bar 67 is established as quarter note=138–142. Immediately the trumpets re-enter to double the strings and right hand of the piano in extending the major chord progressions.

In measure 73, the alternation between pizzicato and arco in the celli and bass recalls both the opening of the finale as well as the second and third movements. Significantly, all pizzicato markings in this section are scored as

Figure 3–11. *Concerto for Orchestra*; V, mm. 60–61.

snap pizzicati, a technique used for the final pitch of the second movement. In measure 83, Higdon continues to recall the string movement through the *col legno battuto* marking; historically, *battuto* indicated guitar strumming[78] and thus serves synonymously to the second movement's marking of *ala guitara*. Additionally, the soli for violas and celli sound ascending major chords, separated by the interval of a major second, to provide the unifying rising contour found throughout *Concerto for Orchestra*. Although moving major chords are frequent in Higdon's compositions, this specific instrumentation reflects the numerous appearances of similar scoring in the third movement to make this passage instantly recognizable. The summation of previous musical ideas culminates in the percussionists' reference to the preceding movement. Percussionists one and two are instructed to "PLAY THE RIM OF ANY DRUM"[79] while the third plays sandpaper blocks to evoke the fourth movement simply through timbre. The section closes with an accelerando in measure 91 that increases the tempo to quarter note=142–150.

In measure 93, the harp plays a figure that correlates to the marimba in measure 24. When the pattern first appeared, it served as accompanimental material to the solo woodwinds; here it complements the string soli. The two passages are undoubtedly related because the string soli imitate the woodwinds. While the violins, viola, and celli present the solo material of the woodwinds, the bass solo continues the pizzicato and arco alternation. To complete the instrumentation, the piano oscillates between B and F, the tritone so significant in this work (Figure 3–12).

Figure 3–12. *Concerto for Orchestra*; V, mm. 91–96.

In measure 101, the strings return to tutti scoring with content based on the $OCT_{1,2}$ scale. The momentum increases through an imitative and rapid dialogue between the violas and celli. Of great significance, in measure 107, the horns present, almost identically, the opening motive from measure two of the first movement while the piano and glockenspiel play descending augmented and perfect fourth intervals to further reference the *Concerto*'s opening.

Measure 118 initiates the final change in tempo to quarter note=160–180. After a plethora of accelerandi sprinkled throughout the fourth and fifth movements, this increase places the tempo at twice the initial speed of the finale's opening for a riveting conclusion delivered through an explosion of instrumental color. Maintaining the trend set thus far, the closing section continues to develop material from preceding movements. Higdon's characteristic employment of an ostinato returns in the bass clarinet, celli, and double bass that emphasizes the pitches of B, Bb, and F. Although less prominent, the viola's countermelody places a degree of significance on B and F assisted by the glockenspiel and piano. Additionally, the trumpets resume here after a prolonged silence and the sudden entry provides exuberance to an already electrifying aural palette. One may reasonably anticipate the composer's characteristic major chord progressions in the trumpets but Higdon is rarely predictable and the sonorities are varied. The majority are indeed major, but she also includes minor and augmented chords to combine fresh sounding music with the familiar. The primary melodic material, however, is presented by the violins with content derived solely from $OCT_{1,2}$.

In measure 134, the marimba and harp recall the duet in measures 24 and 93 but in this final appearance, Higdon combines the timbres of the two previous statements. The ongoing experimentation of instrumental color displays once again, the composer's great emphasis on the joy of sound. In measure 140, an entire earlier section is referenced while maintaining emphasis on the pitches B and F. The woodwinds, strings, piano, and vibraphone sound various patterns of these notes that resemble the material at measure 52. The connection to the corresponding earlier passage is further strengthened through an identical major chord progression presented by the trumpets while the trombones vary only slightly (Figure 3–13). In measure 151, the piano and second violins return to the alternating figure initially presented in measure 52. Rather than shifting between B and F, however, Higdon transposes the music to G and Db to foreshadow the final, unexpected tonality.

Beginning in measure 153, the piano and the bassoons introduce a forte motive derived from $OCT_{0,1}$ in accented eighth notes that lasts precisely one measure. This brief rhythmic line returns twice separated by the strings'

Three. Concerto for Orchestra

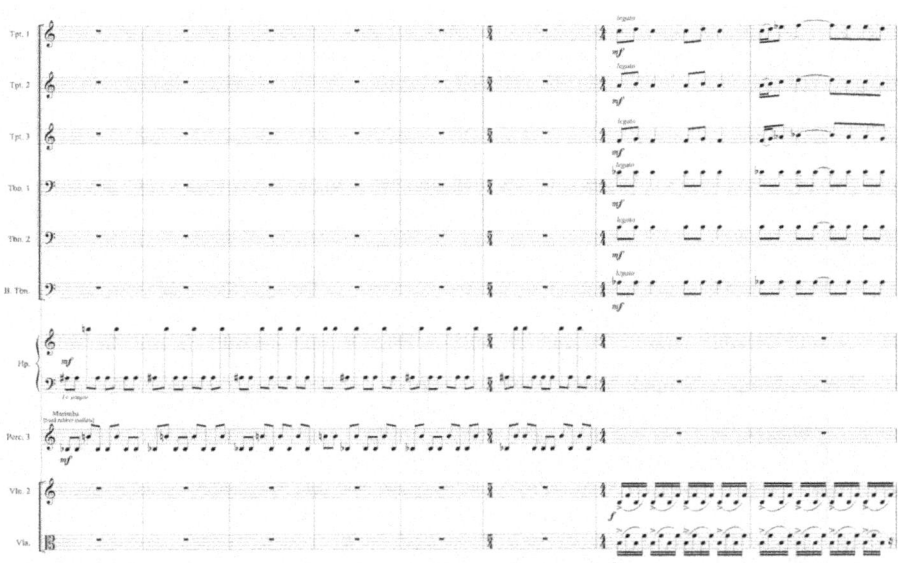

Figure 3-13. *Concerto for Orchestra*; V, mm. 134-141.

major chords in a slow harmonic rhythm. As quickly as it appeared, the motive vanishes by measure 162 only to return in the concluding measures. It is worth noting, in placement only this resembles the concertmaster's solo from movement three that also reappeared in the final measures of that movement.

In measure 164, the strings recall the opening bars of the third movement through a descending, expressive portamento figure followed by a pizzicato. These paired techniques figured prominently throughout the third movement in both the introduction and transitional material; thus, it is not surprising that the composer references this material in the finale even if only for a brief two measures. Here, however, Higdon scores a snap pizzicato with the celli and bass presenting descending tritones while the violas present a descending augmented 11th to serve as unifying devices (Figure 3-14).

Beginning in measure 166, the woodwinds present a flurry of sixteenth notes primarily based on the $OCT_{0,1}$ scale while the remainder of the ensemble revisits earlier material in numerous ways. The first and third horns recall the tail of their own motive from measure 69 but Higdon does not simply restate the material. She incorporates considerable variation in the rhythm that culminates in a polyphonic dialogue with the second and fourth horns. Most recognizable in this passage is the material in the strings: two major chords separated by a major second interval scored nearly identically to the

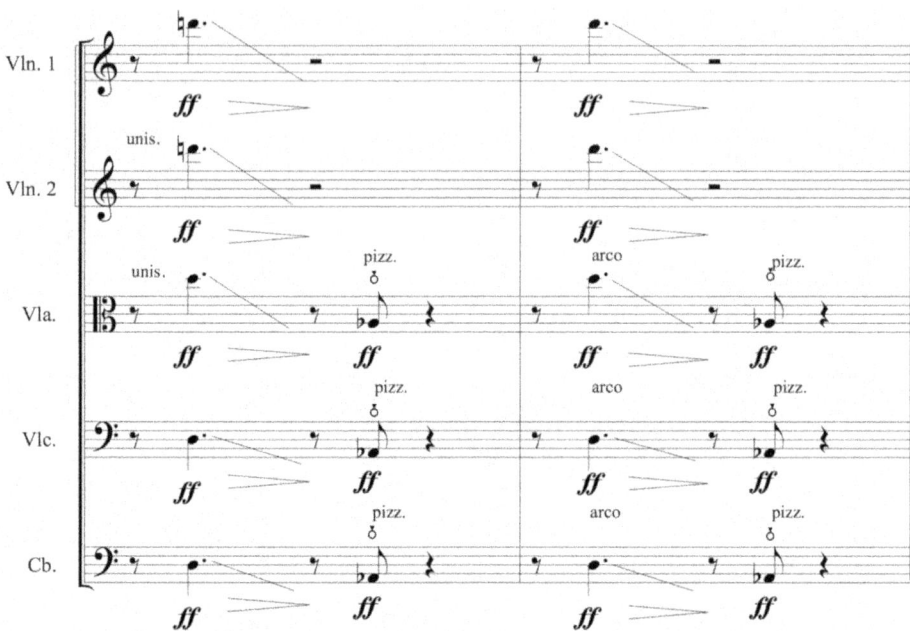

Figure 3-14. *Concerto for Orchestra*; V, mm. 164–165.

opening movement's A section with minor sixth intervals in the first violins and perfect fifth intervals in the seconds and celli. Finally, but of no less significance, the percussion return to the non-pitched instruments featured in the fourth movement.

As expected of an orchestral multi-movement work, all instruments combine to end the composition with great bravura. In measure 181, the unison strings present a brief, stepwise ascending line and upon subsequent repetitions, the material is truncated and rises in pitch at faster intervals to enhance the intensity. The incorporation of rising sounds is significant in this conclusion and its frequent appearances in the previous movements have already been noted. The steady increase in momentum provided by the strings is additionally explored through frequent meter changes and a consistent, driving rhythm in the timpani. Also, the piano returns to densely textured major chords doubled in the wind and brass instruments. The bitonality frequently employed in earlier piano passages is noticeably absent in preparation for a harmonious conclusion. The chords here do not encompass a discernible pattern but the progression in measure 183 (Bb-F#-B-F#) remains noteworthy in the roots of the chords, pitches which have figured substantially throughout the work. One may reasonably anticipate an answer to this harmonic ambiguity that dominated the composition but Higdon does not offer any solutions and in the end, opts for an unforeseen tonality altogether.

In the final bars, the piano and bassoons return to its earlier assertive, rhythmic motive from bar 153 while in the pickup to the final measure, the timpani sound the interval of an augmented fourth that connects the material to the *Concerto*'s opening. The full ensemble sounds the closing major chord progression (G-G-G-F-G), which curiously concludes on a G major chord, an unutilized tonality thus far. Due to the prominence placed on the pitches of B, Bb, and F throughout the five movements, the final key is unexpected. The keen observer will notice, however, that this was foreshadowed briefly in measure 151 in the alternating pitches of G and Db. This pattern originated with the pitches B and F in measure 52, and reemerged in 140 but the transposition to G and Db in measure 151 is vital in foretelling the ending tonality.

Critical Reception and Conclusion

Since the premiere of this work in 2002, Higdon's *Concerto for Orchestra* has garnered performances by several of the United States' leading ensembles. Although this composition contains many of the elements that contributed to the success of *blue cathedral*, it remains unclear why *Concerto for Orchestra* is programmed less frequently. This author can only speculate. One undeniable obstacle is that the severe technical demands of this work far exceed those of *blue cathedral* which explains the lack of performances by second tier and collegiate orchestras but is hardly applicable to the nation's leading ensembles. Commenting on this issue, Higdon stated:

> I think the primary reason *blue cathedral* has so many performances is because it's a smaller work in duration and instrumentation, and that makes it easier to program the work at the beginning of the concert (It fits a standard concert format of opener, concerto, but old symphony at the end). Duration is the prime factor. Also, it's not nearly as hard as the *Concerto for Orchestra*, which is very difficult.[80]

Due to the absolute nature and length of the work, it is plausible that symphonic programmers are unsure of audience reaction. The continuing decrease in funds for the arts may also be a contributing factor. Often forced to cater to the perceived, although not necessarily accurate, tastes of an art music audience, programmers may consider a modern composition of this size a risk for orchestras already in financial peril. Higdon commented, "I can't tell you how many orchestras are performing the Brahms Symphony No. 4. Now I see it on a program and I roll my eyes. I don't deny its genius, but [...] do we have to do the same thing over and over again?"[81] The composer staunchly believes

> that orchestras that stick to the standard lit are the ones driving people away from the concert hall ... if they choose, they could completely make orchestral music irrelevant by just doing old standards. For young people wanting a concert experience, it is death. I can't tell you how many times I've had people say they're not interested in the evening's concert because they've heard it before, so they go to some other form of entertainment.[82]

Higdon's music, however, has consistently found favor with a broad range of audiences and therefore, offers few programming risks.

As mentioned previously, the immediate success of *Concerto for Orchestra* stems partly from the attendance of the American Symphony Orchestra League members at the premiere. Since that auspicious beginning, the work has continued to receive favorable reviews. For example, *The Classical Voice of North Carolina*'s Jeffrey Rossman writes, "When one sees the title 'Concerto for Orchestra,' most people would immediately associate it with Bartók. Well, move over Béla, you're going to have some competition from now on, because Jennifer Higdon has usurped your title and may surpass even you."[83] Perry Tannenbaum from the highly regarded *American Record Guide* also looked on the work with great favor and wrote, "Higdon is so brilliant a colorist that her music teems with beguiling ideas. It would be churlish to criticize. A rigorous sense of purpose sparks this concerto from the outset."[84] And finally, Andrew Clark's assessment states:

> This was its UK premiere [...] and a fine impression it made, thanks to Higdon's tingling sonorities, her superb technical confidence and the bright, blazing energy of her idiom. Although the five-movement concerto lasts 35 minutes, Higdon uses her material with such variety and resourcefulness that nothing outstays its welcome. She is not afraid to wear debts on her sleeve—English string tradition in the first two movements, flash-brass Bernstein in the finale—but she recasts their sound-world in her own upbeat image. The heart of the concerto is its middle movement, a kaleidoscope of spangled colours and solo turns, framed by a recurring glissando motif for strings; but Higdon's coup de graceis [sic] the fourth movement, a magical merry-go-round of tuned percussion, harp, triangle and bells. The challenges she sets her musicians are so pleasurable it must have seemed like a day out for the BBC Symphony Orchestra.[85]

Robert Spano conducted the Atlanta Symphony Orchestra in a commercial recording of the work that also features Higdon's *City Scape*. This release contributed significantly to *Concerto for Orchestra*'s popularity and in 2004, the disc garnered four Grammy nominations in the categories of Best Classical Contemporary Composition, Best Orchestral Performance, and Best Classical Album and won for Best Engineered Album, Classical. The critical reception of the album was highly favorable and as Mark L. Lehman opined in the *American Record Guide*, "This new Telarc release [...]

confirms her arrival as a bright new star in the compositional firmament."[86] The *Chicago Tribune* likewise had a positive review and stated about the *Concerto for Orchestra*, "Its driving, restless outer movements begin where Bartok's famous work of the same name left off, framing a bounding scherzo for strings alone, a haunting central sequence of instrumental solos and a delicately woven section for tinkly, woody percussion."[87]

This composition was intended to be performed in its entirety but after the work became popular, several ensembles wanted to program only the second movement. The composer reformatted this movement and called it *String* to simplify programming information; however, it is not a separate work. *String* has been performed by the Nashville Symphony, the California Chamber Orchestra, the Gulf Coast Symphony, as well as several youth ensembles.[88]

Attesting to this work's popularity, the Boston Crusaders, a drum corps international (DCI) ensemble, included music of Higdon in their 2006 show entitled "Cathedrals of the Mind" that featured arrangements of *blue cathedral* and *Concerto for Orchestra*. Each summer, musicians in these drum and bugle corps perform for thousands of people whose demographics differ from traditional symphony attendees. She visited the ensemble during their rehearsal in Madison, Wisconsin, and with great enthusiasm expressed that hearing her music performed by a DCI group was "more thrilling than taking a bow at Carnegie Hall."[89]

blue cathedral may have ignited the figurative flame of the composer's international stardom but *Concerto for Orchestra* revealed that she has undoubtedly arrived and has secured her presence in the contemporary symphonic circuit. With this second large orchestral work, a unique compositional style becomes attributable to Higdon. Such trademarks do not, however, offer a sense of predictability; the composer's subtle use of variation combines the revered traditions of the past with innovative harmonies, rhythms, and colors of the present.

CHAPTER FOUR

City Scape

Immediately following the premiere of *Concerto for Orchestra*, Higdon received an equally significant commission from Robert Spano and the Atlanta Symphony Orchestra that resulted in the three-movement *City Scape*. In great contrast to the previous work, Higdon had only three and a half months to fulfill the October 1 deadline. *City Scape* premiered on November 14, 2002, with the ASO under the baton of Spano, the dedicatee.[1]

The Atlanta Symphony had been noticeably silent since 1996 in its lack of commissions. Spano had assumed leadership of the orchestra in 2001 and his renewed relationship with the composer after conducting *blue cathedral* was largely responsible for this commission. The parameters given for this work were based on programming needs but the "musical portrait of Atlanta"[2] stemmed from Higdon who maintains a special fondness for the city as the location of her earliest childhood memories. She utilized her own experiences as the foundation for the composition. She recalled, "I have so many memories of Atlanta—playing around Lenox [Square], running around the Woodruff Arts Center as a kid. After Bob [Spano] came to me for the piece, I knew I had a lot of inspiration there, in the city itself, and it was a natural fit."[3]

The terms of the commission stipulated that the work consist of three movements that could be performed separately but combined should not last more than 35 minutes. Higdon was given guidelines for each movement, and she found it "intriguing to be given these parameters and then try to match up."[4] The first movement was to function as an opening number on a program and last approximately seven minutes. In the second movement, the entire orchestra was to be utilized for a lyrical, slow tone poem. The final movement was to complement the educational outreach planned for the upcoming school year. That year's theme was form, specifically rondo, and Higdon was required to adhere to that structure with a smaller orchestration to facilitate the ensemble's touring personnel.

Because of the manner in which ASO had planned to utilize the movements, the personnel for each varies. "SkyLine" and "river sings a song to trees" contain nearly identical orchestrations with the exceptions of percussion and harp. The woodwinds in these first two movements utilize three players per part and include the English horn, the bass clarinet, and the contrabassoon. Similarly, the brass features three players for trumpets and trombones, four hornists, and a single tubist. Higdon utilized a timpanist and an additional three percussionists as well for the opening two movements; instruments in this section not scored in the previously examined works include tambourine, water gong, crash cymbal, brake drum, and xylophone. The last movement, "Peachtree Street," requires the smallest ensemble and the instruments omitted are the piccolo, English horn, bass clarinet, contrabassoon, the third trumpet, the bass trombone, and various percussion.

Higdon knew from the beginning that *City Scape* and *Concerto for Orchestra* were to be paired together on a recording and thus composed the former to contrast and complement the latter.[5] She remained cautious that *City Scape* "didn't live in the shadow of the concerto. I was watching at every step to make sure the ASO piece was strong on its own."[6]

The commission occurred only a few months before its scheduled premiere meaning Higdon had to write with great urgency. She also felt considerable pressure because this request appeared right on the heels of the phenomenally successful *Concerto for Orchestra*. Higdon commented:

> I've never written anything this size in so short a time [...] I spent all July and August writing [...] six hours a day, every day. You have to be careful because your brain turns to mush after about four hours. Adrenalin and sheer panic are what kept me going. Thankfully, I never hit a creative block.[7]

Poetic titles appear frequently in Higdon's works. *City Scape* refers to the work in its entirety but each movement carries its own descriptive title as well based on the composer's impressions of Atlanta.[8] Higdon relishes experimenting with not only musical language but also the written language, which explains the separation of the title into two separate words rather than the standard compound word. She clarified, "I like to change words and spellings around, to make them my own."[9] This trend continues in the individual movements entitled "SkyLine," "river sings a song to trees,"[10] and "Peachtree Street."

While composing, Higdon often utilizes some type of imagery and like *blue cathedral*, that used here does not necessarily translate to the audience, nor was it intended to do so. The piece, therefore, is not programmatic but rather an impression of the "'bustle of traffic and the intensity of moving down the street'"[11] and is best described by Higdon in her program notes as a "metropolitan sound picture written in orchestral tones."[12]

Movement One, "SkyLine"

As mentioned in Chapter One, "SkyLine" was written in only five days.[13] In the liner notes of the recording, the composer wrote:

> Over the past four decades I've watched the skyline change and grow, rising up distinctly into its own identifiable shape, projecting an image of boldness, strength, and growth. Every city's skyline is a fingerprint that the rest of the world recognizes at a distance; Atlanta has developed a powerful, distinctively metropolitan image, recognizable around the world.[14]

Her program notes to this movement complement these thoughts:

> Every city has a distinctive downtown skyline: That steely profile that juts into the sky, with shapes and monumental buildings that represent a particular signature for each city. The steel structures present an image of boldness, strength, and growth, teeming with commerce, and the people who work and live there.[15]

During the composer's childhood, her father was contracted by Southern Bell to recreate a model of Atlanta's skyline. She recalled, "Dad did something for Southern Bell—a replica of the skyline out of yards and yards of telephone wire. [It made me] hyperaware of what the downtown skyline looked like."[16] Higdon musically depicts the skyscrapers of the Downtown, Midtown, and Lenox regions[17] and commented on its reflection of the city, "Atlanta's [skyline] has grown very bold in the years I've known it [...] I made the music bold, too."[18] This is evident from the opening measures with a spirited tempo of quarter note=142, loud dynamic marking, and the emphasis on the bright timbre of the trumpets. As with much of Higdon's music, this movement is sectional in form and effectively combines contrast and repetition. The brass opening represents the tall buildings in the title's skyline that are subsequently contrasted by softer, solo sections reflecting the earthbound, human element of the city. Sections of large musical material return that allow the work to be viewed as a ternary form in the following manner:

Measure Numbers	Music	Letter
1–21	Trumpet major chords and fifth intervals in horn separated by a major 2nd; loud dynamic marking, slower note values for majestic effect; 4/4 meter	Introduction: Skyscrapers
21–93	Texture thins, softer dynamic, Motives A and B introduced; Higdonesque scoring for first desk soli in strings, additional soli follow in brass and woodwinds; significant soli represent the earthbound and individuals in the city	A: Earthbound and human element

Measure Numbers	Music	Letter
94–133	Vibrant mood of opening returns, emphasis on trumpets	B: Skyscrapers
134–194	Softer section; unorthodox soli comparable to A section returns	A': Return to Earthbound and human scale
195–238		Conclusion: Skyscrapers

Introduction

The entire work opens with an introduction referencing the vivid and forceful Atlanta skyline. The trumpets initially present consecutive D major chords in root position, a tonality and orchestration characteristic of Higdon. The horns, bassoons, and vibraphone play descending fifth intervals beginning on E and B making the initial distance between these instruments and the trumpets a major second, a significant trait of this composer. The *forte* brass opening is complemented by percussion contributing to the steely atmosphere of skyscrapers through loud punctuations of the suspended cymbal, Chinese cymbal, and bass drum. The first two percussionists playing the cymbals contribute substantially to the assertive mood by stopping the sound immediately after striking the instrument. Major chords and fifths appear subsequently in bar four in the woodwinds later doubled by the strings and brass in measure eight. With the exception of the percussion, the full ensemble performs in homorhythmic texture to provide a clear statement of the composer's opening musical idea. In bar 13, the harmonic rhythm accelerates while another Higdon stylistic traits occurs, rapidly ascending and descending scalar passages in the woodwinds. Without question, the composer has stamped her musical signature on the introduction.

A Section

The A section clearly begins in measure 21 through an immediate thinning of the orchestration, a softer dynamic, and the change in focus from harmony to melody to expose two of the most crucial components of the entire work. The trumpet and piccolo sound a brief, yet significant motive consisting of five ascending stepwise sixteenth notes; this motive appears throughout all three movements and serves a pivotal role in unifying the composition and thus, is subsequently referred to as Motive A. The initial occurrence of Motive A is immediately followed by a repetition and transposition of the same motive. An equally crucial motive appears simultaneously in the timpani employing a rhythm of an eighth note followed by sixteenth note triplets. This rhythm recurs throughout "SkyLine" and returns in "river sings a song to trees" and although absent from the finale, unifies the opening two movements. This rhythmic pattern will be referred to as Motive B (Figure 4–1). Beneath Motives A and B, the string section thins leaving only the violas and celli presenting major chords, scoring so characteristic of Higdon. The function, here, however differs considerably; the harmonic rhythm is not the sustained chords providing the serene ambiance of the earlier works but rather are significant in their contribution to the animated rhythm through syncopations and accents.

Figure 4–1. "SkyLine," mm. 19–24.

Beginning in measure 29, the orchestral texture becomes even sparser in preparation for the string soli. As witnessed in the above analysis, the A sections are the earthbound sections and musically contrast the bold skyline by featuring soft soli which begin in measure 31 for the first desk of the celli and violas. The lower string soloists present Motive A in unison but after a single measure, the celli are replaced by the second violins (Figure 4–2). These brief solo moments are interrupted by the string section presenting slowly moving, forte major and minor chords. When the soli resume in the pick-up to measure 37 the initial pitches of Motive A return to make this appearance unmis-

Figure 4–2. "SkyLine," mm. 31–32.

takable. The sixteenth note triplets of Motive B also occur in these soli but varied so that the original repeated pitches are replaced with ascending and descending scalar passages.

After the string soli cease in measure 41, the celli and violas return with the highly rhythmic major chords in a noteworthy appearance. The celli sound Db major chords while the violas present open fifth intervals (Eb–Bb), thus referencing the movement's opening harmonies transposed down a minor second. The melodic focus, however, is on the bass and bass clarinet presenting a syncopated, *fortissimo* melody in Bb minor. The unison high ranges are not an unusual scoring for this composer. In measure 49, this melody continues with the bass clarinet replaced by the second bassoon and a syncopated countermelody is added in the tuba and contrabassoon. These themes are combined with imitative entries of Motive A in the violins all supported by a typical accompanimental Higdon figure, alternating major and minor second intervals in the second clarinet and flute.

In measure 54, a transition from the string soli to the brass soli begins. The violas, *sans* celli, return to the accented and syncopated open fifth intervals slightly varied from previous appearances. Complementing the strings, the bongos, designated as a solo, present a line comprised in part of Motive B: repeated pitches in triplet sixteenth note rhythms. The melodic material of this passage appears in the woodwinds that continues the syncopated and accented melody heard earlier in the low bass instruments but newly innovative in range and timbre.

By the time the brass soli begin in measure 62, the tonal center has shifted to b minor, outlined clearly in the sustained open fifths of the lower strings. Specific tonalities are rarely conscious decisions with Higdon. She explained:

> When I'm doing sketches, I don't have perfect pitch but something will occur to me and I try to find it on the piano. I never pay attention to the key. People will tell me, "Oh, this is in such-and-such key," I have to go back and look at the score. I don't know. At no point at any time when I'm composing, do I ever think, "This is in the key of...." It's very rare that I plan things out. When it comes to key areas, I never think about that.[19]

B minor is of course the relative minor of D major, the opening tonality found in the trumpets and thus its use here is noteworthy. The woodwinds borrow the imitative texture emphasizing Motive A found previously in the violins but the passage is more complex through an expanded dialog of three voices. Higdon frequently re-orchestrates previous material while introducing new thematic content and such is the case here with the brass soli. The trombones present sustained chords that solidify the b minor tonality while the principal trumpet contains the melody, comprised primarily of second, fourth, and fifth intervals that remain characteristic of this composer. The orchestration, loud dynamic, slow harmonic rhythmic, and major and minor sonorities very briefly recall the movement's opening mood.

In measure 70, the focus shifts to the first and second violins, the former divided into four parts, the latter into three. In order for this to be clearly heard, the texture is reduced considerably. The first violins sound Higdon's characteristic major chords in root position, while the seconds alternate quickly between e minor and D major chords. As evidenced earlier, chords separated by a major second are typical of this composer but the scoring here is unorthodox because such chords generally appear in two different instrumental timbres.

Between measures 75 and 86, Higdon returns to material that is varied yet corresponds in part to measures 41–52. The violins and celli manipulate the chromatic line initially scored for the bassoons in measure 44 through imitation and fragmentation while the bass returns to its earlier syncopated, high range melody now paired with the bass trombone. The meter change in measure 83 is stylistic of Higdon to mark a new musical idea: brief soli for each of the string principals. The texture is thinned drastically for balance and the soli are accompanied only by the guiro for rhythmic underpinning. The concertmaster plays the first solo comprised of material that reappears in measure 147. This solo opens with Motive B's triplet figure that is subsequently imitated in the second violin and viola soli. The eighth note preceding the triplet associated with Motive B is missing from the concertmaster's solo but in the second violin and viola's respective entrances, the eighth note is present, albeit reversed so that the triplet appears first. The second violin and viola present this significant motive numerous times. After brief statements, the string soloists converge in a homorhythmic texture in measure 88 to begin a dialog with the four principal woodwinds. This interruption is unexpected in a passage dominated by strings but confirms the composer's skill in straying from predictability. The string soli conclude in measure 93 with another meter change and brief solo for the concertmaster that closes the A section.

B Section

A new section clearly begins in measure 94 identifiable through a brief meter change. The sixteenth note triplets of Motive B appear in the woodblock and later the vibraphone in dialog with the oboes' descending sextuplet scalar figures, an extension of Motive B. In the A section, the bass, paired with various instruments presented accented and syncopated melodic lines that reemerges here in a different scoring: contrabassoon, bass clarinet, and tuba. Beginning in measure 95, the violas, so often entrusted with purveying significant accompanying material in the music of Higdon, play chord clusters. Although rare, chord clusters are not entirely foreign to this composer's music and these clusters are subsequently followed by Higdon's characteristic *ostinato* figure of fast, alternating second intervals. The tonality is established by the horns and second bassoon through a D pedal tone that suggests the D major tonality of the opening trumpet chords. Finally, in measure 98, the trumpets begin a progression of major and minor chords in root position, first in d minor, the parallel minor of the movement's opening but only two bars later, the chord quality changes to major and the dynamics are increased to enhance the reference to the movement's opening. These harmonies are complemented by the trombones, bassoons, and eventually the lower strings to sound perfect fifth that are separated by a second interval from the trumpets, again clearly related to the beginning.

The brass is temporarily tacet in measure 108 but the major and minor chord progressions continue in the low woodwinds. In bar 116, the D major chords return in the trumpets complemented by quickly alternating major second intervals in the second violins (D and C in this instance) while the *pizzicato* violas revisit the D pedal tone. The key of D major is unmistakable and although Higdon does not consciously compose in specific keys, a frequent use of this particular tonality is evident. She stated, "I noticed D appearing more. The more people like you I talk to, I start realizing when I write, 'There's that D again.'"[20]

The music builds in intensity as the orchestration expands in measure 123 for a stark contrast in texture from the A section; the flutes exhibit the only appearance of motivic material in this passage with repeated sixteenth note triplets. As the movement approaches its climax, the meter alternates each measure which with Higdon, signifies vital musical moments. Here, the climactic point is also emphasized through a fortissimo dynamic and the scoring of nearly the entire ensemble. Typical of her style is the combination of new and returning material that results in music that is engaging yet familiar. Fortissimo trills in the woodwinds and lower strings comprise the new music supported by material borrowed from the introduction found in the horns and first violins. They reproduce nearly identical fifth intervals as the introduction and similarly, are separated by a major second from the trumpets' major chords. The rhythm in these instruments are varied from their earlier appearance through diminution and livelier syncopation.

A' Section

Following this musical peak, the instrumentation is instantly reduced in measure 134 to only the vibraphone and first violins. Violins one and later violins two and violas are divided into threes to produce major chords; the first violins' chords are answered by clarinets, the horns answer the second violins, and finally, the violas' dark timbre is contrasted by the flutes' response. These question and answer passages demonstrate Higdon's experimentation of orchestral color while contrasting the previous flurry of activity with a considerably slower harmonic rhythm. The dynamics in these measures never exceed *mezzo forte* and offers a clear representation of the "more earthbound, human-scale sections in between"[21] the skyscrapers.

As mentioned previously, the concertmaster solo in measure 147 corresponds to measure 83 and repeats three measures later. In measure 148, the first violin section (sans concertmaster) sustains a C major chord, in a continuation of these sonorities from the previous section. The second violin solo in measure 149 functions as an answer to the concertmaster but noticeably absent here are the triplet sixteenth notes referencing Motive B that frequented the earlier passage. Accompanying these soli, the woodwinds initially present major chords but the third of the chord is eventually omitted to exhibit Higdon's stylistic perfect fifths.

As expected in an A' section, Higdon recalls an entire section beginning in measure 152 and although she alters the orchestration, the music corresponds to measure 54. The bongo solo reappears here but the percussion section is expanded to include timpani and medium woodblock in a highly imitative presentation of Motive B. This polyphonic treatment of the percussion constitutes the primary difference between the two sections.

The reference to the previous passage ceases in measure 161 but Higdon immediately incorporates an excerpt from a different place in the A section, measure 29. The unorthodox scoring for the first desks of the strings returns with a new rhythmic ostinato in the guiro and a solo for the principal clarinet. The ascending and descending scalar contour of this line paired with the inclusion of Motive B is unmistakably connected to the strings and provide a change of color. Measure 173 continues to correspond to the previous section through the accompaniment pattern of the woodwinds and accented, melodic bass line identical to bar 41. Higdon continues to toy with the order of musical ideas throughout this passage, but measures 75–82 correspond clearly to 174–180.

Higdon next returns to a separate section quoting measures 49–53 in bars 181–185. Another parallel section follows immediately in measures 186–

193 which closely relates to the brass soli found in measures 62–69. Thus, the entire passage quickly summarizes the movement's primary musical content in whimsical and unexpected orders to conclude the A' section.

Conclusion

After a review of earlier material, the consistent meter changes and fortissimo dynamic markings reveal the great emphasis the composer places on measure 194. Instruments are doubled to produce an orchestral sound full of grandeur and noteworthy musical content. Firstly, the violas and several woodwinds present Motive A using the identical pitches as its initial appearance. Secondly, the major and minor chord sonorities in the trombones and third trumpet (doubled by two bassoons and bass clarinet) revisit the sound of the bold skyscrapers and even begin on the important D major chord. This orchestration differs slightly from Higdon's typical style of placing such chords solely in the trumpets. Earlier when Higdon scored similar sonorities for the trumpets, the horns presented fifth intervals but in this section, they are reorchestrated to appear in the trumpets, flutes, and violins.

In measure 212, Higdon thins the texture by omitting the brass and nearly all of the percussion. This sparse orchestration leads to the final climax four measures later; the concluding musical depiction of skyscrapers is unmistakable through the fortissimo return of the full ensemble and elevated range of the first violins. The trombones present repeated pitches in varied rhythms in measure 216 that recall the celli in measure 15. This link to the introduction is enhanced by a reiteration of identical pitches from the opening: the horns' fifth intervals and the D major chords of the trumpets. As "SkyLine" concludes, the trumpets' chords are doubled by the trombones and violins before the full ensemble closes with a fortissimo D major chord to create a majestic finish appropriate for a concert opener.

Movement Two, "river sings a song to trees"

Higdon rarely begins composing a work from the beginning and this composition was no exception; the central movement was the first to be penned because it had the fewest parameters dictated by its commissioners. Higdon explained in more detail, "I suspect having the most freedom and using the largest orchestra was probably the thing that inspired the ideas here first. And I have quite a bit of history writing works that reflect aspects of nature."[22] "river sings a song to trees" contrasts the outer movements considerably in both mood and tempo (quarter note=60) to reflect the serene, natural beauty prevalent in Atlanta and its immediate surrounding areas.

Pierre Ruhe of the *Atlanta Journal-Constitution* describes this movement as "an homage to the city's arboreal treasures and to the creek that ran through her family's yard on Ferncliff Road in Buckhead."[23] Likewise, Mark Gresham refers to the second movement as a "tone poem, a remembrance of the proliferation of green around their Lenox home, the beloved creek in the front yard, and the woodlands behind a second home on Mason Mill Road."[24] In the same interview, the composer stated, "I thought of the opening as kind of an homage to nature [...] nature is such a prominent thing"[25]; however, the movement derived specifically from her "childhood memories of playing in a creek that ran across her front yard and reflected a multitude of colors from sunlight streaming through the trees."[26] This exploration of colors is realized in the numerous soli throughout the movement.

Higdon expanded in the liner notes that the second movement

> commemorates the Nature that is such a presence in this city. Trees, parks, and streams add a lush carpet to the landscape, infusing the atmosphere with intense and gorgeous greens that connect neighborhoods and businesses. The presence of Peachtree Creek (I used to play in one of the tributaries that ran through my front yard in the Lenox area) reflects moving life and serves as a reminder of the city's having risen from the Earth itself. The creek also symbolizes constant change, under calm water and over powerful currents, doing so with exquisite beauty.[27]

Although not explicitly programmatic, the dynamics, changing tempi, and mood of this movement clearly reflect the above reference to river currents. Higdon continued, "I'm always struck by how many trees are around Atlanta [...] some are really old trees. There are also creeks and rivers. So this movement is about the sounds that a river makes singing its song to the trees."[28]

As with many of Higdon's works and particularly appropriate for a tone poem, the form is paratactic. Each of the smaller sections are unique in musical content eschewing any contrast or repetition found in traditional forms. As such, a large formal analysis of such a through composed movement is not applicable; however, it is certainly worth noting that many of these subsections and changes in mood are preceded by an *accelerando* or *ritardando* to a new tempo which is stylistic of this composer.

The orchestration is similar to Higdon's earlier scores including a full percussion section complemented by a water gong in the opening and concluding measures, an unorthodox addition. Although it has also been used by others such as John Cage and Lou Harrison,[29] the water gong here can be credited to her former teacher, Crumb,[30] as can the reappearance of the bowed vibraphone. The composer explained the opening instrumentation:

I have a water gong. It makes this bizarre, rising sound. Also, the timpani player has certain crotales sitting on the head of the timpani. He strikes the crotale with a hard mallet—not the timpani, but the crotale—and then moves the pedal so that [...] [it's] a weird *wow-wow-wah* sound. You've got a very high-pitched crystal sound [...] [from] the crotale [...] and the waveform is altered by the timpani head being retuned. Detuned and retuned over and over again. At one point, I have a sizzle cymbal [...], which is basically a cymbal with little rivets in it, little screws that vibrate when you touch it. The combination of the three sounds. It sets up the magic of that movement.[31]

Magic is unquestionably the most appropriate adjective to describe the unusual sounds that cause the listener to lean in with curiosity.

After the percussion's mysterious opening, the strings enter in measure eight. The muted violas, celli, and second violins sound trills marked *sul tasto*,[32] another unusual scoring for this composer that contributes substantially to the ethereal environment while creating a rippling, water-like effect. Throughout the entire movement, soli abound for numerous instruments beginning with Higdon's own, the flute, which presents a line that aptly demonstrates the melodic perfect fifths common in her style (Figure 4-3). The river's opening song here is of great significance because elements of the solo return periodically throughout the movement. Subsequent woodwind soli are scored for the English horn and principal clarinet and like the flute, the ranges are narrow. Beneath the woodwinds, the first two desks of the first violins present major chords, beginning with D major, a tonality not unfamiliar thus far in the work. Such scoring for violin soloists are a significant aspect of the Higdon style. Following the decay of the strings' soli, bassoons enter in measure 22 with the principal displaying an eighth note-triplet recalling Motive B.

After the woodwind soli, a metrical change to 2/4 occurs for only bar 35 to signal a transitional passage that is further emphasized by a subtle accelerando and tempo change to quarter note=66. This transition is marked by the previous major and minor chords now sounded by the entire first violin section with increased dynamics and a faster chord progression and solo viola and cello parts that incorporate elements of Motive B. These are

Figure 4-3. "river sings a song to trees," mm. 16–21.

complemented by the woodwinds and in particular, the principal clarinet and bassoon that also incorporate Motive B. True to Higdon's orchestrational style, the motive is doubled by a solo viola and solo cello (Figure 4-4) all of which are accompanied by the lower strings' continued opening trills.

Figure 4-4. "river sings a song to trees," mm. 46-47.

Designating a new section, another accelerando appears in measure 49 that increases the quarter note to 72. Motive B is explored in the clarinets through repeated sextuplet patterns that reference the rippling water of Atlanta's streams. Much of this passage is stamped with many of Higdon's style traits: the second bassoon alternates major second intervals while the three trombones, each scored a major second apart present chord clusters in dialog with the horns' consonant fifth intervals. The viola and cello soli cease and rejoin their sections to present a unison, lyrical melody characterized by double dotted rhythms. A countermelody by the principal trumpet also emphasizes these rhythms to create a mixture of bright and dark timbres in a texture that becomes increasingly complex.

Higdon places a ritardando in measure 63 followed by an extended accelerando that increases the tempo substantially in measure 68 (quarter note=92). The dotted rhythms of the previous passage are transferred to the trombones while variations of Motive B return in the fortissimo horns with unyielding repeated notes. The passage progresses to a moment of great climax and as common in such sections of Higdon's music, metrical changes appear frequently.

The musical climax lasts briefly and in measure 76, a ritardando returns the tempo to quarter note=72 while the dynamics decrease to further enhance contrast. This entire passage is marked by numerous soli throughout the entire ensemble sprinkled with several Higdon stylistic traits, such as the trumpets' major chords in bar 78, uncharacteristically paired with the trombones sounding minor chords a third lower. These muted brass commence a dialog with the first stand of first violins and the principal second violinists that persists until the meter stabilizes in measure 104. The strings alternate between playing a distinct melody in octaves and presenting sonorities in quartal harmonies. While not particularly common in the works of Higdon, the latter function as inversions of her much preferred parallel fifths. Soaring above is a clarinet solo in measure 84 with a limited range that recalls the opening of this movement and is subsequently joined by a bassoon, oboe, English horn, and flute in an explosion of color. A small phrase presented by the oboe, clarinet, and bassoon in measure 88 likewise presents quartal harmonies. Of particular interest is the triplet sixteenth note rhythms of Motive B introduced by the clarinet in measure 92 and imitated a few measures later in the English horn. Following these woodwind soli, the meter stabilizes and elements of Motive B once again become dormant. The numerous instrumental colors utilized here are undoubtedly an example of Higdon's self-described joy of sound that permeates all of her works.

The return to a consistent meter does not conclude a musical section but rather, earlier musical ideas persist. The strings continue to consist primarily of fourths and fifths while the woodwinds return to the instrumentation and quartal harmony of measure 88. In measure 107, string soli return for the concertmaster and principal second violinist and initially, this material does not appear to be of profound significance. The instruments are separated at the octave and simply present two descending intervals; however, in measure 115, the concertmaster solo incorporates Motive B which foreshadows the widespread employment of this motive in the subsequent measures. The accompaniment here represents quintessential Higdon in the employment of perfect fifth intervals in the cello, viola, and woodwinds (Figure 4–5).

Once the concertmaster has reintroduced Motive B, it is then transferred to the remainder of the ensemble. The motive appears occasionally in the woodwinds but it is the strings that feature the rhythm most prominently with the sixteenth note triplets occurring in nearly every measure. Here, the melodic content of the motive ascends by step to contrast the repeated notes of both the initial presentation and the immediately preceding concertmaster solo.

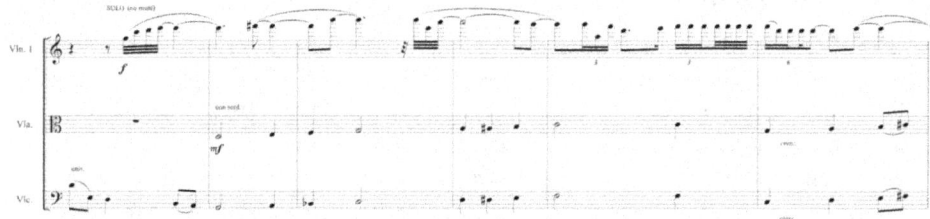

Figure 4–5. "river sings a song to trees," mm. 115–120.

In measure 134, the motive expands to sextuplets. Previous passages that combined these two rhythms often featured the triplet followed by the sextuplet. These measures, however, do not conform to this pattern. In measure 140, a dialog commences between the strings and woodwinds comprised almost exclusively of Motive B. The discourse ceases immediately in measure 146 and woodwind declamations of the motive are separated by their own ascending scalar figures while the strings project a double dotted melody unrelated to that found in measure 50. These jaunty rhythms provide the vitality that defines Higdon's music and as evidenced here, are present even in slower, lyrical movements. Although the focus is undoubtedly on the upper strings during this passage, the low brass feature a legato, homorhythmic countermelody with each part separated by the perfect fifth so characteristic of Higdon.

The entire ensemble returns in measure 154 for a climactic presentation of Motive B that continues to feature numerous examples of this composer's stylistic tendencies. The woodwinds, in a forte dynamic and homorhythmic texture, repeatedly display the sixteenth note triplet motive while the horns exhibit stationary perfect fifth intervals. The timpani alternate between two pitches, another well-known characteristic of this composer. Typically, such passages are scored for woodwinds or strings shifting between second intervals but here, the interval is a minor third.

In measure 158, the dynamics diminish to *pianissimo* and the texture is once again greatly reduced beginning a starkly contrasting section. Although the ensemble is condensed, each of the musical lines represents a significant aspect of Higdon's style. An ostinato pattern appears in the marimba and the harp, an unusual instrumental pairing also explored in *Concerto for Orchestra*.[33] The marimba line is comprised of a single pitch in a variety of rhythms that undergoes augmentation before disappearing in measure 170. Most significantly, the harp, doubled by the second flute and clarinet, presents a unifying link between the first and second movements through four ascending major seconds that somewhat resemble Motive A. This shimmering sound is a clear reference to Atlanta's bubbling streams and tributaries and serves as accompanimental material to the melody, ascending major and minor chords presented by the second violins. Following these chords, the melodic focus moves to the principal bassoon supported by the piccolo presenting Motive B.

In measure 170, the harp ostinato is slightly modified but the sixteenth notes persist relentlessly. At the same time, the violas display a separate ostinato consisting of a repetitive, descending pattern to contrast the initially rising harp line. Although spelled harmonically, Higdon's penchant for major and minor seconds is clearly demonstrated in the violas during this passage. The bassoon melody is transferred to a solo trumpet paired with a countermelody by a solo cello for a continuation of truly unique color combinations.

Following a brief ritardando, a new section commences in measure 179 that increases the quarter note to 92 and is marked *A Piacere*. Ritardandi or accelerandi are stylistic of tempo changes in Higdon's orchestral works but the marking "a piacere" is not and therefore noteworthy. As mentioned previously, meter changes are used by this composer to distinguish musical sections of great significance and here, such changes occur nearly every measure in a foreshadowing of momentous solo material.

The woodwinds begin in a homorhythmic texture that utilize an abundance of expressive two-note slurs. Although filled with metrical changes, this chorale-like passage is peaceful and projects exquisite beauty. Of particular interest is the Higdon fifth that separates the principal bassoon and second clarinet and although the two flutes adhere to this intervallic separation less consistently, its appearance is more than fleeting and worthy of mention. The sextuplets based on Motive B briefly return in measure 183 in the oboe (Figure 4-6) surrounded by rhythms that recall the opening flute solo in measure 18. Similar patterns follow at 189 in the principal clarinet and in a varied context at 197 in the bassoons. Soli for each of the principal strings, doubled by woodwinds, continue the peaceful chorale. In measure 203, the meter becomes consistent and the soli *crescendo* to a fortissimo dynamic. The string soli cease in measure 212 as the texture gradually thickens but this

Figure 4-6. "river sings a song to trees," mm. 183–184.

is not the beginning of a new section; rather, the brass entrance contributes to a soaring climax initiated by the chorale. The horns present their characteristic fifth intervals eventually doubled by the bassoons and clarinets and it is these instruments that are entrusted with Motive B in the ensuing measures with sextuplets and later the original triplets.

The strings continue their homorhythmic texture as the ensemble enlarges to include the low brass and timpani. Noteworthy is the principal trumpet line in measure 213. A descending perfect fourth was also utilized in the trumpet solo found in measures 63 and 187 of "SkyLine" in a nearly identical rhythm, an eighth note followed by a sustained note. This minute detail was neither included purposefully nor composed to serve as a unifying link but nonetheless is an example of her intuitive style in making the movements cyclical.

Following another accelerando in measure 222, the tempo increases to quarter note=102, the fastest tempo marking found in the movement. The surge in speed coupled with a fortissimo dynamic a few bars later undoubtedly represents the most climactic section of "river sings a song to trees." An ostinato of repeated notes is scored for marimba and bass that continues until measure 243. These unyielding sixteenth notes provide a rhythmic drive enhanced by the floor tom's continuous sixteenth notes that are interrupted by sextuplets, an ever-noteworthy expansion of Motive B. Significant musical material also occurs in the remainder of the ensemble. The woodwinds and violins project the major and minor chords characteristic of Higdon's style while the trumpets and trombones imitate then invert descending perfect fourth and fifth intervals presented immediately. These entrances appear in rapid succession to provide a textural contrast to the homorhythmic woodwinds and strings. Of particular importance is the second trumpet in measure 225 that presents an ascending perfect fifth, nearly an exact quotation in both pitch and rhythm as the opening flute solo in measure 16 shown in Figure 4–3. The interval is repeated four times to draw attention to its significance and echoed by the trombone and eventually trumpets one and three. Furthermore, the horns present Motive B consecutively in a forte dynamic that draws the listener's attention to this important figure (Figure 4–7).

The second trombone part in measure 255 is also noteworthy as a unifying element between the first and second movements. In measure 120 of "SkyLine," the beat is emphasized by the bass clarinet's rhythm: a dotted eighth note followed by a sixteenth rest. This identical rhythm reappears here, again emphasizing a single pitch that demonstrates Higdon's subtle intuitive style in making the work cyclical.

In Higdon's music, codas typically reference the opening measures as

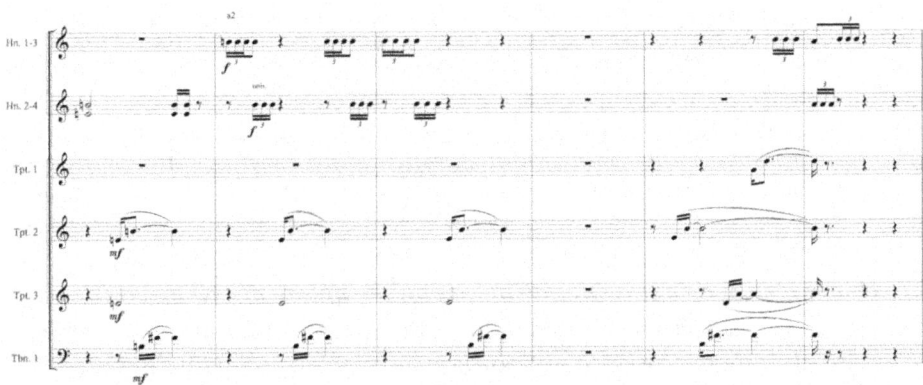

Figure 4–7. "river sings a song to trees," mm. 225–230.

well as other significant sections to bring the music full circle while simultaneously serving as a summation of the entire movement. Here and typical of Higdon, the coda is prefaced by a molto ritardando to return the tempo to the initial quarter note=60. In measure 263, the principal flute reiterates the opening solo from measure 16 and beginning in measure 270, begins an extended emphasis on Motive B. Likewise, the English horn and principal clarinet repeat their opening soli with slight rhythmic variation and as in the earlier appearance, are accompanied by the muted trills of the violins and violas. Solo violin scoring for the first desk of firsts and the principal second references not the beginning but the quartal harmony from measure 81. And finally, measure 273 corresponds to measure 159 in the identical scoring of a harp and marimba ostinato comprised of ascending motives. The ethereal mood of the movement's opening returns through the reappearance of the water gong; thus, the movement closes in the manner in which it began.

Movement Three, "Peachtree Street"

The form of "Peachtree Street" was stipulated by the commission. Higdon commented, "They asked for the last movement to be a rondo, so I knew all I needed to do was find material to fill in the blanks."[34] The "blanks" are episodic material that feature individual sections of the orchestra. Since the premiere, "Peachtree Street" has served as an example of form on children's concerts[35]; however, because of its very design, the movement may also serve as an excellent pedagogical tool to introduce the variety of timbres within an orchestral ensemble.

The title derives from one of the main streets in Atlanta and as a native of this city, Higdon's familiarity with the urban landscape is present in the liner notes:

> The final movement is "Peachtree Street," in honor of this primary artery that runs through the city. With its narrow lanes and winding character, this street is so full of life and energy, forever changing and growing, moving slowly and moving fast, that it serves as a reflection of us. Every turn brings something new and different, and carries us to places and people that have meaning in our lives.[36]

The music adheres strictly to this description with the "new and different" serving as the episodes; the contour of the winding lines in these sections reflect the programmatic content and are surrounded by the "life and energy" of the rondo theme.

"Peachtree Street" utilizes many of Higdon's compositional traits combined with unorthodox elements of her style. The orchestration needed to be smaller for touring purposes and thus features a reduced percussion section, highly atypical of this composer. She explained that although the instrumentation was provided by the ASO here, she is always mindful of practical performance needs while composing.[37] Another anomaly of the movement is the strict and unchanging tempo coupled with a lack of accelerandi and ritardandi, frequently used in Higdon's works to transition between large sections. Lastly, traditional forms are not common with Higdon but this exception, of course was part of the commission's parameters and while the refrain never returns identically, the content remains recognizable through the orchestration, harmonies, and ever present sixteenth notes in the trumpet. The episodes are distinct through consistently alternating meters between 5/4 and 4/4. The movement is analyzed as followed:

Measure Numbers	Music	Refrain/Episodic Content
1–29	Rondo theme	Refrain 1
30–44	String fugato	Episode 1
45–56	Rondo theme, truncated	Refrain 2[38]
57–72	Woodwinds	Episode 2
73–82	Rondo theme, greatly truncated	Refrain 3
83–99	Percussion	Episode 3
100–118	Rondo theme, melodic material is varied considerably	Refrain 4
119–134	Brass	Episode 4
135–150	Rondo theme	Refrain 5
151–178	All previous episodic material explored in order of appearance: strings, woodwinds, percussion, and brass	Episode 5
179–188	Rondo Theme	Refrain 6

Refrain 1

The full presentation of the rondo theme occurs only at the beginning and is truncated significantly in subsequent appearances. The brisk tempo of the finale is designated as quarter note=142–152. The movement opens with a brief but rapid crescendo of repeating notes for the trombones and snare drum followed by the rondo theme with the full ensemble. The orchestra presents the refrain in homorhythmic texture with the exception of the trumpets' sixteenth notes, a significant hallmark of this section. The ensemble's doubling is dependent on range with the lower pitched instruments beginning on a C major chord while the higher instruments sound D major, a favored chord with this composer. The trombones and bass also allude to this tonality through a repetition of the pitches A and D, a V–I progression. The fortissimo rondo theme abounds with syncopation to create the rhythmic vitality so often associated with Higdon's music.

Although the general mood of excitement prevails throughout all of the refrains, a slightly subdued portion of the theme begins in measure 20 where the dynamic marking diminishes from fortissimo to forte. The melody is scored for only half of the second violin section creating a thinner texture while descending two-note slurs provide a contrasting lyricism. The opening material returns in measure 26 and in comparison to Higdon's other orchestral compositions, the scoring in the brass at this point is unusual. The composer frequently entrusts major chord progressions to the trumpets but because this movement is orchestrated for only two trumpets, such scoring is impossible. Higdon slightly alters the instrumentation to two trumpets and the principal trombone to present the major sonorities. Recalling the immediately preceding passage at measure 20, the chords are comprised of descending, two-note slurs; thus, the lyrical quality and rhythmic intensity of the rondo theme are masterfully combined to conclude the first large section of the movement.

Episode 1

Measure 30 marks the beginning of the first episode and as noted previously, meters alternate continuously in these passages. The first episode is reserved for a string fugato comprised of tremendously important material beginning with the celli's two bar, unaccompanied subject; the length of this soon-to-be imitated theme means all subsequent entrances will also begin in a 4/4 bar. The celli's subject opens with two statements of Motive A (Figure 4–8). Although the episode is not a true fugue, the second violins enter two measures later with a tonal answer followed by the violas in measure 34

Figure 4–8. "Peachtree Street," mm. 30–34.

initially avoiding the subject altogether. The first violins enter in measure 36 with the majority of the subject and as expected, on the downbeat; however, when, the violas eventually present Motive A in the same measure, the material is no longer confined to opening on the downbeat. Curiously, the bass do not participate in presenting the subject and are nearly tacet the entire episode. Upon their eventual entrance in measure 42, the material includes Motive A but not the fugato subject. A crescendo culminating in a fortissimo dynamic leads to the return of the refrain in measure 45.

Refrain 2

Typical of Higdon's style, she does not simply repeat the opening. Upon the re-entrance of the full ensemble, the meter returns to a consistent 4/4 but the section is a truncated and slightly varied presentation of the refrain. In the original statement, the rondo theme extended 29 bars while here, the material lasts only 11. Subtle orchestration changes are also present but do not detract from the distinctive qualities of the rondo theme and the arrival of the material is unmistakable.

Episode 2

The woodwinds are featured in the second episode beginning in measure 57 where again, the meter alternates and all significant solo entries occur in a 4/4 measure. As with Episode 1, the homorhythmic, densely textured rondo theme is contrasted by lyrical soli, initially presented here in unison by the principal bassoon and clarinet. Accompanimental material and harmonic underpinning are provided by the second flute and second bassoon, respectively, with the former representing pure Higdon: alternating pitches separated by a second interval.

In measure 61, the opening solo is echoed by the principal flute with additional accompanying material varied considerably. The principal bassoon presents a repeated pitch that replaces the alternating seconds of the flute while the clarinets, in thirds, sound ascending two note slurs. An independent, lyrical oboe solo follows in bar 65 distinct through an expressive line with slower note values that gradually evolves to the consistent sixteenth note rhythms characteristic of the episodic soli. The section concludes with the unyielding sixteenth notes typical of Higdon's woodwind orchestration.

Refrain 3

As expected, the rondo theme along with a stable 4/4 meter follow in measure 73. Rather than quoting the syncopated opening, Higdon reintroduces the material from measure 20 that utilized only half of the second violin section. This appearance contrasts the original with an orchestration and texture that is greatly expanded through the scoring of double stops in both violin sections. The bustling sixteenth notes of the trumpets, however, are unmistakable and clearly allude to the refrain. In measure 79, the highly syncopated part from measure 16 returns newly paired with material that is pure Higdon: the trumpets and principal trombone in ascending major chords. Curiously, descending major chords appeared in this instrumentation in measure 26 of the original rondo theme. Truncated even further, this refrain spans only ten measures.

Episode 3

The percussion episode, scored for timpani, glockenspiel, and xylophone, begins in measure 83 with a return to the alternating meter. Between measures 83–85, the timpani present a continuous eighth note rhythm comprised primarily of Higdon's characteristic perfect fifth and major second intervals which also comprises the timpani's immediate subsequent material.

The glockenspiel and the xylophone present an imitative dialog, a hallmark of each episode. Marked forte, these higher ranged instruments present extremely brief motives that soar above the timpani. The dynamics are greatly reduced in the final measures for a seamless transition to the gradual return of the full ensemble. Additionally, in the episode's closing bar, the snare replaces the glockenspiel to present the sixteenth notes found in the opening to the rondo theme's first entrance.

Refrain 4

In measure 100, the ensemble gradually reenters beginning with the strings, the principal oboe, and the percussion from the preceding episode. Several aspects of this refrain are noteworthy. First, the oboe presents two pitches an octave apart in eighth notes, a stark departure from Higdon's usual style of alternating second intervals in sixteenth notes. Secondly, the horns sound the repeated sixteenth notes previously associated with the trumpets and despite the change in orchestration, these rhythms are absolutely essential in connecting this material with the refrain since little else of the rondo theme is revisited. As in the opening of the movement, the higher ranged instruments are doubled and present major chords while the lower instruments display major chords a second lower. The harmonies are different than those used earlier but the bitonal idiom remains similar. This relaxed section is brief and the mood is quickly altered through rising pitches and an extended crescendo that culminates in a fortissimo dynamic in measure 104. An additional increase in dynamics heightens the volume to *fortississimo* in measure 108. The texture becomes denser by the return of the trumpets and trombones doubling the strings and woodwinds and the entire ensemble presents the homorhythmic texture characteristic of the rondo theme. This refrain is one of the longest in the movement but typical of Higdon, she constantly varies the material.

In measure 113, the instrumentation is reduced to woodwinds, one percussionist, and half of the cello section to segue to the next episode. This material is comprised, in part, of the percussion episode's timpani line now orchestrated for celli and bassoons. The opening articulation and the orchestration for only half of a string section simultaneously recall measure 20 (Figure 4-9). The upper woodwinds provide the primary melodic content, an augmentation of the violins' progression in measure 109 but the volume decreases and the expanded rhythms create a natural ritardando. These sustained, descending major chords in the flutes and oboes are paired with separate, faster moving major chords in the clarinets and principal bassoon. Although Higdon frequently juxtaposes major chords separated by a second, this is not the case here; the lines are clearly independent.

Figure 4-9. "Peachtree Street," mm. 113-115.

Episode 4

The brass episode begins in measure 119 and continues the transition's soft dynamics. The tuba, second trombone, and three horns open the passage as expected in a 4/4 bar but in a stark contrast to earlier polyphonic episodes, the texture is homorhythmic. The second trombone and horns 1 and 3 present the melody in thirds while the tuba and remaining horns consist of major and minor chords, a clear hallmark of this composer. Similarly, the tuba part in measure 120 displays a Higdon stylistic trait of alternating pitches separated by a major second that serves as an accompanimental pattern to the primary melodic material: the trumpets' highly rhythmic ascending line. By 125, the entire brass section has entered. The third horn alternates between minor seconds in bar 125 but unlike earlier examples, an abundance of rests are incorporated to foster intensity. More importantly, the principal trumpet introduces a motive comprised of four ascending sixteenth notes beginning initially on the pitch of B, resulting in a nearly identical quotation of Motive A's initial appearance, even in instrumentation, simply transposed down an octave. This motive serves as the basis for subsequent imitation by the horns in measure 129 while simultaneously linking the finale with "SkyLine." (Figure 4–10) In preparation of the returning refrain, horns one and three present triplets in the episode's final measure, a rhythm and orchestration found in earlier accompanimental passages of the rondo sections.

Figure 4–10. "Peachtree Street," mm. 125–129.

Refrain 5

The entire ensemble returns to a greatly truncated refrain section in measure 135 and curiously, the meters continue to alternate until bar 137; however, the rondo section unquestionably begins in 135 with the full ensemble. In measure 137, the musical content returns in transposition to bar 26. Four measures later, Higdon again transposes the material and repeats the passage with several variations, one of which is the consecutively accented

D in the violas, a noteworthy tonality with this composer. To segue to the final episode, the transitional material from measure 113 reappears in 145 with minor changes including a newly descending melodic line in the principal flute. At the close of this transition, the augmented rhythms from bar 113 are retained but to enhance the dramatic elements, Higdon includes a molto ritardando absent from the earlier passage.

Episode 5

The final episode is greatly expanded and features each orchestral section entering in a 4/4 measure with their earlier, respective episodic material in a display of great compositional skill. In order for this music to function effectively both individually and combined, Higdon composed this most complicated episode first. She explained:

> I did compose that section first, in an attempt to make a complicated texture work well, then I deconstructed it. When doing that, one has to make sure that the musical materials are interesting for each section on their own ... so there's a lot of going back and forth while working on the final section (first) and then on the individual sections.[39]

The strings begin in measure 151 with the celli recalling Motive A (Figure 4–11) followed by the first violins' answer. The passage is severely truncated from Episode 1 and lasts only a brief six measures before the woodwinds commence in measure 157 presenting material from Episode 2 with a few minor alterations. Unlike the earlier passage, however, the woodwinds are not featured alone; the strings continue below in a nearly identical repetition of measure 151. The woodwind section is also condensed considerably lasting only four measures before repeating. In this passage, one can truly see the genius of Higdon in the combination of the different episodes that simultaneously present contrast and repetition.

As the instrumentation expands, the texture becomes more complex. The strings continue to present content derived from Motive A with the exception of the violas that double the clarinets beginning in measure 165. Thus, the string section blends its previous episodic material with that of the

Figure 4–11. "Peachtree Street," mm. 151–153.

woodwinds. Measure 165 also marks the entrance of the percussion restating the material from Episode 3 in the earlier instrumentation of timpani, glockenspiel, and xylophone.

Following the initial order, the brass enter last yet unassumingly in measure 169 initially in an accompanying role before being featured in measure 173. Unlike the earlier passage, the trumpets are paired with the trombones to present major chords while the horns sound different chords separated by a major second, one of the most stylistic traits of Higdon.

Measures 177–178 function as a brief transition to the concluding refrain. The meter returns to 4/4 and the majority of the ensemble exhibits homorhythmic texture, a defining trait of the refrain sections. The exception lies with the sixteenth notes of the trumpets and principal trombone that substitute the repeated notes found in the rondo theme with major chords in ascending and descending runs; these rhythm and timbre are undoubtedly a reference to the refrain while simultaneously exhibiting one of Higdon's most stylistic traits.

Refrain 6

The final rondo theme commences in measure 179 with a near exact quotation of the movement's opening. Soon after and customary of Higdon, the material varies immediately and once again the refrain is considerably truncated from its original statement. The meter in the penultimate measure changes to 5/4, a time signature associated exclusively with episodic material and curiously the entire work closes in this meter. In this same bar, a homorhythmic descending scalar figure by nearly the entire ensemble assists in providing a mood of closure to precede the final *sforzato* D major chord, a concluding tonality prevalent in Higdon's orchestral works. Unquestionably, *City Scape* ends with the excitement and intensity characteristic of multi-movement finales.

Motives A and B unify the three movements which are evident only in a complete performance; however, individual movements have been equally well received and during the compositional process, Higdon actually envisioned the work in both ways.[40] Orchestras of high distinction have programmed *City Scape* either in part or in full including the Baltimore Symphony Orchestra, Atlanta Symphony Orchestra, BBC Scottish Symphony Orchestra, Melbourne Symphony Orchestra, the National Symphony Orchestra, and the Houston Symphony Orchestra.[41] Although each movement is musically interesting enough to stand alone, the work as a whole produces a more comprehensive understanding of the composer's stylistic tendencies.

Critical Reception and Conclusion

The reviews of this work are favorable and particularly noteworthy is the detailed level of musical commentary so often lacking in contemporary reviews. Following a complete performance of the composition with the National Symphony Orchestra in 2007, *The Washington Post*'s Robert Battey wrote:

> Higdon's music is lithe and expert [...] there is no empty note-spinning, and her snazzy pieces stick in the mind. She is particularly expert in her percussion writing [...] and "City Scape" features extremely imaginative passages for an extensive battery in all three pieces. The percussion does not simply add color and flavor to the orchestra; it has its own idiomatic themes as part of the music's basic material.[42]

David Patrick Stearns regularly publishes reviews and articles on Jennifer Higdon's music. About "river sings a song to trees," he commented:

> This music is frankly and unabashedly beautiful, but it never seems like a concession to audience conservatism. It's sincere stuff—and unlike similarly inviting works ranging from Gabriel Fauré to Lowell Liebermann, the ear doesn't grow sated early on. There's so much variety, so many beguiling sounds that you've never previously heard, that you can't tear your ears away.[43]

Battey's impression of the movement is likewise positive and he stated, "'river sings a song to trees,' is particularly original; fluttering, shimmering sounds gradually give way to several haunting, primal-sounding themes building to a well-developed climax."[44] After the premiere and recording with the ASO, the ensemble performed the second movement again in 2007, which prompted Pierre Ruhe to write:

> It's remarkable as a standalone work, conjuring many images of Atlanta, from sprawl to a sort of Buckhead pastorale of backyard forests and twittering birds. Higdon manages to charmingly evoke her own semi-urban domain without sinking into hoary cliches of city and nature.[45]

Since the unifying elements provide a coherence that is unattainable when only individual movements are performed, *City Scape* should be performed in its entirety. True to Higdon's style, these cyclical motives are never stated blatantly rather, they are imbedded deep within the texture. Additionally, the movements complement each other while maintaining musical autonomy; thus, when performed as a triptych, *City Scape* provides a rewarding and meaningful experience for the listener.

CHAPTER FIVE

Concerto 4–3

Bluegrass, a rich tradition of Appalachian music, is one of the few genres that can be classified as uniquely American. Curiously, its exclusive string instrumentation lends itself well to combining this vernacular style with the Western art tradition's symphonic orchestra as uniquely demonstrated in Higdon's *Concerto 4–3*. This unusual concerto is a mixture of styles and cultures reflecting the diversity of the United States and her people while maintaining Higdon's stylistic elements.

Concerto 4–3 was composed for Time for Three, a string trio known for its exploration of eclectic styles including bluegrass. The original members met as students at Curtis[1] and consisted of violinists, Zachary DePue[2] and Nicolas Kendall with Ranaan Meyer on double bass. While the members are conservatory trained, each of their backgrounds contain experiences outside of art music.[3]

The commission of *Concerto 4–3* originated with a meeting between Time for Three and Christoph Eschenbach, the then music director of the Philadelphia Orchestra. The conductor suggested a concerto by Higdon which immediately resonated with the trio since they knew her from Curtis and in the case of DePue, from far earlier. Higdon had studied with DePue's father, a music theory professor at Bowling Green State University, during her undergraduate studies.[4]

The composer generally does extensive research when writing a piece in a new genre but because she had composed numerous string works and concerti previously, her efforts were redirected to studying Time for Three's various musical styles. She recalled, "The idea was to write something that kind of captured their energetic personality because they're three real characters."[5] Higdon explained further in the recording's liner notes, "Being aware of all of the types of music that they play (bluegrass, rock, Bach, Beatles) gave me a starting point of inspiration for creating a piece that would spotlight their joy in performing, soulful musicality and prodigious skill."[6]

The trio provided Higdon recordings of their arrangements[7] to acquaint her intimately with their styles and with the composer present, recorded the various sounds effects they can produce in a Curtis practice room on the program Garageband.[8] DePue explained, "These are things a classical musician wouldn't do right off the bat. Bluegrassers approach the instrument differently. They're not about full, round tone, they're more physically percussive."[9] These sounds cannot be notated traditionally and in some cases, symbols were invented by Higdon.[10] An accompanying compact disc is available through Lawdon Press where each technique is listed with a number and identifying phrase based on bluegrass, traditional string techniques, or in the case of "Bradford," coined by Zachary DePue.[11] In the score, these sounds are also referred to by number and phrase. The ten effects are as follows:

1. Mouse & Light Chuck
2. Ricochet
3. Chuck-Hi & Low
4. Mouse Switch-Back
5. Falling Harmonic Trem.
6. Bradford-B/F
7. Bradford-Fast
8. Bradford-Open String
9. Bradford-Triplets
10. 2 Harmonics[12]

Although *Concerto 4–3* incorporates vernacular elements, it undeniably belongs to the genre of art music. Higdon had much to say about the role of bluegrass here as well as her experiences with this tradition. She explained:

> It's fascinating because I'm so trained in classical but I grew up in East Tennessee and there was a lot of bluegrass around and it's what we call true mountain music where none of the people will actually read the music. And so I had to really stop and think back, "All right, what was it like to experience this early bluegrass? What is that exactly and how do I make that into a piece that would fit on a classical concert" […] so I thought about what makes bluegrass bluegrass. There's a certain feeling to it that sounds like a celebration of joy in music and life. I thought about the fact that there's an emphasis on the offbeat and there are a lot of interesting slides. That comes usually from the tradition because the people who are playing are not used to tuning. They're just different languages, that's what I discovered when I really started thinking […] there are just little characteristics within bluegrass that fit within the classical realm, you just have to bend the notes differently, the rhythms are a little different, the timing […] but it is possible to do.[13]

Comparable statements are found in the work's program notes:

> "Concerto 4–3" is written in the Classical vein, with certain bluegrass techniques incorporated into the fabric of the piece: emphasis on offbeats, open strings, and slides. But the language is definitely tonal, 21st Century and American-sounding in style.[14]

While Time for Three was familiar with the musical language and style of bluegrass, Higdon knew that the musicians in the orchestras were less likely to have similar experiences. She explained:

> You never know what kind of orchestra you're walking into, and you kind of have to be careful how much you deviate from their norm. Bluegrass is so communicative. But the chord progressions are much simpler, and that doesn't always play well in an orchestra setting. You want to incorporate enough of the things that bluegrass uses ... and that was hard. Really tricky, actually.[15]

As typical of Higdon, this work was composed in reverse order beginning with the third movement and finishing with the first. Viewing the movements from this perspective, the music progresses from the art music tradition of the finale to the extended techniques discussed previously in the first movement with far more emphasis on vernacular styles.[16]

The solo writing in *Concerto 4–3* was conceived specifically for the premiering musicians. It is this precise quality that contributes to Higdon's continuously evolving compositional individuality because each piece captures a singular musician or ensemble and style; however, such writing never precludes other musicians from performing the work.

Although Higdon's earlier concerti eschew colorful titles (*Oboe Concerto, Piano Concerto*, etc.), this work is named to reference the premiering musicians (*Concerto 4–3*, Time for Three). The three movements also bear individual titles of rivers in the Smoky Mountains: "The Shallows," "Little River," and "Roaring Smokies." The composer explained, "I wanted to reference the Smokies, because East Tennessee was the first place that I really experienced bluegrass."[17] She expanded:

> Those names are all related to bodies of water [that I have been around] that run through and around the Smoky Mountains [...] I wanted some sort of name for the movements (as opposed to I, II, III), and it occurred to me that the last movement is very much like some of the roaring rivers that run through the mountains (unpredictable, fast, and all over the place). The opening movement's "sounds" reminded me of the sound you hear when you are down in the river, and the water is moving along the rocks ... there's a certain sizzle. I was struggling with finding the name for the middle movement, when I was sitting out on the porch of a barbecue place in Townsend [Tennessee] (Little River Bar-Be-Que [...]). This porch is literally along Little River, and the spot there is quiet (because it's deep) and peaceful, and that made me realize that the 2nd movement is like that area of the river (and quite the contrast to the other two movements).[18]

Prior to the world premiere, Time for Three conducted a read-through with a makeshift orchestra comprised of Curtis students. Experiences such as these are particularly helpful for new works because it allows the soloists to hear the orchestral parts and how their lines fit into the musical fabric. Although Curtis may be the training ground of some of the world's best musicians, college students are still just that as Kendall explained, "A lot of friends were willing to chip in. We had pizza."[19]

Concerto 4–3 was a co-commission between the Philadelphia Orchestra, the Pittsburgh Symphony Orchestra, and the Wheeling Symphony Orchestra.[20] The orchestration is comparatively smaller than what Higdon typically utilizes, particularly in the woodwinds which eschews timbres frequently explored in the composer's earlier works, notably the piccolo, English horn, bass clarinet, and contrabassoon. Additionally, the harp is excluded and only two percussionists along with a timpanist are required.[21] As the composer explained, the only parameters from the commissioning ensembles was an approximate duration; she determined the orchestration and form of the movements. Regarding the former, Higdon stated:

> The deciding factor for the instrumentation was the consideration of cost for orchestras to have to pay for doubling on those wind instruments (it would be more expensive, therefore not as many orchestras could afford to perform the work), and I didn't feel those colors were needed.[22]

Movement One, "The Shallows"

The composer's program notes provide a brief commentary to explain the imagery and techniques of each movement; however, these notes do not make the work programmatic. Consistent with Higdon's previous concerti, *Concerto 4–3* belongs solely to the realm of absolute music. The composer writes that "The Shallows"

> incorporates unique extended techniques (a manner of playing beyond the normal way of playing these instruments) that mimic everything from squeaking mice to electric guitars. These sounds resemble parts of the mountain rivers that move in shallow areas, where small rocks and pebbles make for a rapid ride that moves a rafter quickly from one side of the river to the other.[23]

The form of the first movement is far from traditional although the trio of soloists and returning motives are reminiscent of the Baroque concerto grosso and ritornello form. The A sections are those that utilize the entire ensemble with the soloists and include elements of the returning thematic motive in different key areas. Contrastingly, the B and C sections are scored almost exclusively for the soloists with no appearance of the primary motivic material and thus serve as episodes. Highly unusual is the lack of accelerandi, ritardandi, or meter changes, strategies used by the composer to separate large, formal sections. The analysis is provided below:

Measure Numbers	Music	Letter
1–14	Solo trio, extended techniques	Introduction
15–30	Primary motive of movement featured initially in trio, then orchestra	A
31–54	Reduced texture to trio and primarily percussion; return of extended techniques from introduction	B
55–67	Primary motive returns, full orchestra	A'
68–79	Trio featured, prominent bass solo	C
80–108	Soloists with primary motive; full orchestra	A"
109–115	Solo trio transitions to optional cadenza	Conclusion

Introduction

The opening tempo of quarter note=86 is deceptive; the rhythms, syncopations, and subdivisions immediately create the energy expected of a concerto's opening movement. There is no orchestral exposition or introduction, rather the work begins with only the first violin soloist producing Bs an octave apart. This is listed in the score to be played with a "unique scrub sound"[24] and designated on the accompanying CD as "1. Mouse & Light Chuck," a playing style that returns throughout the movement. The unpredictable emphasis of notes provides another layer of rhythmic vitality to the music. Initially, the first violinist stresses beats one and three, then every beat, and eventually syncopations. The second violin begins in measure five, contrasting the first by playing on beats two and four with effects labeled "2. Ricochet" followed subsequently by "3. Chuck-Hi & Low." Finally, the bass enters in measure six with the instruction of "slap E string against the fingerboard"[25] (Figure 5-1). This is directly related to the bluegrass style since such string

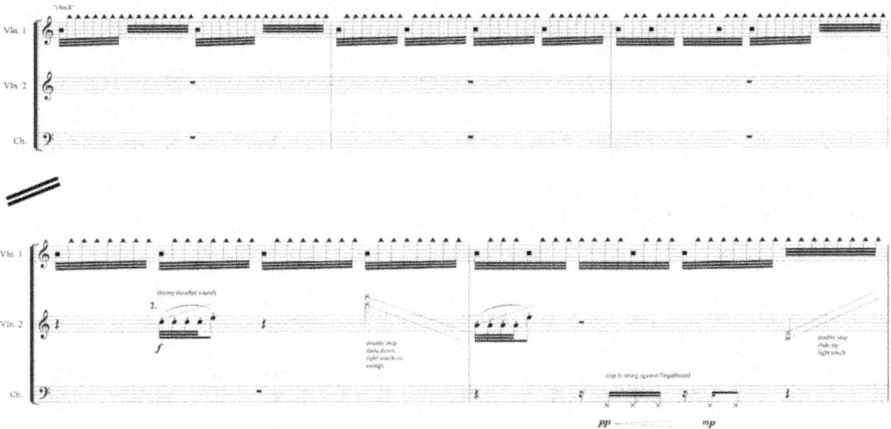

Figure 5-1. *Concerto 4-3*; I, mm. 2-6.

ensembles never include a drum but, and as is the case here, obtain percussive effects through other means. The introduction builds quickly in intensity as the second violin and the bass become progressively more animated.

The second violinist's part in the introduction is comprised initially of an open sting ascending fifth followed by a descending portamento double stop, both indicative of bluegrass; however, the returning ascending fifth in subsequent transpositions prevent the use of open strings. Finally, Higdon scores pizzicato for the bass, the exclusive manner of playing the instrument in bluegrass. As with the second violinist, the part is comprised of portamento double stops but with perfect fourth intervals. While fourth and fifth intervals remain stylistic traits of Higdon, the function is starkly different than the sustained, accompanying intervals found in her earlier works. Their purpose here serves solely as a figurative nod to vernacular traditions.

As the introduction nears its conclusion, two additional extended techniques appear: in measure 13, the second violinist presents "5. Falling Harmonic Trem." and in the subsequent bar, the first violinist alternates from the "1. Mouse & Light Chuck" of the opening to "4. Mouse Switch-Back." The introduction closes in measure 14 aided by the suspended cymbal entrance that crescendos into the A section.

A Section

Higdon eschews all extended techniques for the soloists at the beginning of the A section to facilitate blending with the ensemble upon their entrance. The passage opens with an arco dialog between the violinists comprised primarily of double stop sixth intervals accompanied by moving pizzicato sixteenth notes in the bass. This leads to the primary motivic material of the movement introduced by the first violin at measure 17 (Figure 5–2). Immediately following, the violin parts are reversed from the opening: the second presents the syncopated repeated Bs while the descending portamento double stops are found in the first. The motive reappears with great emphasis through its unison octave scoring in all three soloists at measure 20 immediately prior to the ensemble's entrance.

Figure 5-2. *Concerto 4-3*; I, m. 17.

Although the texture is sparse upon the tutti entrance in measure 21, several Higdon compositional traits emerge. First, the low strings and principal bassoon present a brief *basso ostinato* consisting of numerous fifth intervals. Secondly, the violas and second violins, doubled by the clarinets, present the major chords characteristic of Higdon's works. These hallmarks are complemented by continuing descending portamento figures in the soloists emphasizing a b diminished chord. In the subsequent measure, the initial motive returns in the solo violins while the bass is notated with a solid black line outlining a general contour with the instructions "slide up and around, rising, in 32nds. sul pont[icello]"[26] (Figure 5-3). This is followed in measure 25 by an exchange of a small fragment of the primary motive.

Figure 5-3. *Concerto 4-3*; I, mm. 22-25.

In measure 26, the solo violins return to the double stop sixth intervals that opened the A section. The tutti violins and principal flute provide a subtle reference to the primary motive, echoed by the violin soloists two measures later. A fast crescendo to fortissimo by the soloists followed by a descending flourish in the woodwinds and tutti violins at measure 31 lead directly into the B section.

B Section

The B section features the trio prominently with a sparse, yet rhythmic accompaniment in the horns, marimba, viola, and celli. The horns double the violas with consistent repeated sixteenth notes on A. This same pitch is sounded in the marimba in 32nd notes followed by a half rest while the celli augments the rhythm presenting the pitch on the beat. The orchestration ceases in measure 36 to shift the entire focus to the trio soloists.

When the orchestra becomes tacet, the trio exchanges 32nd note double stops and while not comprised solely of the earlier sixth intervals, the energetic atmosphere remains similar. This flows into a passage beginning at measure 38 filled with extended techniques, some of which have been featured previously but on a much grander scale that requires additional instructions from Higdon. The section begins with the return in the first violin to the "1. Mouse & Light Chuck" manner used for the opening's repetitive Bs. This is subsequently transferred to the second violinist where the style continues through the beginning of the A' section. Also similar to the introduction, the bass provides a percussive element but far more extensively with different pizzicato types. At measure 40, Higdon only notates the bowing and rhythm for the first violin soloist with "extreme sul pont.[icello]."[27] In measure 42, this is changed to a solid black line that outlines a melodic shape; the composer instructs, "Improvise, tremolos or scales or slides or trills, in either bowed trem. or in varied rhythms (or any combination of), all sul pont. <u>Feel free to vary dynamics through here</u>"[28] (Figure 5-4).

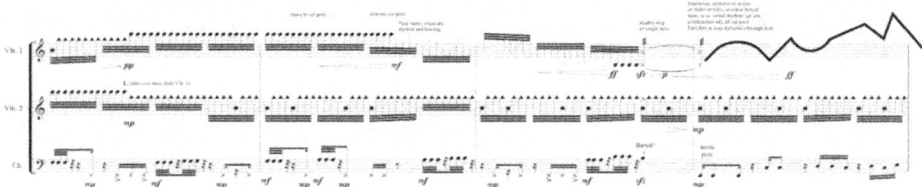

Figure 5-4. *Concerto 4-3*; I, mm. 39–42.

Beneath the first violinist's new melodic line, the second violinist and bass return to varied material from the introduction. It is certainly not unusual for Higdon to alter earlier content but previously, such passages were not joined by a new line; however, and certainly notable, this technique reappears in two of *Cold Mountain*'s arias. Whether or not this demonstrates an evolution of Higdon's style remains to be seen.

The prominent use of percussion, a significant element of Higdon's orchestration, is aptly demonstrated in this passage beginning with the sandpaper blocks in measure 41 followed quickly by the guiro, tambourine, egg shaker, and timpani. Of particular interest is the two beat pattern in the timpani between measures 49 and 53, comprised partly of the b diminished chord featured earlier in the soloists. In measure 53, the third of the chord is eliminated leaving only alternating Bs and Fs. These pitches are doubled and presented harmonically in the first violin soloist with an effect labeled "6. Bradford"[29] that also oscillates through the beginning of the subsequent section. For additional emphasis, the same interval is presented through portamento figures by the solo bass (Figure 5-5).

Figure 5-5. *Concerto 4–3*; I, mm. 53–55.

A' Section

The A' section begins in measure 55 with a return of the ensemble, initially sparsely orchestrated with only the second violins and the upper woodwinds presenting the primary motive. This reduced ensemble balances the trio's continued alternating tritones of the first violinist and bass and the repeated Bs from the second violinist. The extended techniques in the trio combined with the contrasting traditional style of the ensemble create a fascinating blend of vernacular and art traditions.

The tritone interval remains a significant focus creating much harmonic tension until it is temporarily eased in measure 57. At this point, the interval either ceases entirely or is replaced by a perfect fifth, a fundamental interval in Higdon's harmonic language. This coincides with another significant Higdon compositional trait in the tutti violins and woodwinds: major and minor chords. Short lived, the tritones return in the subsequent measure with great emphasis in the descending, syncopated, double stop portamento figures of both the trio and ensemble. This also marks one of the few places in the entire work where the tutti strings participate in any bluegrass performance styles (Figure 5–6).

As witnessed previously, an essential element of Higdon's style is to vary earlier material in subsequent sections. Thus is the case in the tutti strings from measures 59 to 63 which features the primary motive reorchestrated from the soloists; however, Higdon also adds a new line for the bassoons and marimba. The solo trio become temporarily tacet beginning in measure 60 as the texture gradually increases leading to one of Higdon's most characteristic traits, major and minor chords in the trumpets. This lasts only two

Figure 5-6. *Concerto 4-3*; I, mm. 57-58.

measures before the orchestration is reduced to balance the reentering soloists' presentation of the primary motive. Condensing the texture even further, the activity of the remaining tutti strings slowly diminishes before becoming tacet altogether at the close of the passage.

C Section

The C section, featuring the trio soloists exclusively, opens at measure 68 with an exploration of perfect fourth and fifth interval double stops. Most importantly in measure 72, the bass presents an extended solo for the first time in the movement with a range so extensive, three clefs are required for the notation. The solo contains several noteworthy elements including the appearance of the primary motive in measure 73 followed by a return of the sliding B-F portamenti.

Accompanying the bass solo, the second violinist presents fifth intervals in harmonics with quickly moving 32nd note rhythms. This material continues through the remainder of the passage. The first violinist initially alternates between a pizzicato pedal F and open fifth intervals but in measure 75, a new pattern played entirely pizzicato and marked *quasi guitara*[30] emerges. The quadruple stops performed in this manner is comprised of two seventh intervals (Figure 5–7) and the rhythm becomes progressively more animated until the section concludes.

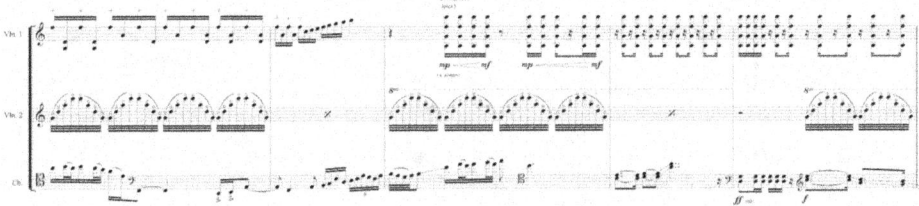

Figure 5–7. *Concerto 4–3*; I, mm. 73–77.

A" Section

The final A section opens in measure 80 with a continuation of the solo violinists with their preceding material. The only other instruments scored in this section's beginning are the timpani alternating third intervals and the tutti violins in pizzicato. In the pickup to measure 81, Higdon designates a solo for the trio's second violin leaving no doubt of the line's musical importance. Indeed, the melody features the primary motive that defines each of the A sections; however, this is complemented by a double stop which functions as a drone common in the vernacular style. As the passage progresses, the soloist's rhythm is augmented while the first violin becomes tacet. This brief respite from the musical excitement prepares the listener for the final climax of the movement.

Thus far, the full ensemble has been featured minimally throughout the work but beginning in measure 87, the orchestration and dynamics gradually increase and continue to do so until the cadenza at the close of the movement. Horns one and two enter with a rhythmic dialog that recall similar earlier passages for the violin soloists. Immediately following, the orchestration expands to include the full string section and the timpani; the primary motive is presented in measure 91 by the woodwinds doubled by the second violins and viola. In the subsequent measure, the three soloists join in displaying the motive. Of particular interest are the portamento figures at measure 93 in the tutti strings (Figure 5-8) that mirrors the similar content from the A' section in measure 58 (Figure 5-6). As with the earlier passage, this leads directly to the primary motive in an unmistakable entrance through the forte dynamic and the unison scoring in the high woodwinds and strings.

Figure 5-8. *Concerto 4-3*; I, m. 93.

Beginning in measure 95, a call and response ensues between the ensemble and the solo trio that also alternates between traditional and extended techniques. The woodwinds and the tutti strings present the major and minor sonorities demonstrative of Higdon's style subsequently answered by the trio. The solo violinists produce fifth intervals on open strings through the "7. Bradford-Fast" technique while the bass, marked sul ponticello, is instructed to produce a "loud, agitated double stop ascent … 32nd notes."[31] The latter is notated in the score with two solid black lines providing an overall ascending contour but in the following measure, the bass's directions change to "Shoot as loud and fast as possible, as high as you can."[32] With the omission of double stops, the notation changes to a solitary black line. Nowhere else in *Concerto 4-3* does the notation and music clearly reflect the distinct stylistic differences between the art and vernacular traditions (Figure 5-9).

In measures 99–100, the orchestra becomes tacet briefly to shift the

Figure 5–9. *Concerto 4-3*; I, mm. 95–98.

musical focus entirely to the trio that present material nearly identical to measures 36–37. The respective earlier passage led to a lengthy solo episode while here, it introduces the full ensemble's majestic fortissimo entrance. This is one of the very few times "The Shallows" features the entire orchestra and its appearance heightens the energy for the following cadenza.

In measure 104, the ensemble becomes drastically softer to balance the trio's reentrance; noteworthy is the sustained A major chord in the trombones, a sonority and orchestration characteristic of Higdon. The solo first violinist utilizes an effect labeled "9. Bradford-Triplets" with fifth intervals on open strings while the remainder of the trio returns in the subsequent measure with the second violinist introducing the final effect, "10. 2 Harmonics." The orchestral texture continues to thin leaving only the high woodwinds that diminish in both volume and rhythmic activity before ceasing altogether in measure 109. In the final bar of the A" section, the first violinist produces open fifths labeled "partial Bradford" while the remaining soloists present Es in differing rhythms. Their music is marked *col legno battuto* for a more percussive sound reminiscent of the movement's opening. Higdon concludes the section softly through dynamics of varying shades of piano.

Conclusion and Cadenza

The ensemble is tacet beginning in measure 109 entrusting the soloists to transition to the improvised, optional cadenza. The notated conclusion is rather brief; however, Higdon incorporates elements from the introduction that bring the movement full circle. Beginning in measure 110, the first violinist returns to the same pitch and "1. Mouse & Light Chuck" effect of the opening which continues through to the cadenza. The second violinist and the bass maintain the col legno style and Es of the previous section with gradually augmented rhythms and increasingly softer dynamics eventually leaving only the first violinist. The optional cadenza follows with no marks or directions from the composer. In fact, the only parameter Higdon provides is to conclude with a bass solo that will subsequently open the second movement. Thus, "The Shallows" and "Little River" are performed attacca. Meyer explained that as in bygone eras, the soloists "take the thematic material and use it as our jumping off point."[33] The cadenza is improvised anew in each performance.

Movement Two, "Little River"

The second movement is slow (quarter note=66) and expressive in contrast to the surrounding energetic, outer movements. In the program notes, Higdon wrote:

> The second movement, "Little River," is slow-moving and lyrical, very much in hymn-like fashion. This movement reflects the beauty of Little River as it flows through Townsend and Walland, Tennessee. At times there is a real serenity and a majestic look to the water, with no movement obvious on the pure, glassy surface.[34]

"Little River" offers unique rhythmic challenges to the performers as explained by the composer, "Nothing occurs on the beat. If it does, there's nothing more square or hideous."[35] DePue echoed that notion and described the movement as "a beautiful, broad and harmonious movement that hints to very simple music but isn't."[36]

The form is of great interest because it contains elements of a Romantic era chaconne where a basso ostinato serves as the foundation for the movement[37] but Higdon replaces the ostinato with a chord progression featured only in the A sections. When asked if she conceptualized the movement around this progression, she responded, "I think I did ... upon reflection, it would seem so (it's amazing how a composer's brain releases this [information] ... when moving on to other pieces). I'm guessing that I thought it might be a good 'touch stone' to return to throughout the movement."[38] It is interesting to note that while "Little River" maintains chaconne-like elements, only later does the fully realized form appear in the aptly titled "Chaconni" movement of this composer's Pulitzer Prize winning *Violin Concerto*. The form of "Little River" is outlined below:

Measure Numbers	Music	Letter
1–8	Conclusion of bass solo from cadenza	
9–47	Eight measure chord progression (chaconne) introduced in soloists, chaconne continues in soloists paired with oboe duet; soloists paired with brass, chaconne in low woodwinds with soloists, closes with oboe duet	A
48–67	Full ensemble with frequent meter changes, chaconne absent	B
68–100	Passage for soloists who are subsequently paired with the strings' presentation of the chaconne, A material returns slightly varied (soloists first with brass, then with chorale in low woodwinds)	A'
101–118	Meter changes, earlier material returns from B reorchestrated in fuller texture, chaconne absent	B'
119–135	Soloists paired with oboe duet and lower strings	Coda

A Section

As mentioned previously, movements one and two are connected by an improvised cadenza that as specified by Higdon, concludes with the bass; this solo opens the second movement with a "length to be determined."[39] Notation returns in measure nine with an eight-bar chaconne in chorale-like texture and slow harmonic rhythm. This chaconne (Figure 5–10), presented first in its simplest form, reappears throughout the A sections in varied orchestrations and serves as the foundation of the entire movement.

Figure 5–10. *Concerto 4–3*; II, mm. 9–16.

In the pick-up to measure 17, the oboes present a lyrical duet joined by a countermelody in the solo bass with the repeating, albeit somewhat varied chord progression in the violin soloists. This chaconne concludes with an accelerando increasing the quarter note to 70 at measure 25 that coincides with the entrance of the trumpets and trombones. Characteristic of Higdon's compositional style, these instruments present major and minor chords and although the chaconne is absent, the mood is maintained through the chorale texture and slow harmonic rhythm. The melodic interest of this passage lies in the lyrical unison octaves of the soloists that exude the serene calmness referenced in the composer's program notes. A very slight poco ritardando returns the tempo to the original quarter note=66.

In measure 34 appears the final chaconne of the A section in the lower woodwinds which although slightly varied, remains recognizable. This progression is paired with a continuation of the trio's earlier lyrical content expanded from the unison octaves to a separate melody in the bass. Following this chaconne, the woodwinds are replaced by an oboe duet reminiscent of the earlier passage to bring the A section full circle.

B Section

The B section, beginning in measure 48, differs from the surrounding material in almost every conceivable manner. First, the full ensemble's majestic power is on display and the loud dynamics and texture provide a striking contrast from the chamber-like A sections. Secondly, the character of the music changes through the livelier rhythms and alternating meters, initially between 4/4 and 2/4 but later including the more unorthodox 5/8 and 5/4. An example of the vibrant rhythm can be found in the triplet motive of the violas, doubled by the clarinet, that begins in measure 48 and becomes progressively more insistent (Figure 5–11). Finally, and most importantly, the B sections are distinct through the complete omission of the peaceful chaconne.

Figure 5-11. *Concerto 4-3*; II, mm. 55–56.

The soloists are active from the beginning of the section. One moment of particular interest can be found in measure 58: the trio present the primary motive from the first movement (Figure 5–2) in unison octaves (Figure 5–12). Although brief, the moment is unmistakable through the unison, homorhythmic writing. Soon afterwards, the soloists become tacet and remain so until the next section.

With the exclusion of the trio, the musical focus shifts to the ensemble for the first time in "Little River." Subsequently, major and minor chords appear for the third trumpet and second and third trombones. The conclud-

Figure 5-12. *Concerto 4-3*; II, m. 58.

ing measures of the section feature the full ensemble in homorhythmic texture paired with a decrescendo and ritardando in preparation of A'.

A' Section

The A' section begins in measure 68 and is distinct in several ways: the soloists re-enter, the ensemble becomes tacet, and the meter stabilizes to the opening 4/4. Initially, the chaconne is omitted but in measure 76, the muted tutti strings enter softly with the progression transposed. The lyrical countermelodies of the trio and accompanying chaconne conclude with a very slight accelerando to quarter note=72 in measure 84.

Following a single presentation of the chaconne, Higdon returns to the brass chorale from measure 25. The soloists' material is likewise comparable to the earlier passage although somewhat varied. At the close of this section in measure 91, Higdon eliminates the brass leaving the trio to introduce the new melodic content. The concluding bars of A' present a lower woodwind chorale unrelated to earlier progressions; however, the mood is comparable to the chaconne passages through the sonorities and slow harmonic rhythm. The latter gradually increases in preparation for the subsequent section.

B' Section

The last large formal section begins in measure 101 and corresponds to the first B section reorchestrated for a fuller texture. The meter alternation, the featuring of the entire orchestra, and the return of the triplet motive remain comparable to the earlier passage and most importantly, the chaconne is absent. Also similar, the soloists are tacet in the latter half and the section likewise concludes with a decrease in dynamics, tempo, and texture.

Coda

The second movement closes with an extended coda reminiscent of the A and A' section through an oboe duet with the soloists and the slow moving chords in the low, muted strings. While neither the oboes nor the strings present earlier material, the timbres in the slow harmonic rhythm unique to these passages create a sense of familiarity. "Little River" ends unassumingly with harmonics for the soloists before closing with a single, sustained note for the bass, the instrument that introduced the movement.

Movement Three, "Roaring Smokies"

In a typical concerto, the finale is frequently the shortest in duration and while also fast, less serious than the opening movement. Thus is the case for "Roaring Smokies" designated with a tempo of quarter note=142–152. In the program notes, Higdon explained:

> The third movement, "Roaring Smokies," is a rapid-fire virtuosic movement that shifts and moves very much like a raging river (those wild mountain waters that pour out of the mountains). It is fun to swim in those cold waters, but your attention must always be alert, as danger lurks … the water goes where it wants and will take you with it.[40]

The movement can be separated into four sections, each beginning with the primary melodic theme; however, these sections neither follow traditional forms nor are they entirely paratactic since musical material returns briefly at times. As such, utilizing numerals in lieu of letters will suffice:

Measure Numbers	Music	Section
1–68	Primary theme introduced in measure 15, small sections of frequent meter changes featured, secondary theme presented accompanied by major chords in strings and woodwinds	1
69–117	Primary theme paired with new countermelody, orchestral soli designated for principal clarinet and first stand solo of tutti violins	2
118–142	Cadenza-like passage for second violin soloist reminiscent of primary theme paired with improvisation by remaining soloists in an exploration of Lydian mode	3

Measure Numbers	Music	Section
143–216	Earlier material returns from section 1 combined with new content, work closes with meter changes and secondary theme in tutti violins	4

Section 1

The movement begins with only the concerto soloists in sustained rhythms that briefly retain the mood of the second movement. The bass and second violin present unison octaves but curiously, the bass is scored an octave higher than the violin. While the bass sustains the opening pitch, the violins begin a dialog exchanging portamento figures which are subsequently featured in the bass at measure six. This activity coincides with faster rhythms to create the illusion of an accelerando.

The portamento figures are replaced in measure nine by staggered entrances of rushing sixteenth notes in no discernable pattern that enhances a sense of unpredictability. In measure 14, the soloists return to the opening pitches in much faster rhythms followed a measure later by the introduction of the movement's primary theme in unison octaves (Figure 5–13). Orchestrating the theme in this singular manner places great emphasis on the content and facilitates its recognition in subsequent entrances. At the close of the melody, the rhythmic action ceases with a fortissimo quarter note followed immediately in measure 21 by a repetition of the theme. As expected with Higdon, the theme is not simply a restatement of earlier material: the temple blocks enter and the soloists present only the opening two beats before the material is somewhat varied.

Figure 5–13. *Concerto 4–3*; III, mm. 15–20.

In measure 25, alternating accents between the soloists emulate the shifting currents of the mountain rivers in Higdon's program notes. These are featured in a 3/4 meter for two measures before being interrupted by a unison passage in sixteenth notes in a 4/4 meter. The abrupt change in texture complements the time signature in portraying the program's imagery (Figure 5–14).

Figure 5-14. *Concerto 4-3*; III, mm. 25-27.

Meter changes between 3/4, 4/4, and 5/4 populate the subsequent measures.

A 4/4 time signature stabilizes in measure 32 that coincides with Higdon's characteristic major chords in the trumpets echoed by similar sonorities in the trombones. As the soloists continue their relentless sixteenth notes, the orchestration gradually expands with the strings and woodwinds replacing the brass with chordal punctuations that never overpower the trio.

Meter changes resume in measure 41. In the subsequent bar, the first solo violinist introduces the brief secondary theme which is reinforced by the pitches echoed in the second violinist. They merge together in octaves at bar 44 which momentarily requires unorthodox notation (Figure 5-15). Immediately following Figure 5-15, the soloists return to unison material in octaves reminiscent of the primary theme; the content varies and the meters continue to alternate, however, the scoring and running sixteenth notes remain similar. Accompanying the soloists are major and minor chords in the trombones, a restatement of harmonies found in the low strings at measure 40. The soloists continue their unison material until measure 51 when

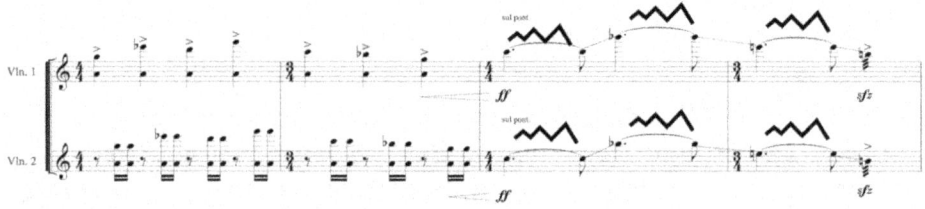

Figure 5-15. *Concerto 4-3*; III, mm. 42-45.

the violins become temporarily tacet. At this point, the same progression in the low strings at measure 40 returns twice in a reorchestration for the lower woodwinds and horns. Upon this chord progression's repeat in measure 53, the violin soloists reenter with the secondary theme.

The meter stabilizes to 3/4 beginning in measure 58 and the orchestration is also greatly reduced to feature primarily the soloists supported only by the marimba, glockenspiel, and pizzicato violins. The violins explore high but indistinct pitches in a specified rhythm (Figure 5–16). Higdon explained the notation in more detail:

> Rather than designating specific pitches, which would make this more difficult, I wanted very high sounds that would squeak. It was a way to keep the rhythm going for the soloists, while creating an unusual color. This technique is sometimes notated in scores with an arrowhead, meaning the highest note possible. But because I wanted them to shape each small fragment, I used the X and moved it up and down a bit (while removing the ledger lines).[41]

The passage culminates with a crescendo that leads to the subsequent section.

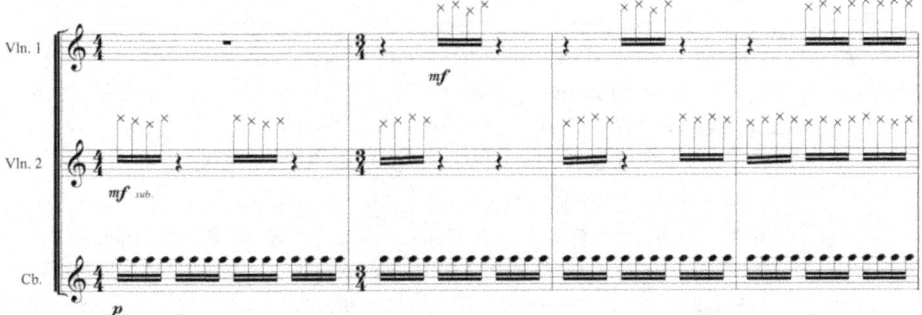

Figure 5–16. *Concerto 4–3*; III, mm. 57–60.

Section 2

A characteristic manner for Higdon to designate large formal sections is through a meter change which begins section two in measure 69. The violin soloists present transposed material from measure ten accompanied by a sustained minor seventh chord in the strings and woodwinds. Three measures later, the primary theme follows, also in transposition and doubled by the solo bass. Although somewhat varied from the original, its appearance is unmistakable since it is accompanied only by sparse percussion. The theme is separated between the two soloists rather than the unison octaves of its initial presentation in Figure 5-13 (Figure 5-17). The quoted material from section 1 continues through measure 77.

Figure 5-17. *Concerto 4-3*; III, mm. 72-77.

Although soft orchestral entrances begin in measure 78, the focus remains on the soloists' alternation between unison sixteenth notes reminiscent of the primary theme and new musical twists and turns reflective of Higdon's program notes. Several elements remain noteworthy in this passage. In measure 88, the trumpets and trombones present major chords in a slow harmonic rhythm. These are initially paired with rushing sixteenth notes in unison octaves in the tutti violins and violas that create a dialog with the soloists. The soloists' response is comprised of major and minor sonorities in sixteenth notes paired with major chords in the woodwinds. In the second statement, the tutti strings are again paired with major chords in the brass; however, in the third and final presentation, the brass chords are replaced by the trumpets' open fifths, an interval of great significance in the works of Higdon.

Section two features one of the very few designated orchestral soli of *Concerto 4-3* with the Bb clarinet in measure 94. This provides a stark contrast to the concerto soloists scored in high ranges while simultaneously demonstrating Higdon's exploration of color. The material in the solo violins derives from measures 79 to 80 with a highly embellished bass solo but unlike the earlier passage, the meters alternate. Although Higdon traditionally varies returning material, new countermelodies such as those found in the clarinet and bass, were not present in her earliest works but occur in more recent compositions such as *Cold Mountain* as noted earlier in the chapter.

The clarinet solo is replaced in measure 99 with the tutti strings and soloists in unison featuring a rush of sixteenth notes in a continually turning contour that reflects the shifting water currents in the program notes. The soloists become briefly tacet in measure 104 replaced by the full ensemble in loud dynamics. The moment is again concise lasting only a few measures before the rhythm is augmented and the dynamics diminish considerably. The soloists reenter in measure 108 with fast rhythms and a crescendo leading into measure 110. Here, the material is again derived from measures 79 to 80 paired with a new Bb clarinet solo and joined by the first stand of first violins, a uniquely Higdon orchestration. These unison soli present gradually descending rushing sixteenth notes; the falling contour is complemented by progressively augmented rhythms also found in the soloists to quietly conclude section two.

Section 3

This section begins in measure 118 and features the soloists with percussion. The second violinist opens with a pattern reminiscent of the primary theme but the accidentals initially imply a tonal center of Bb minor, the relative minor of the Db major featured subsequently, with a rather conspicuous appearance of several G naturals. The soloist is joined in measure 122 by several rhythmic motives in the temple blocks, an orchestration that recalls the movement's opening.

In measure 127, the bass enters with instructions from Higdon: "improv. Key of Db/use G natural sometimes."[42] The G natural, a raised fourth in Db major, suggests the Lydian mode. As noted in Chapter One, she does not consider keys while writing and the same is true here; her intent was not to consciously use Lydian mode but to relate the soloists harmonically.[43] The texture expands when the cabasa joins the temple blocks in measure 127 followed 8 bars later by the first violinist's entrance. Beneath the soloists, the percussion continually increase in volume and rhythmic intensity until the conclusion of section three in measure 143.

Section 4

The final section begins softly with only the soloists and the trumpets presenting the material from measures 32 to 39 but the texture increases through the quoted passage. In measure 151, Higdon instructs the second violinist to improvise loudly for four bars followed by another section of continuously alternating meters that once again suggest the unpredictable waters in the program notes. The solo bass replaces the second violinist's improvisation in 157 complemented by high, repeated pitches in the violin soloists and major chords in the trombones.

Measures 164–167 features a return of the secondary theme in the solo violinists with a much more active solo bass line. The melody is transposed a second higher in measure 168 and again in 172. Two bars later, the secondary theme is replaced by the primary theme in the principal Bb clarinet which immediately repeats an octave higher in the second clarinet. The latter is paired with a notation of a solid black line for both the solo first violinist and bassist that suggests only a melodic contour while the solo second violinist presents energetic octave Bs, reminiscent of *Concerto 4-3*'s opening.

The soloists return to traditional notation in measure 182 which recalls bar 13, material featured immediately prior to the primary theme and indeed two bars later, the trio present this theme in unison octaves. New however, is the orchestration of the major chords in the trumpets subsequently replaced by the trombones. This is followed by a different repeated section: measures 191–196 are transposed and slightly varied from measures 88 to 93.

Beginning in measure 200, the solo violinists and marimba are provided with a notation of x replacing the notehead, which was explained previously in its initial occurrence at measure 57. It bears noting that no other connection exists between the two passages. The previously excluded marimba is given additional instructions by Higdon: "Any notes in key of C at top of marimba range."[44] Following a dramatic, sweeping portamento, the trio become temporarily tacet in bar 204 to allow a final bravura passage for the ensemble. Of particular interest are the alternating meters maintained through the final measures, major and minor chords in the trombones, and the less frequent sforzando major chords in the trumpets. The melodic material of the passage, however, is the secondary theme, initially featured in measures 42–43, in the tutti violins doubled by the flutes.

The trio re-enter initially in unison octaves at measure 210 doubling the woodwinds' ascending scalar passages but two measures later, the soloists' notation changes to a single line indicating free improvisation.[45] The full ensemble, scored in a homorhythmic texture and gradually increasing in volume, presents the major chords so pivotal to Higdon's style and a resounding and cheerful D major chord concludes the work.

Critical Reception and Conclusion

Each of the commissioning ensembles performed *Concerto 4–3* in 2008; the Philadelphia Orchestra presented the world premiere on January 10 at the Kimmel Center for the Performing Arts in Philadelphia, Pennsylvania, led by Christoph Eschenbach. A month later, on February 22, André Raphel Smith conducted the Wheeling Symphony Orchestra in the Wheeling premiere at the Capitol Theatre in Wheeling, West Virginia. Finally, on December 5, the trio performed with the Pittsburgh Symphony Orchestra with Leonard Slatkin at Heinz Hall in its Pittsburgh premiere.[46] Lewis Whittington reviewed the world premiere in great detail:

> Jennifer Higdon's *Concerto 4–3*, which electrified the almost-sold-out audience at Verizon Hall [...] will go down as one of the musical highlights of the year. One thing that impresses is the immediacy of the music, the past compositional theory and the fertile

American musical terrain she explores. The propulsion and the poetic gliding thrills continue for the work's three movements, and Higdon exploited the trio's furious fiddling and virtuosic clarity. The rustic ambience Higdon conjures is a bursting tonal landscape, every bit as evocative and transporting as the urbane metropolitan tour she offered in her 2004[47] work, *City Scapes* [sic]. Higdon's non-derivative style [...] contributes to the understanding of hybrid classical that is distinctly American.[48]

The trio performed the work again with the Philadelphia Orchestra under the baton of Marin Alsop at the Saratoga Performing Arts Center in August 2008. *American Record Guide*'s review was penned by Joseph Dalton:

Higdon launched the piece with the trio's battery of sound effects—including scratching, tapping, and the like—allowing two fully improvised cadenzas, and otherwise alluding often to bluegrass fiddling, tender folk song, and even some rhythmically charged hints at jazz and rock. There was also plenty of old-fashioned American sentiment and traditional orchestral gestures.[49]

Andrew Druckenbrod from the *Pittsburgh Post-Gazette* reviewed the work's Pittsburgh premiere and recognized that the work "creates the illusion of a free-wheeling jam in front of the orchestra. Yet, with the exception of the cadenza, it is all Higdon."[50] Druckenbrod singled out "Little River" as "gorgeous music, played tenderly by all and crafted well by Slatkin."[51]

Reviewing *Concerto 4–3* at the 2009 Ravinia Festival, John von Rhein from the *Chicago Tribune* opined that Higdon:

Finds ingenious ways to integrate violinists Zachary De Pue [sic] and Nicholas Kendall, and double bassist Ranaan Meyer with the orchestra while allowing their personalities to shape and color the musical dialogue. Higdon also gives full sway to their ostensibly improvised interplay in the extended cadenza that links the first two movements. The sounds suggest everything from an electric-guitar jam to a madly onrushing freight train.[52]

In 2011, in Madison, Wisconsin, Time for Three performed the work with the Wisconsin Chamber Orchestra under conductor Andrew Sewell. *The Capital Times*'s Lindsay Christians reviewed, "It took off at a sprint, integrating well with the orchestra in fierce rhythmic passages. The second movement, 'Little River,' filled up with long, full phrases, swells from the winds lulling back into calm again. The Finale, 'Roaring Smokies,' zipped along, alternating tempos for a fiery finish."[53]

Several years later, *American Record Guide* again published a review of the work, this time penned by Jeff Dunn, from the performance at the Cabrillo Festival in 2014 with Alsop again on the podium. He pronounced:

The best work in the Festival was [...] Jennifer Higdon's *Concerto 4–3* [...] supremely skilled at their instruments, these three [Time for Three] injected onlookers, including orchestra members, with gallons of happy juice. Furthermore, Higdon's original and energized, bluegrass infused licks kept everyone on his [sic] toes in the outer movements. The middle movement's respite replaced toe-tapping infection with heart-massaging harmonies.[54]

Alsop, long familiar with Higdon's works, commented:

> I think there's no better composer than Jennifer Higdon to write a piece featuring such an eclectic group. It features all different styles of string playing from bluegrass from [...] old-timey fiddling to the Appalachian waltz kind of approach, very mellow, [...] down by the river kind of playing.[55]

When Alsop performed the work at Carnegie Hall with the Baltimore Symphony, Anne Midgette reviewed the performance, "Higdon takes the energy that's characteristic of all her music and tries it out with different accents, folksier twists and plenty of fiddling for the equally energetic young players."[56] Tim Smith also reviewed this conductor and ensemble:

> Time for Three took every advantage afforded by the concerto to show off brilliant technique and seamless synchronization, with each player burrowing into the folksy themes. Had the closing moments been taken any faster, smoke would have started coming out of the instruments.[57]

Since its premiere, *Concerto 4–3* has been performed numerous times by an array of orchestras. In addition to those mentioned above, the work has been programmed by the Indianapolis Symphony, the Chicago Symphony, the Phoenix Symphony, and the Wichita Symphony; international performances include the Shleswig-Holstein Festival and the Sydney Symphony.[58] *Concerto 4–3* was recorded on the album *Take 6*[59] by the Fort Worth Symphony Orchestra in live performances at the Nancy Lee and Perry R. Bass Performance Hall in Fort Worth, Texas, between October 9 and 11, 2009, with conductor Miguel Harth-Bedoya.[60] The two-disc set, released in 2012, celebrates the ensemble's centennial by featuring their composers in residence for the six years prior to the recording.

With the departure of DePue from Time for Three and the ensemble already on its second member to replace him, it's difficult to predict the future of the trio. *Concerto 4–3*, however, remains unique and significant in the canon as a bridge across the ever-increasing gulf between high art and vernacular music. As such, the composition appeals to wide ranging demographics, inclusive of the diversity that defines the citizenry of the United States.

Chapter Six

Violin Concerto

Higdon's *Violin Concerto* premiered in 2009 and in its short life has been performed by several violinists, recorded on a major record label, and won the Pulitzer Prize, achievements that suggest the work will enter into an already full canon. The composition was commissioned for and premiered by Hilary Hahn, one of the world's leading violinists and a Curtis alumna. Her relationship with Higdon stems from a 20th century music course taught by the composer. Hahn recalled, "She would play the music of a composer for most of the class, then tested us on what we heard and noticed [...] I learned so much from her and knew she would do something substantial when I commissioned the concerto."[1] Likewise, the composer had fond memories and remembered Hahn "devoured the information in the class and was always open to exploring and discovering new musical languages and styles."[2]

The parameters of the commission were purposely broad stipulating only an approximate duration of 30 minutes and that the work be "substantial."[3] In preparation, Higdon asked about violin concerti Hahn enjoys playing to gauge her musical tastes. The composer recalled:

> We discussed the various concerti that she has played through the years, with me asking various questions such as, "Are there concerti where you feel you have to fight the orchestra for balance? Are there works that you just enjoy playing for the sake of playing?" We talked about how she loves the use of the G string, but that I should make sure I'm using the entire violin.[4]

Hahn wanted:

> a little bit of polyphony, [...] and I wanted her to approach the violin not as an instrument with limits, but as the means for whatever she wanted to write. I told her early on that she should push what she thought the violin could do and not worry about it, and I'd tell her if it was not possible. I don't like for people to self-edit along the way.[5]

When it came time for Higdon to compose, the violinist wanted to stay in the background. Hahn explained, "I don't get too editorial when I work with composers; I want them to write what they want to write [...] I don't want to take credit for anything, because it's not my piece, it's her piece."[6]

Because both musicians maintain a whirlwind travel agenda, the premiere could not be scheduled immediately which was helpful. Higdon expanded, "With this particular piece, I actually think I allowed six or seven months [for composition] because I realized I really needed to think about what would work for you [Hahn]."[7] Higdon began composing this work after *Concerto 4-3*[8] but since the soloists and the styles between the two works are so different, she had no concern that they would sound similar.

Since the composer already has a wealth of music that utilizes strings including *Concerto 4-3*, her preparation for the *Violin Concerto* consisted of familiarizing herself with Hahn's playing. Higdon listened to the violinist's recordings, notably the concerti of Arnold Schoenberg and Edgar Meyer, the latter composed specifically for Hahn. At Curtis, Higdon also heard her perform Britten's *Violin Concerto*.[9]

The violin concerti canon spans centuries and includes nearly all of the significant figures in the history of music. This grand tradition was not lost on Higdon who commented:

> Writing with the weight of music history bearing down on a specific genre-especially string music, which is so rich-can be very difficult. It's best for composers to not think about that too much. The one wonderful aspect of writing for today's performers has to do with the fact that the players are so phenomenal. I don't think there has been a time in history when players have had this high a level of playing.[10]

She continued in a separate interview, "I had to work hard to get around ... awareness of history. That made the composing process way more intense."[11]

The *Concerto*'s three movements were each written "to highlight a different aspect of her [Hahn's] playing."[12] Hahn remarked on having pieces composed specifically for her:

> It completely changes how you view your own playing [...] I know what I'm trying to do when I play, but I don't know what comes through to people and when a composer writes, it's a very honest account of what they hear in your playing because they're writing to what they perceive to be your strengths.[13]

This personalized composition has certainly not been an obstacle to other violinists performing the work since its premiere.

As discussed previously, Higdon rarely begins writing from the beginning and in most of her multi-movement works she starts with an interior section with the first movement usually composed last. Such was the case here; the composition began with the middle movement, "Chaconni," followed by the finale, and then the first movement, "1726."[14] Throughout the process, she sent the movements electronically to the touring Hahn. Because Higdon's music is known for its difficulty, she was surprised when Hahn suggested even more technical challenges. Higdon explained, "She would tell me that it could be harder [...] it would be her job to learn it."[15] Higdon worried the demanding cadenza, the very last portion of the concerto to be composed, was not even possible. Hahn reviewed it and agreed that it was challenging but as the composer recounted, Hahn stated, "It was her job to learn it. I think every composer's dream is to have the opportunity to work with soloists like that."[16]

Composing the *Violin Concerto* took the approximately six months Higdon had reserved for herself. Curiously, Zach DePue, a former member of Time for Three, is the concertmaster for the Indianapolis Symphony Orchestra, the ensemble that premiered the work. Higdon's recent experience with DePue's playing in her *Concerto 4–3* resulted in several significant soli for him in the *Violin Concerto*.[17]

This work follows several other concerti by Higdon for instrumental soloist or soloists: *Oboe Concerto, Percussion Concerto, Soprano Saxophone Concerto, The Singing Rooms, Piano Concerto, Concerto 4–3,* and *On a Wire.* The *Viola Concerto,* premiered by Roberto Diaz and the Curtis Chamber Orchestra in Washington, D.C., in 2015, has since been added to this list.

Higdon's *Violin Concerto* was co-commissioned by the Indianapolis Symphony, the Toronto Symphony Orchestra, the Baltimore Symphony Orchestra, and the Curtis Institute of Music. The work was also made possible through the support of LDI, Ltd., the Lacy Foundation, and the Randolph S. Rothschild Fund. The score was published by Lawdon Press, the composer's own publishing company and is dedicated to Hahn "with great admiration and enthusiasm."[18]

Because of the extensive history Hahn and Higdon have with Curtis combined with the fact that the conservatory was a co-commissioner,[19] the piece was workshopped there on September 10 and 11, 2008.[20] Violist Milena Pajaro-van de Stadt recalled the experience with Higdon, "She actually changed instrumentations on the spot [...] she would hear something live and say [...] I think that wasn't what I intended."[21] Hahn explained the value of these experiences in her blog, *Postcards from the Road*:

> We're running it [Higdon's *Violin Concerto*] through with the Curtis [...] Orchestra to make sure all of the notes are in the right places and it sounds like everyone has imagined it would. The premieres aren't until the spring, so this will give us plenty of time to make adjustments.[22]

Benjamin Beilman, who later performed the work as a soloist, was a member of the Curtis Orchestra during the workshops that provided him with a thorough comprehension of the work. He commented:

> Hilary, Jennifer, and the Curtis Orchestra workshopped this piece just sort of to get a sense of balance, what type of pacing things worked, what didn't work, and I was actually sitting

> at the very front of the second violin section, I was principal second violin [...] and so I got to see firsthand, Jennifer's ideas about the piece [...] I was also part of the premiere performance in Philadelphia, Hilary gave it with the Curtis Orchestra [...] I've been a part of a performance as a part of the orchestra. Undoubtedly, it gives you a behind the scenes look at everything [...] I think that this is probably the most well rounded approach I could possibly have to a concerto, I've seen it from all possible angles at this point.[23]

Hahn recalled in the recording's liner notes the accompanying feelings of those present at the workshop:

> The first complete reading came with the Curtis Orchestra, in Curtis Hall. After a thorough day of rehearsal, with Jennifer Higdon revising the score as we progressed, we began the final, complete run-through. Instantly, all fatigue disappeared. Every moment brought something new, and every note felt electric. In the end we were exhausted, but we were also thoroughly elated.[24]

The orchestral personnel is standard for Higdon particularly the harp and extensive percussion. In addition to the timpani, the percussion includes the five-octave marimba, glockenspiel, bass drum, Chinese cymbal, suspended cymbal, one rute, sizzle cymbal, chimes, and crotales. The composer's well known fascination with sound is further demonstrated by her sparing but effective use of the English horn.

The program notes penned by the composer open with an introductory paragraph:

> I believe that one of the most rewarding aspects of life is exploring and discovering the magic and mysteries held within our universe. For a composer this thrill often takes place in the writing of a concerto ... it is the exploration of an instrument's world, a journey of the imagination, confronting and stretching an instrument's limits and discovering a particular performer's gifts.[25]

Movement One, "1726"

Higdon explained that the first movement:

> carries a somewhat enigmatic title of "1726." This number represents an important aspect of such a journey of discovery, for both the composer and the soloist. 1726 happens to be the street address of The Curtis Institute of Music, where I first met Hilary as a student in my 20th Century Music Class. As Curtis was also a primary training ground for me as a young composer, it seemed an appropriate tribute. To tie into this title, I make extensive use [of] the intervals of unisons, 7ths, and 2nds throughout this movement.[26]

Although unmentioned, she also makes abundant use of the sixth interval to further complement the title. During the composition process, however, Higdon did not singularly focus on those intervals; she recalled:

> I kept it in the back of my mind but I never overtly thought about it. There's kind of an emphasis on some of the leaps on those intervals, but other than that I wasn't consciously

thinking of it. If I had a choice between possible intervals.... I would opt to use maybe a seventh.[27]

Large intervals are one of Hahn's unique strengths due, in part to being double jointed. She explained that her hand is tremendously flexible and that in comparison to other violinists, she can "contort a little bit more."[28]

The first movement is sectional, as is typical of Higdon's large works, with divisions clearly distinct through contrasting tempi resulting in an ABA'B'CA" form as outlined below.

Measure Numbers	Music	Letter
1–53	Quarter note=82; harmonics in soloist with glockenspiel and crotales played by knitting needles, sparse orchestration	A
54–164	Tempo doubles to quarter note= 164; tutti sections featuring Higdon major chords, various orchestral soli in scoring such as first stand strings particularly characteristic of this composer	B
165–215	Original tempo and mood; return of glockenspiel and crotales and various orchestral soli, soloist alternates between pizzicato and arco	A'
216–282	B tempo; large sections of B material return in varying order	B'
282–317	Solo Cadenza, features second and seventh intervals	C
318–360	Original tempo and mood, combines elements of A and A'	A"

A Section

The work begins unassumingly in a moderate tempo, quarter note=82, with the unaccompanied soloist presenting harmonics in a mezzo piano dynamic (Figure 6–1). This curious and highly unusual opening was inspired by Hahn's recording of Schoenberg's *Violin Concerto*. Higdon recalled:

> I had just listened to your Schoenberg recording which is stunning [...] you have all these great harmonics in it and that's actually the opening of my concerto [...] it was kind of like a leap of inspiration from your performance of the Schoenberg. That's where the opening came from.[29]

The first five measures present significant material that returns throughout the movement, beginning with the interval of a major 7th that alludes to the title and closing with the perfect fifth intervals that define Higdon's style. Because of the harmonics, the range is naturally very high and with the

Figure 6-1. *Violin Concerto*; I, mm. 1–5.

ensemble tacet, the composer draws the listener in immediately. Higdon has not included any musical directions, outside of tempo and a single dynamic for the soloist which allows much freedom in the interpretation. It is worth noting that this opening phrase ends with perfect fifths on the pitches B and F#, which will subsequently be prevalent.

In measure six, the glockenspiel and crotales enter striking their instruments with knitting needles. These soft, curious sounds contribute to the mysterious opening initiated by the soloist. The percussion dialog also features the intervals referenced in the title but ends five measures later with typical Higdon perfect fifths.

A meter change in measure 11 introduces a new subsection. The only instrument sounding is the timpani whose instructions are "Place crotale upside-down on drum head. Strike with mallet while silently moving pedal … in continuous 8th-note pattern."[30] When the meter returns to 4/4 in bar 13, the crotales and glockenspiel repeat their earlier material while the soloist explores a lyrical melody in the instrument's lowest range. This theme is comprised almost exclusively of the title's intervals but also demonstrates Higdon's incorporations of Hahn's preference for playing on the G string. The slow moving, low melody provides a rich contrast from the opening's high range. In less than 15 measures, Higdon has exhibited the expansive range of the violin.

Individual string soli in this composer's orchestral works are not at all unusual. Such soli are frequently scored for the first stand of musicians but as mentioned earlier, Higdon knew the concertmaster of the premiering ensemble; thus, in this work, the concertmaster alone is entrusted with significant solo material beginning in measure 13. While the concerto soloist explores its lower range, the first violin solo echoes the opening harmonics.

In measure 20, the ensemble is tacet while the solo violin displays again the title's intervals complemented by the inclusion of sextuplets and septuplets, rhythms that also reference these significant numbers. Four measures later, the chamber ensemble returns to the material's opening with the addition of the harp to provide counterpoint. This content continues through measure 34 where a meter change occurs, always indicative of a new subsection in Higdon's music.

In measure 35, the harp and timpani are replaced by the string section in a manner most stylistic of this composer: fourth and fifth intervals in the lower strings and unorthodox soli in the violins. The concertmaster continues the harmonics in dialog with the concerto soloist but three additional soli for the assistant concertmaster and second stand present major and minor sonorities. The focus on the string section here is particularly noteworthy within a violin concerto and simultaneously demonstrates Higdon's compositional traits and individuality. The flutes enter as the A section comes to a close in measure 47 in a nearly exact restatement of the percussion's opening. In the penultimate measure, the meter changes to signal a new section is on the horizon while the dynamics diminish and the texture is thinned to eventually leave only the soloist.

B Section

The B section unmistakably begins in measure 54 with the meter change and the doubled tempo to quarter note=164, an increase that is complemented by the rhythmic excitement that so frequently defines Higdon's music. First, the marimba opens with Scotch snaps in a highly rhythmic passage that repeats itself six bars later. The percussionist plays only a single pitch, an Ab that is doubled by pizzicato second violins and violas in their own rhythm. Above these ostinati, the concerto soloist's syncopated line is marked legato and comprised of a narrow range consisting primarily of varying second intervals that undoubtedly reference the title.

In measure 66, the pizzicato Ab is transferred to the celli and basses while the soloist begins a brief dialog with the woodwinds allowing Higdon to experiment with various ranges, tone colors, and qualities of second intervals. The soloist initiates the conversation with triplets echoed by the oboes and clarinets in unison. In the subsequent measure, the soloist is echoed by the high woodwinds and the following phrase explores the low woodwinds.

At the cessation of this dialog in measure 73, the principal trumpet enters. Highly rhythmic, the line is comprised almost exclusively of second intervals while the soloist performs fast, scalar passages sprinkled occasionally with double stops. This section erupts in measure 78 with a *fortissimo* dynamic and the inclusion of nearly the entire ensemble. Noteworthy are Higdon's stylistic major and minor chords scored for three trumpets, although here doubled by the first trombone and atypically the violins. The *tutti* section finishes succinctly at measure 80.

The concerto soloist reenters to introduce a dialog with various solo strings in measure 82 beginning with the first stand of first violinists. At first, the triplet exchange recalls the earlier woodwind passage but these rhythms are fleeting and the association quickly disappears. Small soli for the first stand of the celli, violas, and the second stand of first violinists follow in quick succession. In measure 89, the concerto soloist and the first two stands of violins present a line in call and response comprised of *portamento* double stops figures that are accented and *fortissimo* emphasizing "1726"'s intervals.

Measure 94 is a particularly noteworthy section. Below the staff are instructions for the soloist that read "vary dynamics widely and wildly"[31] coupled with a notation of a solid line that traces only the melodic contour. Higdon directs the violinist: "Bowed tremolo, fast and furious, moving along the general lines of the graph, ending up at the very top of the range."[32] Such nontraditional notation is atypical of this composer but not entirely without precedent as evidenced in *Concerto 4–3*. The result lends itself to an aleatoric quality in which each performance will differ somewhat. An excellent contrast to this unpredictability are the ostinato patterns present in the harp and glockenspiel: two-beat patterns comprised of second, sixths, and seventh intervals. The reduced texture in this passage also includes piccolo, timpani, and crotales. The orchestration of the crotales and glockenspiel here recall the A section where these instruments were prominently featured. The crotales and piccolo present the minor second intervals connected to the title in varying rhythms while the timpani sound perfect fourths and subsequently fifths, always an identifying trait of Higdon (Figure 6–2).

When the solo violin ceases at measure 98, the texture increases and the remainder of the ensemble gradually enters. Because the full orchestra has seldom been heard up to this point, it is immediately apparent that the mate-

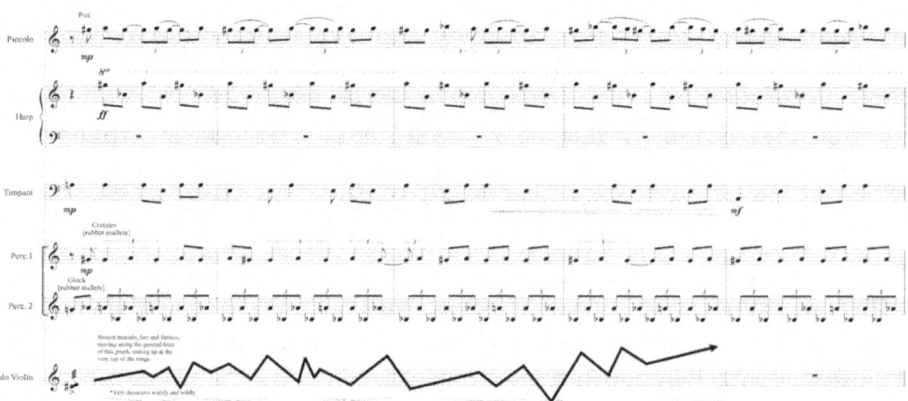

Figure 6–2. *Violin Concerto*; I, mm. 94–98.

rial is familiar; the chords of the trumpets and trombone in measure 103 are identical to those found at 79. As is typical with Higdon, rather than just repeating the passage, she pairs this returning progression with new material, ascending figurations in the woodwinds and strings. The tutti section is also brief here and the texture thins beginning in measure 105 to feature the principal trumpet with the concerto soloist.

At bar 109, the oboe presents a tiny solo that leads to meter changes, an indication of a new subsection. The passage opens with Scotch snaps in the marimba, an identical rhythm and orchestration to the beginning of the B section. The celli and viola return to music from later in the B section at measure 73, the latter presenting a reorchestration of the previous trumpet line. The concerto soloist's line also incorporates its earlier material combined with new content that is based exclusively on scalar passages and second intervals.

As the B section continues, in measure 115, the principal trumpet presents a transposed version of its earlier solo ending with triplets that recall the dialog between the soloist and the woodwinds; however, here the triplets are unanswered and lead to another very brief moment for full ensemble in measure 123. Although the music is not identical to previous tutti passages, the rhythms and the major chords in the trumpets and trombones evoke the earlier sections and likewise cease after only two measures.

The triplet dialog hinted at by the trumpet returns in measure 126 as a solo for the first clarinet, subsequently replaced by the principal bassoon. Both of these instruments are paired with the concertmaster and as with the earlier section, answered by the soloist. The rhythms are not solely comprised of triplets but expanded to sixteenth notes and sextuplets complemented by the soloist's major seventh double stops to connect the passage to the title.

In measure 141, the soloist initiates the ascent to the climax of the B section through repeated, fortissimo high Dbs followed by the return of the full ensemble. The marimba part returns to the two beat glockenspiel ostinato from measure 94 with the timpani also presenting alternating fourths from the same earlier passage in differing rhythms. Combined with this previous material are new ostinati in the violas doubled by the principal clarinet and the celli doubled by the second clarinet. The oboes also remain noteworthy in their display of intervals connected to the title: sevenths, sixths, seconds, and even unisons. Simultaneously, the trombones present major chords, a variation from Higdon's traditional trumpet orchestration; however, in measure 143, these sonorities are, in fact, transferred to the trumpets in a repetition of the chords found in measure 79, and as in the previous passage, doubled by the violins. The horns present separate major and minor chords in slower harmonic rhythms than the other brass that aptly demonstrates Higdon's counterpoint of textures as defined in the opening chapter (Figure 6–3). In measure 146, the composer uses one of her most characteristic scorings, two major chords separated by a second interval. The trombones, horns, and principal trumpet play one chord while the strings and upper woodwinds present a chord whose root, initially, is a minor second away. Although it is

Figure 6–3. *Violin Concerto*; I, mm. 141–142.

tempting to place this intervallic distance in relation to the title, it is a defining trait of this composer and certainly not specific to this work. To extend the tutti passage in measure 149, Higdon returns to material from measure 141: the two beat marimba passage, the celli and viola ostinati doubled by the clarinets, the exploration of the title's intervals in the oboes, and the major and minor sonorities in the brass. These all cease in measure 151 as quickly as they began and by measure 153, any hint of bitonality in the brass also disappears leaving only the chords in the trumpets doubled by the violins.

Beginning in measure 157, the meter change marks the transition to the A' section. Higdon decreases the dynamics to *pianissimo* and reduces the texture in bar 159 to leave only the upper woodwinds and strings. Descending soli in progressively slower rhythms are scored for both the principal bassoon and the clarinet complemented by a *molto rit.* that returns the music to the hallmarks of the A section: quarter note=82 and smaller orchestration.

A' Section

The A' section begins in measure 165 and true to Higdon's style, this is not simply a repeat with a few variations. Outside of the tempo, mood, and sparse texture, the musical content is starkly different. Gone are the opening harmonics for the soloist replaced by a low ranged pizzicato line, a far cry from the movement's opening. This melody, comprised exclusively of second intervals in reference to the title, is complemented by a sustained F for the first stand of the first violins, a characteristic Higdon scoring. In measure 169, the concerto soloist presents arco triplets on this same pitch before repeating the pizzicato melody. These triplets will reappear in the A" section to unify the movement but here they appear consistently on the pitch of F and introduce new instruments into the texture beginning with a piccolo solo in the subsequent measure. This woodwind solo also begins on an F, an exceedingly low range for the instrument. Hearing this pitch successively in three different timbres combines what Schoenberg referred to as *klangfarbenmelodie* with Higdon's own self-described "joy of sound."[33] Throughout this entire passage, the piccolo repeats a five measure phrase that steadily incorporates ascending minor seventh intervals in connection to the movement's title. The concerto soloist repeats the triplet figure in measure 174 to introduce the remainder of the first violin section that presents the sixth and seventh intervals (Figure 6–4). The tone-color-melody continues to be explored when a second violin solo and harp enter at measure 179 on the same F. The former utilizes the triplets to introduce the celli repeating the initial pizzicato line of the concerto soloist.

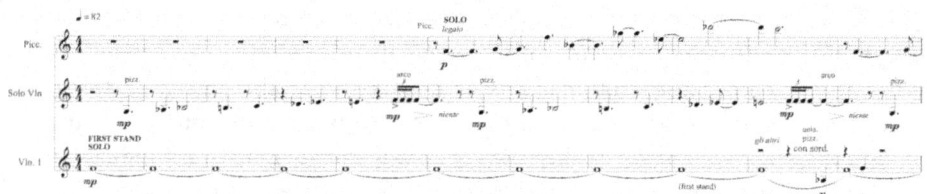

Figure 6-4. *Violin Concerto*; I, mm. 165-175.

In measure 174, the first stand, first violin soli are joined by a countermelody presented by the remainder of their section and several measures later, the soli's sustained F is transferred to the second violins. Noticeably absent thus far are the glockenspiel and crotales that were featured so prominently in the first A section. These percussion instruments' eventual return in measure 190 is introduced by the recurring F triplets.

In the movement's opening, the only soloists were the concerto soloist and four first violins; however, in the A' section, soli in addition to those discussed previously are found in both clarinets, principal oboe, flutes, viola, three celli, and three first violins. The composer has also increased the texture and variety of sounds by including the marimba and two trumpets instructed to play with a bag over the bell. Two consecutive meter changes herald the opening of the B' section and as occurred previously, the concerto soloist closes the A' section although here, accompanied by major chords in the celli.

B' Section

The B' section is unmistakable at measure 216 when the tempo returns to quarter note=164. Unlike A,' this passage revisits much of the earlier content but in typical Higdon fashion, this is combined with new material and does not follow the same order as the initial B section. The Scotch snaps that opened the B section return in the marimba, as does much of the ensemble's music. The solo part is entirely new, however, but similarly focused on second intervals in a much faster rhythm. Original material can also be found in measure 221 in the dialog between the soloist and concertmaster.

Measures 228-267 contain material found primarily between bars 66-102 with several noteworthy additions. The motivic exchange between the concerto soloist and the woodwinds returns in transposition but the rhythmic trumpet line that followed is reorchestrated for the cello. As with the earlier section, the ensemble enters briefly in measure 241 with a transposition of bar 78. A new, melodic solo for the principal trumpet in measure 243 is paired with the soloist's returning material from measure 80. This leads to a typical

Higdon scoring that continues through measure 256: first stand soli for the first violin section subsequently joined by the first stand of celli, viola, and finally, the second stand of the first violin section. Immediately following this passage in the B section, the notation for the concerto soloist changes to a solid line but here the violinist presents material from measure 134 and in several places, a measure is added that does not correspond to the earlier section. The remainder of the ensemble continues to present the ostinati initially found in the glockenspiel, crotales, harp, and piccolo from measure 94.

The soloist is tacet beginning in measure 268 in preparation for the cadenza while the entire ensemble gradually enters hinting at previous material. In measure 280, as the B section closes, the texture becomes homorhythmic in a fortissimo dynamic that builds anticipation for the cadenza. The two meter changes in the final bars remain typical of Higdon as a way to separate formal sections.

In the Classical period, a cadenza followed the recapitulation and was preceded by a second inversion tonic chord presented by the ensemble. Higdon neither utilizes functional harmony nor is the first movement in sonata allegro form and yet the cadenza appears after a large musical section is repeated, akin to a recapitulation. Curiously, the *tutti* ensemble sounds a B-major chord in second inversion prior to the cadenza in a figurative tip of the hat to a tradition centuries old.

C Section

Higdon's notated cadenza was the last section written of the entire piece. She recalled, "I wasn't absolutely sure it was going to be playable, so I wrote a note to Hilary: 'Look, if this is too hard, let me know and I'll write another cadenza.'"[34] The cadenza is to be played "in strict tempo; with ferocity"[35] which suggests that this is not intended to be lyrical but a display of sheer virtuosic bravura. Beilman played the cadenza for Higdon during his performance preparation but she told him it was too musical and that he should play it so the audience thinks, "He's going to break his instrument, it is about to fall apart, something is going to snap."[36]

The opening of the cadenza includes prominent use of second intervals sprinkled with descending seventh double stops that contrast the many rapid scalar figures. The first half of the cadenza is also dominated by a rhythmic motive of three eighth notes and a triplet (Figure 6–5). In the latter half of measure 299, Higdon incorporates a very brief instance of non-traditional notation through a solid line, a technique examined earlier in the movement. As the cadenza closes, it is worth noting that the intervals of the final two

Figure 6-5. *Violin Concerto*; I, mm. 288-290.

measures are also seconds. The dynamics decrease steadily and the rhythms are augmented for an unassuming transition to the A" section.

A" Section

Following the cadenza, the opening tempo and mood of the earlier A sections return in measure 318. As noted above, the thematic content of A and A' were dissimilar and comparable in only tempo and mood and thus, the resulting combination of the disparate sections here demonstrate Higdon's compositional genius. First, the second stand of the second violins present a sustained G, a slight variation from the earlier F sounded by the first stand of the first violins in the A' section. The soloist begins in unison with the violins but after several beats alternates pizzicato and arco that also recall the A' section with one significant difference: the arco notes are harmonics from the movement's opening. As with the A' section, the triplet rhythm serves to introduce instruments into the sparse texture, initially the violas echoing the pizz and arco concept from the A' section. The scoring, however, is reminiscent of the concerto's opening dialog between the concertmaster and soloist (Figure 6-6).

Figure 6-6. *Violin Concerto*; I, mm. 318-327.

In the pickup to measure 329, the second stand of second violins' triplets introduce the crotales and glockenspiel, an orchestration associated with the opening. As the movement nears its conclusion, the *con sordino* string passage from measure 35 returns in bar 339 with three first violin soloists presenting major and minor chords. The final measures leave only the harp, timpani, celli, basses, and the concerto soloist with sustained pitches while the first violins present harmonics to bring the movement full circle. The closing orchestration omits all wind instruments allowing for a stark timbral contrast when the second movement opens with these instruments.

Movement Two, "Chaconni"

The slow, central movement derives its title from the pluralized word chaconne, a form whose characteristics have changed over time but here refers to two separate, repeating and alternating chord progressions. The idea of two interchanging chaconnes was not part of Higdon's original concept; initially she composed the harmonies and the form eventually followed.[37] As one may expect with Higdon, upon each repeat, the music varies. She explained in the program notes:

> The excitement of the first movement's intensity certainly deserves the calm and pensive relaxation of the 2nd movement. This title, "Chaconni," comes from the word "chaconne." A chaconne is a chord progression that repeats throughout a section of music. In this particular case, there are several chaconnes, which create the stage for a dialog between the soloist and various members of the orchestra. The beauty of the violin's tone and the artist's gifts are on display here.[38]

The composer expanded to Hahn in an interview, "I was thinking about your tone in the second movement. I actually pondered this a great deal and [...] I just love your sound and I love your low notes and I love your high notes. [...] It's the extremes [...] so that's the whole focus of the second movement."[39] Although certainly not identical, this form retains elements found in the slow movement of *Concerto 4–3* that utilized a singular repeating chord progression and likewise paired the soloists with different ensemble instruments.

In the opening measures, Higdon presents the two chaconnes successively and it is important to note their differing functions throughout the movement. Chaconne I reappears in single statements and with the exception of the concerto soloist, rarely features orchestral soli. In contrast, Chaconne II repeats consecutively in varying orchestrations that serve as the harmonic background for numerous duets between the concerto soloist and members of the ensemble. Because the movement is structured in this manner, the formal analysis can be best explained by examining which chaconne is present as demonstrated here:

Measure numbers	Music	Chaconne
1–6	Woodwind chorale in 4/4 meter	Chaconne I
7–61	String chorale in 3/4 meter; orchestral soli appear in the following order: cello with English horn, oboe, return of cello, Bb clarinet with viola, and flute.	Chaconne II

Measure numbers	Music	Chaconne
Measure 35	Chaconne transferred to horns, concerto soloist enters paired with instrumental soli as follows: oboe, trumpet, Bb clarinet, cello, concertmaster, and English horn	
61–64	Return to 4/4, reorchestration of Chaconne I for strings	Chaconne I
65–103	3/4 meter with woodwinds presenting Chaconne II, concerto soloist re-enters paired with concertmaster	Chaconne II
Measure 78	and solo viola. Chaconne moves to brass, concerto soloist paired with	
Measure 87	horn. Chaconne returns to strings, concerto soloist paired with trumpet followed by Bb clarinet. Tempo fluctuates through accelerandi and ritardandi.	
104–109	String soli present chaconne I in 4/4 meter and closes with a ritardando	Chaconne I
110–142	Meter remains in 4/4 and although not an exact restatement, Chaconne II is recalled in the woodwinds. Concerto soloist paired with instrumental soli in the following order: concertmaster with principal cellist, horn, flute, and trumpet.	Chaconne II
143–151	Subito tempo change to return to opening quarter note=52 featuring Chaconne I in woodwinds. Concerto soloist paired with concertmaster and cello. Measures added to expand Chaconne.	Chaconne I
152–195	Meter in 3/4 and Chaconne II returns in horns, strings (ms 160) with ww doublings (170), then brass (180). Concerto soloist joined by solo instruments in the following order: English horn with concertmaster and cello, oboe, flute, and bassoon. Accelerandi employed throughout the passage but closes with a ritardando returning music to original tempo	Chaconne II
196–220	Chaconne I in woodwinds, concerto soloist in brief duet with concert-	Coda featuring Chaconne I and II
Measure 202	master. Transition to remnants of Chaconne II in strings, with material from measure 110 reorchestrated.	
Measure 215	Final return to triple meter	

Chaconne I

The movement opens with a tempo designated as quarter note=52 featuring a mezzo piano woodwind chorale in 4/4, an unusual meter for a chaconne (Figure 6–7). The harmonic content is pure Higdon since the instruments present two different harmonies. Usually when this occurs in her music, the chords are triadic and separated by the interval of a second but here, the chords in the flutes and first clarinet are triadic while those in the bassoons and second clarinet are quartal.

Figure 6–7. *Violin Concerto*; II, mm. 1–6, Chaconne I.

Chaconne II

A cello solo links the two chaconnes and continues as Chaconne II unfolds. This solo is the first of many darker timbered instruments featured in the movement and it is worth noting the cello's opening interval is a minor third. This interval will be significant in subsequent soli, a stark contrast to the dissonant intervals featured in "1726." Following a meter change in measure seven, Chaconne II is presented in the muted strings complemented by a basso ostinato in the harp. The passage is marked pianissimo, in the typical 3/4 meter with a slightly increased tempo of quarter note=60. The progressions in this chaconne are triadic but non-functional (Figure 6–8). Presenting the two chaconnes consecutively with different orchestral sections allows the listener to hear them clearly in their purest forms before adding soloists.

In measure ten, the solo cello is paired with the English horn which is subsequently replaced eight bars later by a principal oboe solo beginning on a descending minor third. Following the oboe, the Bb clarinet, doubled by a

Figure 6–8. *Violin Concerto*; II, mm. 7–10, Chaconne II.

solo viola, embarks on its solo initiated by an ascending minor third. Finally, in measure 27, a flute solo opens with an ascending minor third while the cello and viola become tacet. During these woodwind soli, Chaconne II remains scored only for the strings and repeats in four measure intervals. With the exception of the oboe and the viola, the soli begin and end to coincide with the chaconne's four bar phrases.

In measure 35 when the concerto soloist first enters, Higdon contrasts the previous orchestration by moving Chaconne II to the four horns, instruments that had been silent thus far in the movement. The soloist's opening interval is the significant ascending minor third in a low range filled with expressive markings that demonstrate the aforementioned lyricism of Hahn. This solo is paired with the oboe in measure 36 and as with the same instrument's earlier solo, it begins with a similar rhythm and a descending minor third. It briefly appears that the oboe is repeating its earlier theme but it soon becomes apparent this is not the case. The concerto soloist's line slowly ascends and when the oboe ceases in measure 44, the violinist is paired with a solo for principal trumpet that opens with a descending minor third. The oboe and trumpet soli do not coincide with the length of Chaconne II and the progression's return to the strings occurs in the midst of the trumpet solo in measure 47. The harp also reenters here with a variation on its Chaconne II ostinato. At the close of the trumpet solo, the violinist continues its lyrical melody now paired with a Bb clarinet solo that begins with an ascending perfect fourth, an interval inverted and echoed in the solo cello three bars later. The Chaconne II passage closes in a similar manner to which it began, with an English horn and string solo. Rather than the cello heard in the opening, the concertmaster doubles the concerto soloist an octave lower but the instrumentation brings the section full circle.

Chaconne I

The meter change at measure 61 signals the return of Chaconne I scored for strings. The violin soloist is tacet and the English horn is replaced by a second oboe since the former is a timbre associated exclusively with Chaconne II. The return of Chaconne I is not an identical repetition of the opening. The rhythms are in diminution allowing for the progression to be heard in less time and while the celli and second violins begin with identical pitch content as the bassoons and second clarinet, respectively, after the opening measure, these are varied. The essential element of this chaconne remains: distinct quartal harmonies paired with triads. This succinct statement closes with a small ritardando at measure 64.

Chaconne II

Measure 65 features a return to triple meter and Chaconne II in the lower woodwinds. The concerto soloist is paired with the concertmaster and principal viola in octaves that begin with the significant descending minor third intervals. The orchestral string soli ceases at measure 78 where the first accelerando appears to increase the tempo to quarter note=72. Here, orchestration of Chaconne II is transferred to two trumpets and two trombones, while the concerto soloist begins a duet with the principal horn. This scoring for Chaconne II partially coincides with a Higdon stylistic trait: major chords in the trumpet. As seen in earlier works, the inclusion of the trombones in such sections do occur on occasion; however, the omission of the principal trumpet here is curious but its absence can be explained by its solo immediately following in measure 89.

Another accelerando occurs in measure 87 moving the tempo to quarter note=84 while Chaconne II returns to the strings. As mentioned above, a trumpet solo is featured with the concerto soloist and the fast rhythms and assertive dynamics of the latter are complemented by an increasingly rhythmic horn part. When the passage nears its close, the concerto soloist plummets to its lower range with rhythms in diminution accompanied by a brief solo for the Bb clarinet in measure 102 that opens with the reappearing minor third interval. A ritardando creates a sense of finality to the conclusion of this section.

Chaconne I

A meter change in measure 103 to 4/4 indicates the return of Chaconne I which reappears in the strings in the subsequent measure. Two elements make this passage noteworthy: the concerto soloist is featured, the first time this has happened with Chaconne I thus far and the progression is presented by soloists from the string section. The triadic and quartal harmonies are scored for the first stand of the first violins with principal second and first stand of the celli with principal viola, respectively. The remainder of the orchestra is tacet producing a chamber-like sound within this large Neo-Romantic ensemble. Another brief ritardando at the close of this chaconne brings the tempo to quarter note=66. Typical of Chaconne I, it is presented only once.

Chaconne II

Chaconne II is recalled in the woodwinds in measure 110; although neither an exact replication nor in triple meter, the chordal qualities and harmonic rhythm are comparable. The concerto soloist is paired with the concertmaster doubled by the principal cello opening with the recurring third interval, although major in this instance. Relatively brief, the orchestral soli cease in measure 114 to feature the concerto soloist in a remarkably difficult, contrapuntal passage. String soloists return in measure 117 scored for the first stand of violins one and two, the first stand of celli, and a single viola, an unusual orchestration but highly stylistic of Higdon. These soli double the woodwind chaconne but in the subsequent bar, the woodwinds become tacet to allow the numerous soloists to be heard clearly. The string accompanimental passage is another fine example of Higdon's counterpoint of textures. The violins present major chords in a flowing harmonic rhythm with ties over the bar line to obscure the downbeat while the viola and celli present separate major chords in slower rhythms that change on the first beat of each measure (Figure 6–9).

In measure 122, the horn is replaced by the principal flute and for the first time in the movement, neither of the chaconnes are readily apparent. The major chords in the lower string soli are changed to tutti parallel fifths

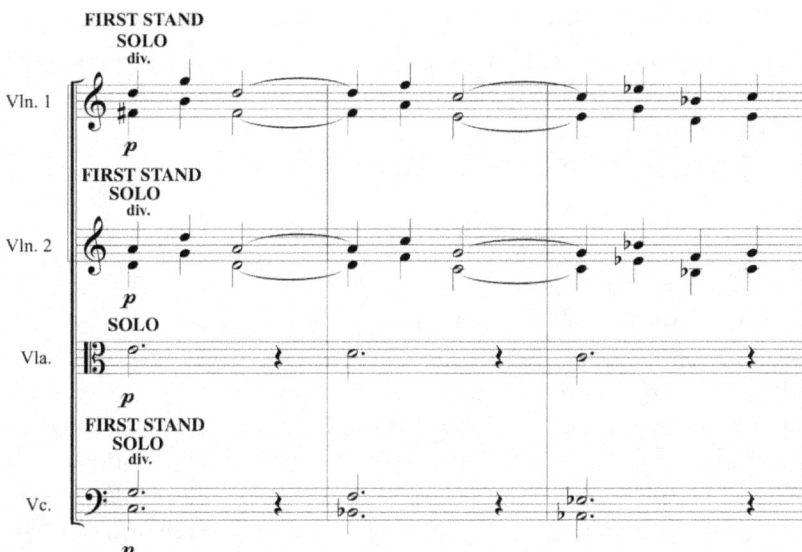

Figure 6–9. *Violin Concerto*; II, mm. 118–120.

here, one of Higdon's most prominent compositional traits. The harmonic rhythm of all the strings increases so substantially that no remnant of Chaconne II remains. The texture also becomes more dense and by measure 127, the mood has changed considerably. The concerto soloist performs at a fortissimo dynamic and is paired with a highly rhythmic solo for the principal trumpet while the lower woodwinds present major chords. This is particularly interesting because such sonorities are generally scored for the trumpets; because the principal trumpet is featured as a soloist, this is not an option. Higdon has scored this passage for the highest and lowest sounding instruments that make the ensemble seem fuller. A very brief accelerando in measure 131 increases the tempo to quarter note=69. The major chords in the lower woodwinds are transferred to the violins doubled by the flute, oboe, and clarinet. In measure 133, another brief *poco accelerando* increases the tempo to quarter note=72. The musical tension continues to grow until it eventually erupts in measure 138 with the entire ensemble demonstrating full chordal sonorities to create the musical climax of the movement. The concerto soloist is tacet with the focus solely on the ensemble.

Chaconne I

In measure 143, Chaconne I returns in its original tempo and woodwind orchestration with extra measures added by Higdon. The concerto soloist reenters but this passage also features orchestral soli not found in earlier Chaconne I sections. The first is the concertmaster in measure 146, a solo that opens with a minor third and followed by a solo cello three bars later. The extra measures added by the composer create opportunities to clear the texture for these soloists.

Chaconne II

In measure 152, a triple meter returns with Chaconne II in the horns and a solo for the English horn, a timbre associated exclusively with this progression. Additional soli include the previously separate concertmaster and cello that converge to present a single line in octaves. The Chaconne is transferred from the horns to the lower strings in measure 160 where an oboe replaces the English horn. It is interesting to note this order of soli also occurs in Chaconne II's initial appearance and similarly, the oboe melody begins with a minor third; however, the subsequent musical content is far different. The woodwinds continue duets with the concerto soloist, first the flute then the bassoon in measure 166, the latter beginning on a descending minor third. This bassoon solo is accompanied by an accelerando that leads to quarter note=72 by measure 172. The new tempo coincides with a reorchestration of Chaconne II in the lower woodwinds and strings with a brief respite from the flurry of activity for the concerto soloist.

When the soloist is silent, the focus shifts to the tutti ensemble with no orchestral soli. In measure 179, another accelerando increases the tempo to quarter note=84, the fastest tempo of "Chaconni." Paired with a fortissimo dynamic in the strings and woodwinds, the movement reaches its final climax. Major chords linger softly in the trumpets and trombones, an instrumentation characteristic of Higdon and reminiscent of Chaconne II.

Coda

The coda begins in measure 196 preceded by a substantial ritardando that returns the tempo to the original quarter note=52. Higdon alternates the meter between 5/4 and 4/4, stabilizing with the latter in bar 202. Chaconne I is featured first in the woodwinds and although the rhythms are altered slightly from their initial appearance, the sonorities and instrumentation make the reference unmistakable. Likewise, the chords are not identical to the original, particularly in the higher woodwinds but the overall harmonic scheme remains: upper woodwinds featuring triads paired with quartal harmonies in the lower woodwinds. Unlike the beginning, the concerto soloist is included with a lyrical theme that initially explores the instrument's lower range. The line quickly soars and in measure 200, is paired with a concertmaster solo that serves as a transition to the second chaconne which is found in the strings in bar 202. Similar to its appearance in the B' section, this is not an exact replication of Chaconne II but rather a reorchestration of content from measure 110. The concerto soloist's part, technically difficult through the double stops and counterpoint, mirrors briefly its previous line from the same passage.

The ending measures feature a final return to triple meter, a very thin texture, and a progressively slower harmonic rhythm that presents sustained chords in the strings. Augmented rhythms are scored for the concerto soloist near the top of its range for a beautiful, yet unassuming conclusion that greatly contrasts the outer movements.

Movement Three, "Fly Forward"

According to Higdon, the final movement is, "a tribute to the speed and accuracy of her [Hahn's] technique"[40] and demonstrates "her incredible ability; her fingers moving at high speed, [...] and her ability to maintain a rhythm even [...] [while] moving through these different meters."[41] As with many of Higdon's large orchestral works, the movement does not adhere to established forms and is best described as sectional. Typical of this composer, elements return from earlier passages in new guises so that contrast and repetition are simultaneously explored. The returning material rarely appears identically and thus, may be considered in multiple ways; however, the analysis below will be used in the subsequent discussion:

Measure Numbers	Music	Letter
1–52	Frequent meter changes and opens with tonal center of B; concerto soloist presents thematic material	A
53–76	Meter stabilizes and tonal areas include Eb minor,	B
Measure 69	f minor and	
Measure 73	F# minor	
77–99	Partial return of A material but largely truncated from original presentation	A'
100–120	Soli for orchestral strings	C
121–128	Scalar passages for concerto soloist based on opening of A	Transition
129–160	Return of measures 53–79	B'
161–174	Return of measure 18–29	A"
175–198	Based on A	Coda

The finale, from start to finish, is a demonstration of pure bravura beginning with the spritely tempo, quarter note=152–160. Unlike the preceding movements, the orchestra is less of a partner and functions primarily in a supportive role with the focus exclusively on the soloist. The physical stamina required of the violinist was partly inspired by the runners in the Olympics. Higdon explained, "I realized I was working on this when we were approaching the Olympics [...] that last movement moves very fast, so you have to imagine Hilary flying forward across the racing tape at the end of the race."[42] The descriptive title of the movement undoubtedly references the soloist's speed. The composer continued in her program notes:

> The third movement, "Fly Forward," seemed like such a compelling image, that I could not resist the idea of having the soloist do exactly that. Concerti throughout history have always allowed the soloist to delight the audience with feats of great virtuosity, and when a composer is confronted with a real gift in the soloist's ability to do so, well, it would be foolhardy not to allow that dream to become a reality.[43]

A Section

As a post-tonal composer, Higdon rarely utilizes functional harmony and thus detailed discussions of key areas are omitted; however, in several earlier works, the final chord was D major. "Fly Forward" continues this trend and thus it is worth noting that unison Bs, the relative minor of D major, open this movement.

The movement begins with a two-beat crescendo from pianissimo to accented fortissimo by the trombones, horns, and bassoons that coincide with the soloist's entrance marked "with intensity."[44] The ensemble becomes temporarily tacet so the soloist, in its lowest register, can be clearly heard but throughout the opening, the orchestra repeats their emphatic unison pitches. The soloist's theme is nearly exclusively comprised of second intervals that recall the first movement, a connection further enhanced by the glockenspiel sounded by knitting needles. The theme quickly expands to a higher range and faster rhythms as the figurative race begins.

In measure 12, meters begin to alternate continuously between compound and duple (6/8 and 4/4). Throughout this entire passage, the primary melodic content is in the concerto soloist's part and of interest are the double stops that emphasizes b minor and D major (Figure 6–10). Interruptions occur by the principal second violinist in measure 23 that return two bars later. In both instances, the composer utilizes the curious meter of ¼.

As the passage continues, the soloist's double stops expand to include drones on the open strings of D, A, and E implying tonic, dominant, and secondary dominant, respectively, in the key of D major. Simultaneously, the

Figure 6-10. *Violin Concerto*; III, mm. 22–27.

harmonies in the ensemble introduce sonorities indicative of the same tonality, such as C#7 chords (Figure 6-11).

Figure 6-11. *Violin Concerto*; III, mm. 36–39.

The A section closes with a cadence in measure 52 where the meter changes to 2/4. Although the meters have been alternating consistently, the use of 2/4 is significant because it occurred only once thus far and its appearance here signifies the conclusion of a large formal section.

B Section

The B section commences in the pick-up to measure 53 where the meter stabilizes to 4/4 and the texture thins considerably. The tonalities alluded to previously have also been altered from the generous sprinkling of sharps to flats initially suggesting Eb minor. The scoring of the second violin section is particularly characteristic of this composer: she alternates between using half the section for the arco pitches and the full section for the pizzicato markings.

Beginning in measure 57, the concerto soloist briefly explores sustained double stops that provide a moment of respite from the unceasing motion. A crescendo is employed that changes the dynamics from mezzo piano to fortissimo in only two beats. As the passage progresses, the double stops occur in faster rhythms, highly accented, and closer together retaining the Eb minor tonality.

Measure 69 marks a significant change in the melody and harmony of the concerto solo. Gone are the flats and double stops in thirds replaced by octaves with abundant sharps. The harmonies in the lower strings initially outline F minor before shifting to F# minor in preparation for the subsequent section.

A' Section

The A' section begins in measure 77 with a slight variation of the material from measure 34, the latter part of the initial A section. The concerto soloist's part is nearly identical, complete with double stops repeating the tonic, dominant, and secondary dominant harmonies. The music recalls the earlier passage until measure 93 where new material is used to transition to the next section.

C Section

Following a strong cadence, the C section begins in the pick-up to measure 100 with a greatly reduced texture. Arco soli are designated for the principals of the first and second violins, the viola, and the cello creating a momentary string quartet. The concertmaster and principal cellist present a single question and answer phrase during the concerto soloist's rests but the counterpoint changes quickly to homorhythmic texture to produce a unified timbre and the rhythms become progressively augmented. While these string soli unfold, Higdon explores various softly sustained chords in the lower woodwinds, noteworthy because it is highly atypical. Generally, while exploring such sonorities, this composer features the trumpets in much faster rhythms but the changes here were undoubtedly implemented to balance the string soli. These sustained chords are replaced by strings in measure 112 only to cease completely three measures later paving the way for a bravura passage for the concerto soloist. Again, double stops are present prominently featuring the pitches of A and D as drones beneath the highly chromatic melody. Furthermore, the accidentals include nearly exclusively F#s, C#s, and Bbs that suggest a modal mixture of D major and minor.

Transition

In measure 121, the ensemble gradually begins to reenter and while not an exact quotation, recalls the A Section. The double stops of the concerto soloist cease and the rhythms return to triplets with a melody in the lowest range, both which reference the movement's opening. The only exact replication occurs in measures 122–123, a reproduction of measures five to six; however, the accompanying material differs and the remainder of the soloist's part is new. Thus, this passage is best described as a transition rather than a full return to A.

B' Section

Transposed and reorchestrated, the material of the B section returns in measures 129 with the earlier, alternating pizzicato and arco string passage now scored for the woodwinds. Similarly, the ascending figurations originally in the woodwinds are reorchestrated for solo violins: the concertmaster joined by the assistant concertmaster four measures later. Beginning in measure 145, doublings provide a thicker texture than the initial B section but the content and harmonies, including the tonal centers of F minor and F# minor, are maintained from the earlier, corresponding passage. The concerto soloist's part is likewise comparable until measure 156 where Higdon introduces new material as a bridge to the next section.

A" Section

Measure 161 constitutes a return of the A material in the concerto soloist and atypical of this composer, there is no noticeable division that separates the two sections. The content derives from measure 18 with the frequent meter changes that filled the opening with excitement and energy thus closing the work in a similar grand display of bravura. Stylistic of Higdon, variations from the original are present throughout the ensemble but none so severe that would require labeling this passage anything other than a return of A; however, some altered material is particularly noteworthy, for instance the original ¼ meter expands to 4/4 in measure 166. Additional slight variations occur in the solo part, such as an extra measure inserted or repeated, but the material remains recognizable, including the implied b minor and D major tonalities in the double stops.

Coda

The coda begins in measure 175 preceded by fast, ascending rhythms in the woodwinds and concerto soloist. While a meter change coincides with the coda's opening, it does not herald the new section but is amidst the alternating time signatures from the previous section. The fortissimo dynamic and homorhythmic texture of the full ensemble found here are common in the closing of Higdon's orchestral works. The opening pitches are D and A, immediately followed by an F natural suggesting the minor mode, particularly since Bbs appear subsequently, but the moment is fleeting.

The soloist is tacet at the start of the coda but reenters in measure 182 with a momentarily reduced ensemble to balance the sound. Beginning on the second beat, the concerto soloist recalls measures 28–29 interrupted by a fortissimo d minor chord from the full ensemble in measure 184. Here, the trombones present a chord progression answered by major chords in the trumpets, a significant hallmark of Higdon's compositional style. Atypical of these passages are the doublings found in the celli and violas.

In measure 188, the texture is again reduced to feature the concerto soloist which returns to double stops with one pitch consistently a d. The minor mode is suggested through F naturals and Bbs but gradually F#s appear in preparation for the ending D major tonality. These harmonies are reinforced by a i-v progression in the celli and bass while the timpani alternate between A and D, dominant and tonic, of the final key area (Figure 6–12).

Several elements in the closing are of particular significance beginning in measure 192: major chords return in the trumpets, pizzicato Ds in the violins and violas highlight the ending tonality, and the celli quickly alternate major second intervals (Figure 6–13). The latter, stylistic of Higdon, appear consistently through the end of the work but in this context may also be viewed as a link to "1726." Above the ensemble, the concerto soloist's double stops continue to emphasize the D tonality.

The final three measures serve as a cadential extension with great emphasis on D major's tonic and dominant. The violins and viola exclusively sound the pitches of A and D, notes that also continue to be emphasized in

Six. Violin Concerto

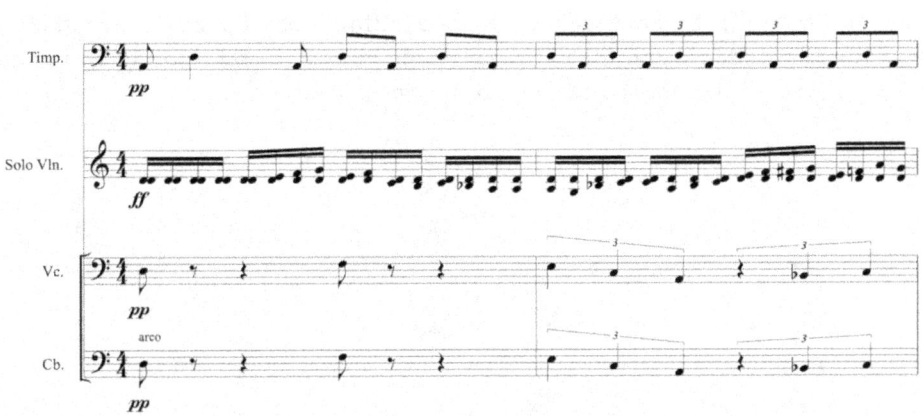

Figure 6-12. *Violin Concerto*; III, mm. 188–189.

Figure 6-13. *Violin Concerto*; III, mm. 192–194.

the timpani. The basses reenter in the penultimate bar to further strengthen this final cadence and the entire ensemble joins in a crescendo to end the work on a triumphant D major chord (Figure 6-14).

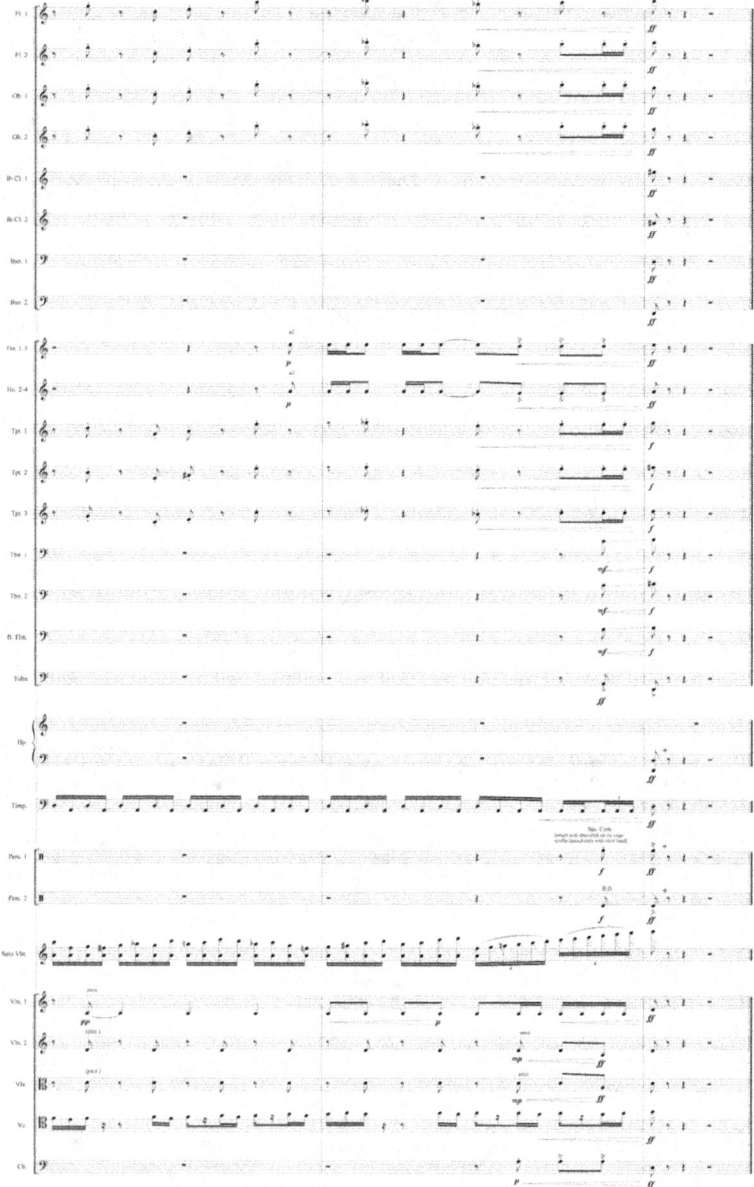

Figure 6-14. *Violin Concerto*; III, mm. 196-198.

Six. Violin Concerto 163

Critical Reception and Conclusion

Higdon's *Violin Concerto* premiered on February 6, 2009, by Hilary Hahn with Mario Venzago conducting the Indianapolis Symphony Orchestra. Subsequent performances by the co-commissioning ensembles were likewise performed with Hahn as soloist in the following order: the Toronto Symphony Orchestra, under the baton of Peter Oundjian, on March 11, 2009 (Canadian premiere), the Baltimore Symphony Orchestra with Marin Alsop on June 4, 2009 (East Coast premiere), and finally, Juanjo Mena and the Curtis Symphony Orchestra on February 14, 2011 (Philadelphia premiere).[45] Due to the fame of both composer and Hahn, the work's premiere provoked great interest from critics and public alike.

Mary Ellyn Hutton reviewed the world premiere performance in Indianapolis for the *American Record Guide* as follows:

> Higdon's Concerto is a brilliant 35 minutes of color, gesture, and pizzazz couched in diatonic harmonies and infectious rhythms. "1726" begins delicately with soft harmonics by the solo violin, joined in the sixth bar by glockenspiel and crotales struck with knitting needles. It unfolds as an expansion and variation on the rhythmic-motif pattern heard at the onset and culminates in a "ferocious" cadenza.[46]

Tim Smith of *The Baltimore Sun* reviewed the Baltimore concert:

> The half-hour concerto makes a grand statement, packed with thematic material and expansive development, all of it delivered with extraordinarily prismatic colors. The opening of the score, [...] is quite the ear-grabber, a wonderful way to begin what amounts to a journey through moods and events, through light and shade [...] Higdon's fundamentally tonal, yet imaginatively spiced style communicates with a refreshing directness. The violin part encompasses an enormous range, technically and expressively, and the orchestral writing is no less substantial. The second movement is especially potent [...] with richly textured chords supporting a slowly soaring melodic line.[47]

The work was equally well received in the UK when it was performed with the Royal Liverpool Philharmonic Orchestra conducted by Vasily Petrenko, the ensemble and conductor who recorded the work. Of the live concert, Hilary Finch wrote in *The Times*:

> Higdon seems to have absorbed and assimilated something from almost everything that exists in the violin repertoire—and yet she speaks with a fresh and confident voice of her own. What enchants the ear [about the first movement] is the way that tiny, icy shards of sound, which start the work so insignificantly that you think the soloist is still tuning, are subsequently voiced by soloists throughout the orchestra. They're heated up, transformed into a spiky dance and a frenzied moto perpetuo, only to return to those initial icicles of sound, and a good old-fashioned cadenza.[48]

In London's *The Daily Telegraph*, David Fanning noted:

> Its crystalline opening, which blends violin harmonics with glockenspiel and antique cymbals, immediately tickles the ear, and the fast invention that follows—and which also

dominates the finale—has something of Prokofiev's bounding energy. In between is a slow movement that floats rhapsodic solo lines over tightly disciplined orchestral writing. Tone colour is imaginative throughout and the instrumental writing impeccably professional, allowing the soloist-dedicatee, the richly gifted Hilary Hahn, every chance to shine.[49]

In the early conversations of the commission, it was determined that the work would be recorded and following the premieres, Higdon made musical revisions that were implemented for the recording sessions.[50] Hahn, of course, was the soloist for the recording with the Royal Liverpool Philharmonic Orchestra under the direction of Vasily Petrenko as noted above. She explained the pairing of the Higdon with the Tchaikovsky *Violin Concerto* in her liner notes:

> I believe that these full-scale, grandly conceived concertos, both connected for me by my time at the Curtis Institute, illuminate each other. While they come from different centuries and compositional worlds, they share a great many qualities: lyrical delicacy, a brooding gentility, energetic abandon, and a fine maturity of spirit. Placed back to back, they suggest the range of musical possibilities open to the violin in the early twenty-first century.[51]

Because recordings are easily accessible, there are far more numerous critical reviews of these than the live performances. In the *American Record Guide*, Lawrence Hansen described the *Violin Concerto* as

> entirely accessible to anybody comfortable with mainstream 20th Century American composers (but not derivative!) and often very demanding of the soloist. Yet it's not difficulty for the sake of difficulty but always for an expressive purpose. There's plenty for the orchestra to do, too, including the percussion section.[52]

Geoff Brown published his review of the disc in the UK's *The Times* and opined:

> This concerto's opening, with the violin's high-register [...] is immediately captivating and a foretaste of beauties to come, especially in the pellucid, shifting tapestries of the slow movement. Yet there's nothing lightweight about the piece's technical demands [...] with Hahn's sparkling display and Petrenko's lively support, the new work easily earns its place as a concerto to listen to, and enjoy.[53]

The critique of Anne Midgette from *The Washington Post* found "Jennifer Higdon's music is energetic and attractive, with undeniable crowd appeal and finger-twisting virtuosity."[54] Finally the *New York Times*'s Allan Kozinn wrote:

> Ms. Higdon's concerto is a showpiece in the classic Romantic style [...] Higdon's chromatic neo-Romanticism and inventive orchestration keep the piece lively and surprising. And it fits Ms. Hahn's interpretive personality perfectly, drawing on both her pinpoint precision in fast, intricate passages and the singing tone she typically produces in slow, long-lined music.[55]

Higdon's *Violin Concerto* was awarded the Pulitzer Prize for music in 2010. Although seemingly another feather in the composer's figurative hat, the prestige around the Pulitzer surpasses all other awards. Receiving this significant honor brought additional publicity to the work, subsequent performances by several violinists, and will undoubtedly secure its place in the canon.

Pulitzer Prizes began in 1917 stemming from the final will and testament of journalist, Joseph Pulitzer and decades later, in 1943, the music Pulitzer was created.[56] The judges for this category consist of three composers, a music critic, and an active musician who meet to evaluate the somewhat vague submission requirements of "distinguished musical composition by an American that has had its first performance or recording in the United States during that year."[57] The 2010 Music Jury was comprised of the chair, composer Joseph Schwantner, along with Chuck Owen, Maria Schneider, Delta David Gier, and John Rockwell.[58]

When announcing the winners in mid–April 2010, Higdon's *Violin Concerto* was described as a "deeply engaging piece that combines flowing lyricism with dazzling virtuosity."[59] The other music finalists that year were Fred Lerdahl's *String Quartet No. 3* and *Steel Hammer* by Julia Wolfe.[60] Higdon's Pulitzer Prize follows a number of prestigious awards and honors including a 2010 Grammy in the category "Best Contemporary Classical Composition" for her *Percussion Concerto*. Undoubtedly, 2010 was a year full of great validation and success.

With her usual good humor, Higdon recalled how she was informed about the Pulitzer, "I turned on my cellphone and I had all these messages and I thought that was unusual [...] I guess I found out a little bit after everyone else."[61] Then she "jumped up and down a little."[62] Higdon later expanded, "I was trying to understand what had happened. It didn't seem real. Other people win it. Many Pulitzer winners phoned to say that the award would change my life. And it did. Suddenly, offers poured in. I was turning down a commission every couple of days."[63]

Fran Richard, vice president and director of Concert Music for ASCAP, stated:

> We are thrilled with the news that Jennifer Higdon has won the Pulitzer Prize. ASCAP's Cia Toscanini and I were the first to let Jennifer know that she had won, and in her usual, wonderful way, she reminded us that it was the ASCAP Foundation that commissioned her first orchestra piece [...] a piece honoring Morton Gould for the Portland Symphony under Maestro James DePriest [sic].[64] In addition to being one of our most treasured members, Jennifer also currently serves on ASCAP's Symphony & Concert Committee, so there is a deep connection between Jennifer and ASCAP.[65]

Asked about her celebratory plans for the evening, Higdon responded, "I'm going to attend my students' composition concert tonight at Curtis—and try not to steal any of their thunder."[66]

And finally, Hahn's response to the announcement must be included:

> I was overjoyed by this news. It was both artistically and intellectually rewarding to collaborate with Jennifer on this concerto, and she put so much energy into the work. She has been a wonderful colleague throughout the whole process, attending nearly every performance of the piece as well as the recording sessions in Liverpool last spring. From a performer's perspective, there's no substitute for that kind of support. Congratulations, Jennifer![67]

After winning the Pulitzer, Higdon used the opportunity to recommend other composers. In her explanation, much is revealed about the kindness and altruism of her character:

> I receive even more commission offers that I can't accommodate, but now I am able to say, "If you like my music, check out this composer." So I know some other composers got commissions and that's one of the best outcomes of winning. It also gave me the chance to thank all of those people who had helped me along the way. A Pulitzer Prize shouldn't just honor the individual who writes the music. It should be something that goes to all the people who have been involved in that person's life.[68]

Higdon has since composed the violin and piano work *Echo Dash* for Hahn's album, *In 27 Pieces: The Hilary Hahn Encores*. Released in 2014, the album received a Grammy for Best Chamber Music/Small Ensemble Performance. *Echo Dash* is truly unique since it may be performed several ways: both parts together, the violin and piano as individual soli, or even pairing the violin with only the right hand or left hand of the piano.[69]

Only three months after the premiere of Higdon's *Violin Concerto*, Hahn stated, "I look forward to the time when this concerto is out there in the standard repertoire [...] and I'll like it not needing me to play it, because that will mean it has its own life and I've done my part."[70] In a few short years, her wish has become a reality with the work being performed several times with different violinists and orchestras.

As mentioned previously, Beilman has performed the *Violin Concerto* and had been intimately familiar with the work from his student days at Curtis. He played the *Concerto* as a soloist with the Philadelphia Orchestra led by Robert Spano in February 2015[71] and with the same ensemble and conductor at the Bravo! Vail Valley Music Festival on July 12, 2015.[72] Another musician who programmed the work was Holly Mulcahy with the Chattanooga Symphony conducted by Kayoko Dan on March 12, 2015.[73] Curiously, Mulcahy solicited bartender Nathan Herron from Easy Bistro and Bar in Chattanooga to create a cocktail inspired by the composition. Amongst the various components of the drink, Herron included Uncle Val's Botanical Gin because it "represented the brightness, freshness, pungent yet radiant chords and energy of the concerto."[74] Other performers of the work thus far include Naha Greenholtz with the Quad City Symphony Orchestra (Davenport, Iowa) with Alasdair Neale conducting in December 2013 and Caroline Chin with the Bowling Green Philharmonia led by Emily Freeman Brown in 2015 at Bowling Green State University's New Music Festival.[75]

In approximately five years, the work has already secured a place in the canon, partly due to the Pulitzer Prize but more importantly because of the quality of the composition. Violinists across the nation continue to express great interest in learning and performing this work. The life of the *Violin Concerto* is only in its infancy but its promising start suggests a longevity rarely seen in contemporary American art music.

Chapter Seven

Cold Mountain

Introduction

From the first thought of writing an opera to the highly anticipated world premiere, the journey of Higdon's *Cold Mountain* lasted approximately a decade. The idea, initially proposed by Robert Spano and Donald Runnicles,[1] Principal Guest Conductor of the Atlanta Symphony Orchestra, percolated while she continued to fulfill obligated commissions.

The earliest step in the process was finding a librettist; knowing such a collaboration would be an extensive, lengthy relationship, Higdon researched and interviewed several possibilities. At the time, she was serving a term on the Board of Directors for the League of American Orchestras whose President was Jesse Rosen, a cousin of Gene Scheer. Higdon asked Rosen for Scheer's contact information and after meeting with him, she believed they would work well together.[2] Scheer is well known in contemporary American opera as an established librettist of works that include Tobias Picker's *An American Tragedy* (2005) and Jake Heggie's *Moby Dick* (2010). Scheer also composes. He penned *American Anthem* featured in Ken Burns's World War II documentary and coincidentally, recorded by Nathan Gunn, the baritone who premiered the opera's leading role of W.P. Inman.

Spano advised Higdon to consider the Santa Fe Opera Company (SFO) and after making contact, she felt certain they were the ideal choice to premiere her first opera.[3] She approached Charles MacKay, the SFO's General Director, about a potential premiere. He recalled their first phone conversation, "She said I want to talk to you about my new opera […] I want to write an opera and everyone says Santa Fe Opera would be the perfect place."[4] They arranged to meet in New York on MacKay's next visit which was scheduled following a stay in Chicago to adjudicate the Metropolitan Opera auditions. MacKay saw Gunn at the auditions and mentioned that the SFO was approached to produce *Cold Mountain*. The baritone responded, "I love that novel […] is there a part in it for me? It hasn't been written yet, right?"⁵ According to MacKay, the rest happened very quickly:

> I looked at him [Gunn], I said, "You are Inman" and so [...] we shook hands on the deal and [...] went off to judge our auditions then, a couple of days later, I met with [...] Jennifer in New York and I said, "You won't believe this but I think I've signed on Inman for our project." And she said, "Really? We haven't even decided we're doing this." And I said, "Yes, we are doing it [...] because Nathan Gunn says he would love to sing Inman in *Cold Mountain*."⁶

Gunn was no stranger to Higdon's music; he had asked her to arrange her *Dooryard Bloom* for a chamber ensemble⁷ which he subsequently premiered in 2013.⁸

All of the principal singers had worked with the SFO previously and were familiar with the company. Leading the enviable cast were Gunn and Isabel Leonard in the starring roles of Inman and Ada, a soprano. Leonard, known primarily as a mezzo-soprano, was adamant that she could sing the role of Ada and sent copies of soprano characters she had performed to Higdon who also heard Leonard perform the soprano lead in a 2012 revival of Thomas Ades's *The Tempest*.⁹ Leonard's persistence proved beneficial and she won the role.

Supporting roles in *Cold Mountain* include Ruby, a mezzo-soprano premiered by Emily Fons, Teague depicted by tenor, Jay Hunter Morris, and finally Stobrod, Ruby's ne'er do well father played by Kevin Burdette, a bass. For practical reasons, a few of the minor roles double as additional characters including an all-male chorus that portrays at various times Confederate soldiers, the homeguard, Federal troops, and a chain gang. Although Gunn was informally cast by MacKay, all other singers had to receive Higdon's approval. Lawson explained that the composer "gave great latitude to Santa Fe in suggesting/hiring because she felt they would know the best singers."¹⁰

The SFO produces operas only in the summer in their outdoor theatre and although their operating budget is comparable to urban companies, staging a grand opera the size of *Cold Mountain* was a new undertaking.¹¹ Opera Philadelphia and the Minnesota Opera were enlisted as co-commissioners later joined by North Carolina Opera (Raleigh, North Carolina) as a collaborator. Because SFO undertook more of the financial investment, they had the honor of hosting the premiere.¹²

Cold Mountain premiered on August 1, 2015, in Santa Fe, New Mexico, at 8:30 p.m. local time with subsequent performances on August 5, 14, 17, and 22 at 8 p.m. The enthusiasm for this work was so great that an additional performance was added on August 24. The Santa Fe productions were dedicated to the memory of Richard G. Higgins, a member of the SFO Board of

Directors since 2008; an engineer, Higgins's interests coincidentally included military history and the American Civil War.[13] Higdon dedicated the score to Lawson.[14]

The core production team consisted of director, Leonard Foglia, Scheer, scenic designer Robert Brill, and Elaine J. McCarthy for the projection design. This was a reunion of sorts since all four had previously collaborated on the Dallas Opera's 2010 premiere of Jake Heggie's *Moby-Dick*.[15] Foglia is known for his work in both operatic world premieres and on Broadway but his involvement with *Cold Mountain* began approximately four years earlier. Scheer had worked with him previously and strongly recommended him as a dramaturge; after meeting Foglia, Higdon approved SFO to hire him in that role and as director.[16] He explained, "In this particular piece, I was hired [...] really before anything is written. I spend time working with the librettist. Of course, the words come first, and the composer comes into it, and I'm there, involved in the whole process from the beginning."[17]

Foglia recognized the challenge of staging a story where the main protagonist travels over lengthy, mountainous terrain and recounted:

> I can't compete with it [the novel] [...] I can't compete with people's imaginations. We have all walked in the woods. We all know what that is. And I knew I couldn't do that, and so I wasn't going to even try. So, I was going to just try to get to [...] the soul of the story [...] he's [Inman] been gutted, is one of the phrases that Charles uses in the book and we use it in the opera [...] I wanted an environment that's been gutted.[18]

The director contacted Brill, whose abstract set featured planks of wood at varying elevations mirroring both the physical destruction of the war and the characters' shattered emotional states. No set changes were required and this design easily accommodated Inman's changing terrain. For the majority of the opera, Black Cove Farm occurred stage left and Inman's travels stage right. The composer was initially scheduled to view the presentation of Brill's set, but she was accidentally excluded and was not present.[19] She described the set as follows:

> It looks like a modern sculpture. It looks like something to me like a bomb fell down into a timber yard and then the boards exploded upwards [...] the director [...] had said that when he was speaking with Robert Brill [...] he wanted a piece of sculpture that might be able to fit in the Whitney in New York so he was looking for something that was very artistic.[20]

Miguel Harth-Bedoya, Music Director of the Fort Worth Symphony Orchestra, was enlisted as the conductor for the premiere. The maestro's relationship with Higdon originated from their student days at Curtis in the late 1980s.[21] More recently from 2009 to 2010, she served as the Composer-in-Residence with the FWSO; coincidentally, it was Harth-Bedoya and his ensemble that recorded another composition referencing Appalachia, *Concerto 4–3* in 2012, the year he was hired to conduct *Cold Mountain*.[22]

Libretto

Choosing a story for the opera was a formidable challenge. The work had to connect with both Higdon and Scheer while being suitable for the operatic stage. The composer took countless suggestions for potential stories.[23] Frustrations with obtaining a source's legal rights continued to mount but eventually Scheer suggested Charles Frazier's *Cold Mountain*,[24] the recipient of the 1997 National Book Award.

Inman, the protagonist, was based on Frazier's great-great uncle whose story he discovered while visiting family in Western North Carolina. His father told him about a relative who fought in the deadliest battles of the Civil War, was injured, and walked home following his desertion. Frazier recalled:

> On the way back to Raleigh, […] I just kept thinking, "I know how to tell that story" […] and immediately dropped the book I had been working on. There were very few details of Inman's life, there were some family stories, the place where he was killed in a gunfight with the Confederate homeguard but a lot of it was just imagining, being from that place, going through that experience and how damaged you would be and yet what hopes you might still have left.[25]

Ada never existed but was created to counteract Inman's war experiences[26]; the casting of Leonard as the lead female won Frazier's approval and he commented, "She looks like Ada just stepped off the page."[27]

The novel is primarily set in the rural, mountainous region of Western North Carolina, very close to where Higdon spent her adolescence in Eastern Tennessee. In Frazier's prose, she realized she "had found home and that was the most important thing for writing."[28] She recalled:

> The minute I started reading it, I thought, "This is it. I can tell that this is the story we're supposed to set" […] it was recognizing the personalities of the characters because I grew up so close to there […] I recognized those individuals despite the fact that it's a Civil War story, there are still people in East Tennessee who are just like those individuals […] It has not changed and I was so blown away by that […] but there was just something about the love story.[29]

Higdon read the novel four separate times[30] but only after the first few did she notice

> that there was a map in the front of the book and I looked and […] I realized the farm I grew up on was actually on the map [in the front of the book] […] I got out Google Earth […] and it was […] 60 miles as the crow flies as we say. But I recognized these people,

> I recognized the language, [...] the way they speak, the way they tell tales and the landscape, the personalities, every single bit of it just resonated for me.[31]

The synopsis of the novel and subsequently the opera is often described as an Appalachian Odyssey during the final months of the Civil War. Inman, a wounded deserter of the Confederate Army, resolves to return home to Cold Mountain where he has left Ada, his love interest. As he walks across North Carolina, he encounters various people and obstacles while the villain, Teague, leads the homeguard in charge of finding and punishing such deserters. Ada is a highly educated and sophisticated woman from Charleston who moved to Cold Mountain with her late father. She is ill equipped to maintain the property in the bucolic region but is aided by Ruby, a formally uneducated woman wise in the ways of the land. Ruby's father, Stobrod, abandoned her as a child and when he re-enters her life, she is torn between resentment and a sense of duty. Stobrod is a fiddler and like Inman, has become a deserter. Curiously, Burdette, who premiered the role of Stobrod, plays the viola[32] and hails from Knoxville, Tennessee, not far from the opera's setting. When Higdon initially met him, he mentioned his string background which led her to compose music for him to play in character.[33] The opera maintains all of these lead roles and storylines but several minor characters were omitted to keep the opera under 150 minutes.

Because the novel was made into a feature film, obtaining the rights to the story became exceedingly complicated. Higdon recalled:

> Getting *Cold Mountain* took 10 months of pushing and taking back avenues to make it work. It was a major ordeal. Miramax, which holds some of the rights [...], was up for sale when all of this was going on, and we had to wait until it was bought.[34]

Despite this hurdle, the opera is based solely on the book rather than the film's interpretation. Higdon had actually purchased the novel soon after publication, but had not read it because:

> My younger brother [Andy] had since passed away and for a couple years I couldn't concentrate on the novel, couldn't concentrate on books at all. I remember seeing the movie when it came out. But after reading the book, I realized parts of the movie are completely different.[35]

She had seen the Anthony Minghella film twice but once the libretto was chosen, she avoided the film so as not to be influenced in any way by its interpretation or the music.[36]

As a native New Yorker, Scheer's exposure to Southern dialect was limited. He traveled to Asheville, North Carolina, to meet with Frazier who drove him through the area including Cold Mountain. Higdon assisted in some of the idiomatic writing because as she explained, Scheer "wasn't sure he could figure out 'Southern speak.'"[37] He sent her large sections of the libretto and she altered some of the dialog's verb tenses and incorporated double negatives and other incorrect grammar for characters who "weren't educated or they might be [from] farther back in the mountains."[38]

The composer and author met in person and the latter was so impressed that he gave her his blessing to adapt the material freely. He related to her creative situation, "I cannot imagine somebody who doesn't know about writing a novel, looking over my shoulder saying, 'I've got 10 great ideas that you need to incorporate.'"[39] Curiously, music is a significant part of Frazier's own creative process. He commented, "I listen to music when I'm working, [...] it's in my head, [...] I have soundtracks for each of the characters."[40]

The structure of the novel contributed to its phenomenal success. Not only are there flashbacks critical to the drama, but the two lovers' stories alternate each chapter with Inman's location continuously changing as he traverses the mountains. Shell-shocked by the horrors of war, Inman has little dialog. The events unfold slowly over the course of an extensive work that provide a rewarding and meaningful experience for the reader but present unique challenges to the librettist in adapting it for live theatre. Scheer explained the role of music:

> Transforming narrative art into an active theatrical form does not mean that the narrator no longer exists. Rather, the narrative voice is reborn in the voice of the composer. Literary details that seem to have been jettisoned reemerge and are reborn in a vocabulary of direct emotion, the vocabulary of music.[41]

Scheer began with an outline and Higdon sketched the synopsis by scene noting the action and singers required. She recalled, "I had to try to visualize it to figure out how to do it. How long do you need for a costume change? We have a flashback, how long will that take?"[42] The composer worked with the librettist to focus on significant sections of the story that would not disrupt the plot or lose the crucial character developments.[43] For Scheer, the dramatic interest was in the changes that each of the main character's experience; therefore, a scene's relevance to the characters' evolution was the deciding factor of its inclusion.[44] One of Higdon's primary concerns was the length of the opera. This resulted in frequent conversations with Scheer about text setting and the use of melisma which can obscure textual clarity and lengthen scenes.[45] Higdon frequently reminded him, "We need only the essential things, only the essential!"[46] Finally, the duo considered the minor roles from a practical, financial perspective doubling voice types for the numerous secondary characters so singers could perform multiple supporting roles.

One significant change from the novel is the role of Lucinda, a slave woman. In Frazier's work, Inman only hears about her and has no direct contact; however, in the libretto, he encounters her himself in one of the most dramatic and universally lauded scenes of the opera. Lawson explained that this role was expanded to "demonstrate mercy"[47] while simultaneously substituting for the goat woman, a character omitted to avoid using live animals.[48] The complexity of the character served several other significant functions as Higdon explained:

> Our first thought was that it would be an extremely dramatic moment; secondly, it seemed irresponsible to create an opera based on events connected to the Civil War and not have someone of color represented; thirdly, Inman needed to be rescued from his "bondage" [he has been momentarily captured and is in chains when the two characters interact] … Lucinda does represent mercy, but also the hope that when given the choice, even those who have suffered for so long at the hands of others might find the compassion to assist. Lucinda represents so many different things, even beyond what I've stated here, that I find it difficult to articulate it all; being a composer, the easiest way for me to describe the depth of that scene is through the music.[49]

As noted above, while Scheer worked on the libretto, Higdon made sketches about the characters, the order of scenes, and number of singers necessary while considering the logistical and practical aspects.[50] Thus when she received the finished prose, some of the musical ideas were already established.[51]

Compositional Process

For her first opera, Higdon researched and studied countless opera scores to study the voice and dramatic pacing. When she struggled with a specific problem, such as balancing the voice with the orchestra, she turned to the works of Puccini, Stravinsky,[52] Mozart, and most importantly, Benjamin Britten.[53] She remarked, "Everyone does it differently but there are little answers buried in all of those scores."[54] She also attended opera premieres of fellow American composers, including the aforementioned Heggie's *Moby-Dick*, Stewart Wallace's *The Bonesetter's Daughter* (San Francisco, 2008), and John Adams's *A Flowering Tree* (Vienna, 2006)[55] amongst several others. During her research, Higdon set two primary goals: "a commitment to textual clarity and a sense of motion, or eventfulness."[56] These parameters support her well established compositional philosophy of maintaining audience interest while communicating effectively. In *Cold Mountain*, this meant eschewing traditional recitatives. She explained:

> I didn't want that, so for me it was about trying to make everything that wasn't one of the set pieces [arias, duets, etc.] sound musical. Opera's more effective when you don't tell people what's happening, you actually show them what's happening, and it makes the opera experience a lot more engaging.[57]

Higdon dedicated her time exclusively to composing the opera, which meant rejecting or postponing commissions and limiting her residencies and travel schedule considerably. She recalled:

> I knew I needed time to study. When I ran up against roadblocks, I should be able to get out scores and look at them and listen and see if I can figure out how to solve the problem. I wanted to make sure we had time to workshop so that I could make changes but it basically was me [...] saying realistically what I think I could do is take three years out.[58]

Once Scheer delivered the libretto, she began composing from the beginning, a most unusual method for Higdon. She elaborated on her process, "By following the libretto, my notes in my notebooks, and the sketchpad illustrations, and then creating sketches on the computer, I was slowly able to work my way through each scene (keeping track of the durations, so that nothing was too long)."[59] Conceptualizing the grand opera as individual, smaller works[60] made the project seem less daunting and more manageable.

With Scheer's permission, the composer made significant changes to the libretto. She explained, "It was a little bit the length of the lines, but it was also changes that helped the music move over the bar line to make it more musical [...] Sometimes a repetition didn't work. Sometimes I would have to shorten a line."[61]

Higdon's adolescence in East Tennessee proved helpful. She remarked that composing the music came "more naturally to me than anything I have ever written and so when I had to write mountain music, [when] I needed to write Southern fiddling, it happened so easily."[62] Foglia's early involvement allowed Higdon to pose questions to him about the timing of logistics such as walking across the stage or costume changes. She remembered, "I'd call [Foglia] and say how much music would be needed for this or that action. And he would say 90 seconds"[63] while other times when she asked similar questions, he said he would simply follow the music.[64]

The composition of *Cold Mountain* lasted approximately 28 months working daily eight hours a day. Focusing exclusively on a single composition for such an extended period of time was new for Higdon. She commented:

> The thing that shocked me was how the characters lived in my head. When I got to the end of the opera, when I put the double bar on, [...] I could see the last character go out of the room, and close the door and it became completely silent for the first time in over two years. And I was lost, confused and celebratory, and exhausted [...] it was like nothing I've ever experienced.[65]

The days of composers finishing the music at the last minute like Mozart are quite different than the business of writing an opera in the 21st century. The SFO required a piano-vocal score of each act, which is not part of Higdon's usual process. She begins composing large works in short score which in *Cold Mountain* meant the voice part(s) and approximately eight instrumental lines. The mandated piano-vocal score meant a very lengthy step had to be inserted between the composition of the short score and the orchestration of the entire opera.[66] As Lawson explained, however, Higdon completed the piano-vocal score of Act I much earlier to submit to Curtis for the workshops[67] and thus the extra step required from SFO was convenient.

Workshops and the Guggenheim Preview

The two acts were workshopped by student singers and a pianist at the Curtis Institute's Lenfest Hall. Higdon's colleague, Mikael Eliasen, is not only the Artistic Advisor to Opera Philadelphia but also the Artistic Director of the Curtis Opera Theatre making the conservatory an ideal setting.[68] Act I's workshop convened from December 3 to 8, 2012, allowing Higdon time to incorporate the feedback into Act II which was then workshopped December 2–7, 2013.[69]

The procedure for each was nearly identical: the singers were given their scores in October,[70] rehearsed with vocal coach Lisa Keller, and then met in December performing scenes in two daily sessions of three hours each. Because all the singers were highly advanced students, the experience was somewhat different than using professionals. Scheer explained:

> Professional workshops frequently happen so quickly that preparation time is lacking. There's a push just to get the music learned, and it becomes a sing-through. You want the material to be done well enough so you can assess if the problem is the material or the performance. If it's done poorly, you could end up cutting things that would actually work. These singers were so good and so well prepared that we got a really honest assessment. It was a great gift they gave to us.[71]

The Act I workshop was attended only by the core creative team (Higdon, Scheer, and Foglia), Eliasen, and the performers conducted by Vinay Parameswaran. Each Act's workshop concluded with a presentation featuring excerpts intended to "give the commissioning opera companies and potential participants (and donors) a glimpse of the work."[72] Both the presentation and the workshops provided opportunities for feedback not only to Higdon but to the entire production team. Act I's presentation was attended by Charles Frazier and his wife, Katherine, David Devan from Opera Philadelphia, MacKay, SFO's Director of Artistic Administration Brad Woolbright, Leonard, Gunn, Morris, a few select donors, and representatives from other opera companies.[73] The experience of having his words turned into an opera was thrilling for Frazier who commented:

> You write a book [...] sit at home for eight years [...] with these things in your head and never imagine that anybody will read the book much less that you then, 15 years later, 16 years later, [...] come and listen to these beautiful voices and this beautiful music with [...] your characters and your story. It's a very overwhelming kind of feeling.[74]

The author further recalled, "I don't remember feeling this way but Lenny Foglia [...] said I looked stunned. I think if I was stunned it was to hear Inman who is so damaged and wounded that he can barely speak sing in a huge, magnificent voice."[75]

Similarly, Act II's workshop was attended by Eliasen, the Curtis singers with Keller at the piano conducted by Joseph Meckavich, along with Foglia, Scheer, and Higdon. The presentation following Act II was not attended by the Fraziers or Morris but otherwise, consisted of the members named above.[76]

Higdon maintained an open dialog with the student singers and solicited their suggestions. In both workshops, Inman and Ada were performed by Jarrett Ott and Rachel Sterrenberg. The latter explained:

> We [the workshop singers and Higdon] had discussions about the tessitura of a soprano and a mezzo and what the difference is; we talked about what a singer can handle, like how many high notes you can sing in a row. We learned a lot about our voices, because we had to communicate that to Jennifer. This was something I've never had to do, because normally music is given to us, and we are expected to be able to learn it. It was a big learning process for us to be able to articulate what singers can do.[77]

Higdon added, "They were like superb music teachers. This opera has a lot of people in distress, and the human voice in distress is at a different pitch [...] I said to them, don't hesitate to tell me if anything is awkward [...] and I want your suggestions about how best to change it."[78] Ott's work secured him a place as a featured Apprentice Singer at SFO where he was the understudy of Gunn. MacKay, filled with confidence in the young singer, said prior to the premiere, "I won't lose a wink of sleep over Inman."[79] Ott also was appointed the understudy for the East Coast premiere in Philadelphia and played the leading role with little notice to great critical acclaim after Gunn's withdrawal due to a family emergency. Sterrenberg performed in this production as well as Sara, a secondary soprano role.

Foglia's contributions to the workshop were from a dramatic perspective. He explained:

> I'm always looking for clarity. Is it in the music? The libretto? The performance? And because an opera score is so complicated, changes other than a clean cut are often hard to make. However, we made a major change in Act II: We moved a scene. Being able to do that, on the spot, with the singers—to flip scenes, and hear it one way, and then another way—was invaluable.[80]

Lawson added more detail:

During the workshop of Act 2, [...] Eliasen [...] and Jennifer met to talk about the dramatic form of the second act [...] Jennifer went into the second day of the workshop and talked with her librettist and the director, and they decided to move one of the scenes to an earlier spot in the opera. It turned out to be a very simple change and took only about 30 minutes to figure it out. They tried it immediately and it worked, so they made a permanent change.[81]

Higdon worked tirelessly through the workshops composing new transitional material for scene changes each morning before the afternoon sessions began. She reflected on the experiences:

> I thought I knew quite a bit about the voice, but I learned so much from hearing my musical lines come out of the singers' mouths and then being able to talk to them about what they were experiencing: what felt like a stretch, what was a strain, what was too much, what was too low, where they were in their tessitura, where their problems were.... I also got a sense of pacing.[82]

On March 30, 2015, the Works and Process series at the Solomon R. Guggenheim Museum featured a preview of excerpts from *Cold Mountain* that marked the first public hearing of Higdon's operatic writing. The music was interspersed with discussion from Frazier, the creative team, and the singers. Due to a scheduling conflict, Inman was sung by Ott with the other leads performed by those scheduled to premiere the roles at the SFO assisted by Keller at the piano. The excerpts were as follows: "The Metal Age," "Listen," "A Fence Is a Good Thing," "I Should Be Cryin' but I Just Feel Numb," and "Come Back to Cold Mountain." The composer programmed the selections out of order because as she explained, "I thought it might be kind of nice to have this love duet at the end. Send people out with a little bit of a smile on their face and a little bit of hope in their hearts."[83] Amongst the members of the press in attendance was David Patrick Stearns who wrote, "The Cold Mountain excerpts performed Monday showed how well Higdon has mastered the musicalization of conflicting but simultaneous emotions among strongly drawn characters."[84] This brief preview of Higdon's work further increased anticipation and excitement about the world premiere.

Rehearsals and Critical Reception of Premiere

To capture the characters' Southern accents, the singers worked with dialect coach Erie Mills, a former coloratura who has served as a diction coach for Opera Theatre of St. Louis, the Met, and previous SFO productions.[85] In early spring of 2015, Mills and Higdon discussed the specific dialects needed and continued to work closely once rehearsals began on location. Although all the characters are from the Carolinas, minute variances were necessary to represent the differing levels of education while Ada's accent needed to sound more urban to reflect her Charleston origins.[86]

As the premiere drew closer, Santa Fe was abuzz with excitement; in connection to the opera, the city had been exploring the Civil War since late spring. The New Mexico History Museum's exhibit *Fading Memories: Echoes of the Civil War* displayed daguerreotypes, books, and other objects from the War Between the States while Collected Works Bookstore hosted gatherings to explore literary works associated with the war. Finally, the Center for Contemporary Arts Cinematheque showed films connected in some way to the opera.[87]

A closed, full dress rehearsal occurred on Thursday, July 30, 2015, at 8:30 p.m. In order to preserve their voices, the singers did not perform at full voice nor were the Spanish and English subtitles available at the premiere in use; however, the clearly enunciated diction coupled with Higdon's syllabic text setting made the subtitles unnecessary. The composer sat in the theatre with the score, a small light, and a pencil making notes. Immediately following Act I at the start of intermission, Higdon dashed down to Maestro Harth-Bedoya in the pit with her notes to rehearse a few instrumental excerpts.

Although an additional performance was added to the world premiere run, the demand remained so high that regular seating and standing room were exhausted. SFO sold tickets for folding chair seats and for those audience members, no subtitles were available.[88] Precisely because of the comprehensible diction and Higdon's focus on textual clarity was such an accommodation even possible.

Outside of the Guggenheim Works and Process preview, the opera had remained highly secretive and thus many curious critics flocked to Santa Fe for the premiere. Stearns, a reviewer for the *Philadelphia Inquirer*, possesses a knowledge of Higdon's music that is the most comprehensive of all critics since he resided in the same city as Higdon and has attended and reviewed numerous recitals featuring her music. He also used to live in close proximity to the composer's residence which houses her publishing company, Lawdon Press. As such and by pure happenstance, Stearns found a misformatted piano-vocal score of the opera in a nearby dumpster.[89] This critic remains the most prolific commentator of the opera and coupled with his unintentional access to the score, his writings are of particular importance and thus are quoted at length below.

One concern worthy of note are reviewers unfamiliar with Frazier's novel or worse, having only viewed the movie. Of course, one need not read the original source of a libretto to understand an opera but making critical judgments on the drama based solely on the film's interpretation is problematic since the opera is based on the book.

Of the reviewers that commented on non-musical aspects of the production, detailed commentary is few. Most found McCarthy's projections, displayed high on the set's wooden planks on stage left, favorable and helpful for flashbacks and Inman's changing locations. Opinions on the lighting were mixed; the *Washington Post* called it "ingenious"[90] and the *Santa Fe New Mexican* wrote that the "lighting guides eyes to where they need to focus at a given moment, [...] and it enhances the activities with appropriate infusions of heat or cold, both physical and emotional."[91] The *Denver Post*'s Ray Mark Rinaldi was less enthusiastic and opined, "At times, the lighting was so dark you couldn't tell what was going on."[92]

The set evoked great controversy; Brill's abstract design, was interpreted by all reviewers as representative of destruction but they differed substantially in their opinions. Rinaldi stated, "Brill's scenery allows anything to happen. There is just one set, consisting of a pile of giant beams and boards that jut out in all directions. They evoke, generally, ruin. But the parts move with agility, allowing the heap to stand in as a farm, a boat, a battlefield."[93] Stearns, however, abhorred the design and believed a new set would be preferable for the subsequent Opera Philadelphia productions.[94]

Foglia's talent as director was lauded universally, particularly in the clarity of the changing locations and flashbacks. James Keller opined, "These issues prove not just manageable but downright coherent, thanks in great measure to Leonard Foglia's cleverly conceived and clearly executed direction."[95]

The libretto, surprisingly, was almost completely omitted in reviews with many failing to mention Scheer's significant contributions. Those that did, applauded him for altering the role of Lucinda. Rinaldi explained that

> words matter in "Cold Mountain" and he [Scheer] is alternately sparse and poetic, and always on point as his characters suffer greatly from their lost conflict and evolve as humans. It's hard to discern the bad guys from the badder guys in this narrative. The ones you end up rooting for are cowards, killers and thieves. Scheer and Higdon mine their dramatic riches without whitewashing their evils.[96]

Stearns commented on Scheer's changes from the novel:

> Cold Mountain maintains the framework of the original book but also dramatically departs from it [...] a few pages, even sentences, are expanded to involve ensembles that deliver visceral gravity—needed in the opera but not the book. The slave Lucinda, mentioned briefly in the novel, appears in Act II with a personality invented by Scheer in one of the opera's best scenes.[97]

Finally, Terry Ponick of *Communities Digital News* wrote that

> Scheer has created a working libretto that transcends opera's generally stage-centric tradition, reimagining the story with a genuinely cinematic sweep and scope. The difference is star-

tling, and succeeds in rapidly drawing the opera audience into the action in an immediate and personal way. It's an approach that, perhaps, may signal a new era for the way new operas are conceived and performed.[98]

Scenes mentioned most frequently in the reviews are found in Act II, particularly the opening scene with Lucinda and Inman ("Is That All You Got?") and the large ensemble number near the end when all the characters Inman has encountered return as he recounts his experiences to Ada ("Tell Her"). On the latter, *The Washington Post* explained that this scene is "why people fall in love with grand opera."[99] Frequent and favorable mentions were also made regarding the all-male Confederate choruses, most notably when they performed "Our Beautiful Country" as the Chorus of the Dead.

The reviews that commented on Harth-Bedoya's conducting and ensemble, an orchestra comprised of the highest caliber of musicians across North America, were overwhelmingly positive. Rodney Punt of the *San Francisco Classical Voice* offered the most comprehensive commentary on the issue:

> Conductor Miguel Harth-Bedoya set unerringly appropriate pacing for his orchestra, enforced clarity and precision in its delivery, and kept his singers properly cued, assuring they could be heard over the instruments. His orchestra sparkled in the first act's ample opportunities for humor and lamented with power and tragic virtuosity as the tragedy set in.[100]

The cast was universally extolled for their combination of virtuosity and acting that brought the characters to life. Stearns referred to Gunn, Leonard, and Fons as "vocally resplendent," while praising Morris for capturing the cruelty of Teague.[101] *Opera Warhorses* acclaimed the leads as follows:

> Gunn's performance, not only beautifully sung, but a fine piece of theater, was the emotional center of the opera. His creation of the role of Inman should be regarded as one of the high points of his important career and a contribution of incalculable value to the opera's future. Leonard performed the high *tessitura* of the role masterfully. Ada's poignantly brief reunion with Inman—their first opportunity ever for an intimate moment—provided a memorable opportunity to observe Leonard's dramatic powers.[102]

Nearly all reviewers mentioned Higdon's prestigious contributions to the symphonic canon; curiously, however, only a few commented on the orchestral writing in *Cold Mountain*. One exception was *Madison Magazine*'s Greg Hettmansberger who declared:

> Higdon's best writing is consistently in the orchestra, and it is remarkable. She is not afraid to turn again and again to sparser, chamber music-like combinations of fascinating variety, but is fully capable of unleashing torrents of instrumental power with equally compelling coloristic combinations.[103]

Ponick noted that her "score, beginning with its thin, almost surrealistic percussive opening to its full-throated post–Romantic finale proved flexible and reflective, moving each of this work's many scenes rapidly and effectively forward while providing each vocalist with interesting and character-based palettes of sound."[104] The *San Francisco Classical Voice* found that

> the score's finest musical moments were, appropriately, in the few character-defining arias, ravishing choruses, time-stopping musical interludes, and reflective epilogue. Higdon's music serves the text with power and grace, yet without ego. Higdon's is tonal music, but it is a thoroughly modern score: Though often elegiac, the music is punctuated with violence and dissonance is almost an orchestral character itself, paralleling the opera's unsettled, anxious mood. It is a score, which, in its sure-handed clarity, accessibility, and inventiveness, marks Higdon as a natural creator for the lyric stage.[105]

East Coast Premiere and Recording

Cold Mountain's East Coast Premiere was produced by Opera Philadelphia between February 5–14, 2016, in five performances with ticket sales reaching the third highest in the company's history.[106] The basic production, including the set and costumes, was transported from Santa Fe but Nason's lighting was altered to accommodate an indoor theatre.[107] Higdon explained another significant change to an enclosed production, "There will be in effect more power inside the Academy of Music because we're not outdoors so the music isn't floating out, we aren't battling the wind, rain [...] extraneous highway sounds [...] so we [...] have the luxury of having more controlled sound here."[108]

The significant roles, with the exception of Emily Fons, were originally to be performed by the same cast as the SFO but in late January, a press release announced that due to a family emergency, Gunn would be replaced by his understudy, Ott. Because of Ott's extensive history with the role, this provoked little concern.

Numerous critics also attended and published reviews of the East Coast Premiere. The *American Record Guide*'s Lewis Whittington's stated, "Higdon's compositional font just pours forth with lucid symphonic narrative in *Cold Mountain*, a work that is on its way to being considered an American classic."[109] David Shengold, writing for *Opera News*, lauded the composer for her "finely textured lyrical orchestration and punctuation"; he also noted that Ott "assumed the part with considerable distinction and often ravishing, airy vocal finish. Ott brought [...] a deep investment in the words. "[110] Shengold's overall assessment of the production was that "Cold Mountain again proved an impressive first opera and a memorable theatrical experience."[111]

The opinion of Peter Dobrin from the *Philadelphia Inquirer* is noteworthy since Higdon has lived and worked for decades in Philadelphia and the music critics there are most familiar with her music. Dobrin opined that Higdon:

is a highly skilled composer. She has a good feel for filling out something in a character's air, motive, or temperament by conjuring, for two seconds or the duration of a scene, corresponding melodic material or orchestral texture. Jarrett Ott [...] seemed vocally and dramatically the right man for the part all along. And Opera Philadelphia did what it does so well, cushioning the work in stunning visuals. Rarely do set and lighting design align as beautifully as those of Robert Brill and Brian Nason, respectively, surrounding characters in light, shadow, and the brawny planks of a central structure that perfectly signals the feel of a life chaotic and askew.[112]

A recording of the Santa Fe production was released in April 2016 by Pentatone, a company in the Netherlands, as part of its new American Opera Series. Philip Kennicott, reviewed the two discs for *Gramophone* and commented that Higdon "writes music with a bracing, gun-metal grey flintiness, using her deft orchestration skills to evoke the novel's mix of violence and reverie."[113] It is interesting to note that a European company recorded an American opera because of a "direct and clear connection to modern society"[114] and thus considers American composers unique in keeping opera relevant in a genre historically associated with Western Europe.

Conclusion

Undoubtedly, the expectations of Higdon's long-awaited first opera were incredibly high; taken as a whole, the critics found the work poignant and original in both story and music. Stearns called *Cold Mountain* "an inevitable success"[115] while the *Washington Post* declared it to be "further proof that we are living in a Golden Age of American Opera."[116] Perhaps most telling was the reaction of Marc Scorca, president of OPERA America, who "left *Cold Mountain* really wanting to hear Jennifer Higdon's next opera."[117] Higdon has, in fact, committed to composing her next opera, a chamber work to be premiered in 2020 by Opera Philadelphia. The resounding success of *Cold Mountain* resulted in two Grammy nominations in the categories of Best Opera Recording and Best Contemporary Classical Composition and culminated in winning an International Opera Award in the World Premiere Category on May 15, 2016, at the Savoy Theatre, London. The subsequent and final chapter examines the significant musical aspects of this work.

CHAPTER EIGHT

Cold Mountain: The Music

Cold Mountain is in two acts and scored for a standard opera orchestra: paired woodwinds (with doublings on piccolo, English horn, bass clarinet, and contrabassoon), four horns, three trumpets (one doubling on piccolo trumpet), two trombones, one bass trombone, one tuba, harp, three percussionists, and strings.[1] Although instruments undoubtedly play a significant role in any opera, for a composer so well-known for her orchestral work such as Higdon, it is surprising that there is no overture and almost no purely instrumental numbers. Rather, the ensemble, when not supporting the singers, accompanies the dramatic action and provides seamless transitions between scenes, a crucial aspect of a synopsis that alternates two very different stories. Throughout both acts, neither the action nor the music cease thus omitting any opportunity for applause.

Although the orchestra is featured less prominently than the voices, Higdon's instrumental compositional traits remain present, perhaps most noticeably in the scoring of string soli for the first stand of sections. Additionally, sustained chords in the lower strings, particularly the violas and celli remain part of Higdon's style. Less prominent are major and minor chords scored for three trumpets (or trombones which infrequently may be the case). This disparity is easily explained in the significant use of the trumpet in *Cold Mountain* to represent Inman and other characters associated with the military.

The instrumentation was left to the composer with the exception of limiting the percussionists to two and a timpanist, which Higdon eschewed in favor of three percussionists. One of the practical reasons for such a switch was because of the severe space limitations of the orchestral pit, particularly in the Academy of Music in Philadelphia. For similar reasons, the percussion instruments utilized are smaller in size, no larger than a vibraphone. Higdon finished writing the percussionists' parts a full year in advance and forwarded the instrumentation to the principal player clarifying specifics such as the types of pitch pipes and thundertubes required. She explained:

Eight. Cold Mountain: The Music

> By the time I arrived [in Santa Fe] they had all of the [percussion] equipment there [...], but they ordered a fancier concert type of Thundertube, and I was looking for the version that is used as a toy, because the sound is better. After the first run through of the score with the orchestra, the principal percussionist and I went online, found the toy, and ordered it. The sound was much better [...] percussionists have to play so many instruments, they're extremely conscientious about checking the instrumentation and really working to find the right instruments in advance. It's very different than playing other instruments, where the individual only plays the one instrument (or two, if doubling).[2]

Because nearly the entire opera is set outside, the orchestral musicians are at times required to create unorthodox sounds on their instruments suggestive of the natural world. The wind and brass players "blow wind through [the] instrument"[3] without producing any actual pitch in three significant places: Act I, Scene 9 ("Listen") when Ruby teaches Ada how to interpret the sounds of nature and twice in Act II, in Scene 3 (the "Orion" duet) and the Epilogue when Ada and her daughter gaze upon the constellation. Without question, the most unusual aspect of the opera's scoring is the onstage fiddling by Stobrod which may also be produced by the concertmaster if future singers in the role do not have a string background. Momentarily, Higdon considered utilizing a mountain dulcimer, an Appalachian instrument, but decided against it for practical reasons.[4] The nontraditional instruments that complete the ensemble include the guitar pitch pipe and thigh slapping.[5]

Throughout his novel, Frazier mentions specific folk songs which Higdon chose not to reference.[6] In fact, the only Appalachian ballad in the opera is *Shady Grove*,[7] performed exclusively by Teague; however, at times the instrumental music purposely reflects the region's folk tradition. In her youth, the composer was exposed to authentic mountain fiddling during Old Timers' Day where such music was common.[8] As documented earlier, enfolding this vernacular language into a Western art context informed the entire concept of *Concerto 4-3* but in *Cold Mountain*, the Appalachian style appears sparingly and only in particular places such as the scenes featuring Stobrod. Higdon explained:

> There was just something about the fact that opera is considered a very elitist sort of musical language. I thought there was something very cool about being able to use bluegrass. And I realized one of the characters in the novel actually plays the fiddle, so it seemed so logical to just use some of the principles of bluegrass.[9]

Bluegrass refers to a commercialized music originating in the mid–20th century with many similarities to the earlier hillbilly, or in less pejorative language, old-time music. The similarities between bluegrass and its predecessor include ensemble string music, improvisation, the fiddle's melodic dominance, open string sounds, syncopations, and faster tempi. The bluegrass sections in the opera were not based on preexisting melodies but rather, were a newly created manipulation of the genre's characteristics that provide a uniquely Higdon result. The style, according to her, is "a little bit different than normal bluegrass because some of it is in 5/4 which is not normal [...] because the bluegrass section is supposed to sound like it's being improvised by some musicians who are trying to figure out what they're doing. I wrote it to be a little bit unusual."[10]

An opera, by design, is sectional through the division and subdivision of acts and scenes. *Cold Mountain* is as well, perhaps even more so than the typical opera through the continuous alternation between characters and locations. Although sectional forms are prevalent in Higdon's orchestral oeuvre, its use here is defined by Frazier's novel. Transitions between sections, or scenes in this case, are not achieved through the *accelerandi*, *ritardandi*, or meter changes common with this composer but rather through orchestral interludes.

Musical Depictions of Characters

Higdon considered several aspects in determining the voice types for each of the characters such as vocal projection and exploration of color, the latter always a significant motivation with this composer. She also contemplated the characters and imagined how their voices would sound.[11] The voice types of the lead characters are as follows: Inman—Baritone, Ada—Soprano, Ruby—Mezzo Soprano, Teague—Tenor, Stobrod—Bass, and Veasey—Tenor.[12] Perhaps the easiest decision was making Inman a baritone since Gunn had already committed to the role. The parts of Ada and Ruby were scored as soprano and mezzo soprano, respectively. Isabel Leonard, although known as a mezzo, premiered the role of Ada in both Santa Fe and Philadelphia due to her great interest in the project as explained in the previous chapter; however, Leonard's participation came well after Higdon had composed the role for a soprano.

The composer considered each character's personality and emotional state[13] and how these could be reflected musically. She commented:

> I thought a lot about every character, what kind of music would fit that character, what kind of development does the person go through in the story? How do they change? Everybody has to have a different kind of music, a different part of the orchestra supporting them and it's flow, timing, and the rhythm of life.[14]

Early in the compositional process, Higdon decided that Inman's music would feature open fifth intervals as a reflection of his emptiness after years of war. She explained that these sounds "represent that damage."[15] Fifth intervals are, of course, a stylistic trait of this composer but their function here serves an entirely different purpose. Throughout the opera, she also paired the trumpet with Inman to connect the character with his recent military experiences.[16]

Higdon found it challenging to compose the scenes with Teague because of his profound flaws. She found the character irritating and immoral and asked herself, "How can I stomach writing an aria for Teague?"[17] She explained her solution in an interview alongside Jay Hunter Morris:

> I used the thought of you [Morris] kind of as the antidote [...] I knew he [Morris] was going to be singing it so I thought to myself, "Here's a good person who's going to play a bad person" but I focused just on your [...] personality, [...] you are legendary for being such a great person to work with so that actually helped me.[18]

Morris reflected on Higdon's vocal, writing, "I think Jennifer's done a really great job setting my character, because [...] sometimes the most [...] unkind acts and words are given with a smile and that's often the case with my guy, [...] I'm singing a little tune that seems harmless enough until I slowly [...] slip a dagger between your ribs."[19] Teague's "little tune" is the aforementioned ballad *Shady Grove* that opens the opera and returns several times. Although the melody is lyrical, the character's onstage presence is often accompanied by a tritone in the lower ranged instruments. This interval, historically known as the *diabolus in musica,* was used purposefully by Higdon[20] to betray the character's villainous nature. Percussion instruments are also associated with Teague. The composer elaborated:

> Teague is a very nasty man in this [...] opera, he's creepy, he's just absolutely creepy, so I made the decision early on that I wanted always to have some sort of [...] sound like a rattle snake whenever he's on the stage [...] kind of warning you that danger was coming.[21]

Lastly, Stobrod's interest in folk fiddling is mirrored in his character's music through the use of a solo violin and open string sounds.

The musical depictions of the female characters likewise reflect their circumstances. In Ada's sections, the orchestration features the woodwinds,[22] timbres long associated with birdcalls and nature scenes. Such scoring references bucolic Black Cove Farm and physical isolation while simultaneously providing a stark contrast between the orchestration of the brass sounds of Inman. Like him, Ada feels an emptiness that emerged from entirely different circumstances. Higdon explained:

> At the beginning of the opera she's a lot more [...] delicate, she wasn't raised to survive which is kind of her journey in this [...] to figure out how to survive when she's lost everything [...] she doesn't know how to farm, she doesn't even know how to cook, and so her personality kind of grows, becomes stronger as it goes through the opera, she becomes more

and more of a presence. She's not much of a presence at the beginning, she's there but she doesn't make as much of an impression.[23]

The composer described Ruby's music as "very energetic,"[24] which complements the character's actions: surveying each situation and quickly devising a to-do list. Higdon summarized, "Ruby is very smart but very hyperactive; she's a survivor. Her music moves at a real clip."[25] There is no specific orchestration or consistent intervals associated with this character but when Ruby is singing, Higdon supplies an animated mood through numerous means discussed subsequently.

While writing, Higdon combined creativity with the objective of maintaining audience interest, all while being mindful of the timing of the action. She explained the blending of these elements:

> At one point, there's a huge gun battle [...] I felt a little nauseous writing it because I realized I was going to have to kill quite a few people in this scene and I felt responsible for it but I also was aware that the music had to be the most violent music I had ever written and so that kind of pushed me to think, "All right, how do I do that with an orchestra?" and I knew it had to be one minute and fifteen seconds, which doesn't sound [like an inspiring way to approach this task, [...] because most people like to think of a composer as being inspired and the music just comes to you and you write it and then everything fits in that way but the reality is [to keep it interesting and functional on stage], you have to actually make all of this happen within a certain time frame [...] I spent more time asking myself questions like, "What do I want the audience to take away from this, how do I want them to feel, and how do I put that into music?"[26]

Due to the size and scope of the opera, detailed discussions of each scene are not possible. The examples included have been chosen with great care to demonstrate the music representative of each character, Higdon's vocal ensemble technique, unifying motives, and excerpts of orchestral interludes that relate to her overall symphonic style.

Act I

Almost without exception, operas begin with an orchestral overture that introduces subsequent melodies; however, this is not the case in *Cold Mountain* which is surprising because of Higdon's extensive symphonic experience. The opera begins unassumingly with Teague singing *Shady Grove* a cappella. On the prowl for a Confederate deserter, he interrogates the soldier's father and when he does not receive any information, he buries him alive to force the soldier out of hiding. It is a remarkable beginning to travel from an unaccompanied folk song to a full orchestra accompanying a murder. Higdon explained how this originated:

Eight. Cold Mountain: The Music   189

Gene [Scheer] and I were talking about it and we realized [...] we needed to establish right off the bat one of the bad characters [... we] were looking for ways to shock people [...] I said, "They're going to expect nice mountain music [...] so what do we need to do?" We looked at each other and I said, "We need to kill someone in the first couple of minutes." It sets the story forward [...] the audience [needs] to know that there [... is] a bad guy on the loose.[27]

Act I, Scene 1, "Peaches in the summertime"

As mentioned earlier, *Shady Grove* is an Appalachian folk ballad, an incorporation originally suggested by Scheer.[28] As with much folk music, the narrow ranged melody utilizes four bar phrasing, is modal, and the contour moves primarily in stepwise motion, all maintained in the Higdon setting. Although the pitches are not identical to the original, the melody is unmistakable; the rhythm is also slightly altered by Scotch snaps which serves two purposes. First, it makes the melody more rhythmically vibrant, a characteristic of Higdon's style and secondly, the music reflects the Appalachian setting, a region settled by Scots-Irish immigrants.

The opera begins with Teague singing the sprightly folk tune that suggests he is not bothered by the despair he inflicts. After he finishes the first verse, the soldier's father, Owens, asks who is there accompanied by the entrance of the cabasa to produce the rattling sound associated with Teague. When Owens realizes it's Teague, the basses present a loud descending *portamento* tritone, another significant characteristic of this character's music (Figure 8–1).

When Owens recognizes Teague as leader of the homeguard, Teague responds with dark humor that he must be a prophet followed by the phrase "Hallelujah! Blessed with vision.... Hallelujah!"[29] The text and music are equally significant because as clarified later in the scene's stage directions,

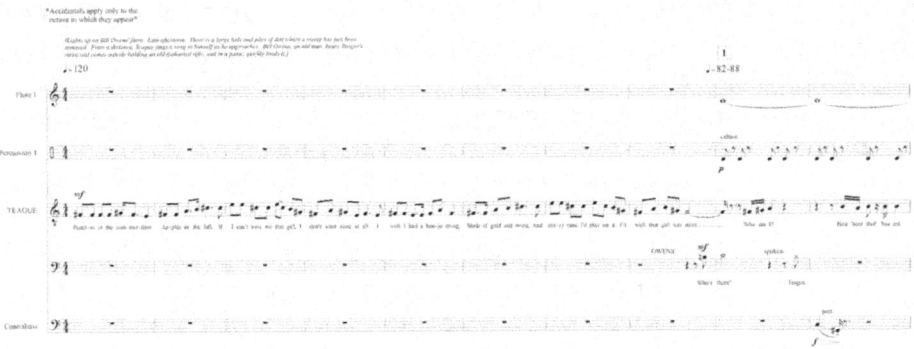

Figure 8–1. *Cold Mountain*; Act I, Scene 1, mm. 1–10.

the phrase "'Hallelujah, Amen' is the signal for his men."[30] The pitches and rhythm on the "Hallelujahs" (Figure 8–2) return in measure 58 when Teague gives the full signal, discussed in more detail below. Throughout the opening scene, the orchestration continues to be sparse through measure 33 when Teague tells Owens that he knows his son is hiding there. This phrase ends with an ascending tritone followed by a meter change, a Higdon hallmark to designate critical sections. Here, it introduces the full orchestra for the first time in the opera. The meter change lasts only a single measure to accompany the sudden appearance of Teague's men who are aiming their rifles at Owens, a dramatic moment heightened by the fortissimo dynamic. The measure closes with another descending portamento tritone in the strings.

Figure 8–2. *Cold Mountain*; Act I, Scene 1, mm. 20–22.

Throughout the opera, Higdon utilizes text painting albeit sparingly. One could argue that the ascending tritone Teague sings in measure 41 on the word "Yankees" reveals his dislike of Northerners; however, the interval also appears in this scene on the words "Owens" and "notion." Although Teague undoubtedly feels no empathy for Owens, the tritones represent the character himself rather than examples of text painting.

In measure 50, the drama on stage and in the music continue to increase as Owens becomes agitated. He sings loudly that if his son were there, he would tell him not to come near which serves as a warning for the son to stay hidden. The measure is marked *senza misura*, an unusual designation for Higdon but occurring with some frequency throughout *Cold Mountain*. The strings, performing *col legno* and unsynchronized, present a diminished chord that begins softly but quickly crescendos to fortissimo. Comparable dynamics are found in the sandpaper blocks and bundle sticks; the orchestration is limited to only the percussion and strings both which are instructed to perform in a "sporadic" manner. Each of the strings is responsible for a single pitch and although the rhythms are thirty-second notes, the notational style is unconventional. After the initial notes, the score has only a thick, black line with an arrow pointing to the end of the *senza misura* measure and a return to a 4/4 meter that coincides with a brief return of the full orchestra.

A meter change to 3/4 occurs at rehearsal six (measure 58) and true to

Higdon's style, this indicates a moment of great importance. Teague sings, "Hallelujah Amen!"[31] signaling his men to stab Owens and as noted above, the phrase is similar to his earlier "Hallelujah" declamation in pitch and rhythm. After the signal, the strings, woodwinds, and trumpets present two tritone intervals loudly to complement the horrendous stage action (Figure 8–3). The "Hallelujah" motive also returns in Act II, Scene 9 when Teague gives his men the signal to shoot Stobrod and his companion, Pangle; its rhythm varies from the original and is transposed but the intervallic content remains identical (Figure 8–4).

The ensuing orchestral interlude accompanies the live burial of Owens by the homeguard. After two measures, the ensemble is reduced to primarily woodwinds and strings that provide an example of Higdon's self-described counterpoint of textures. The woodwinds present

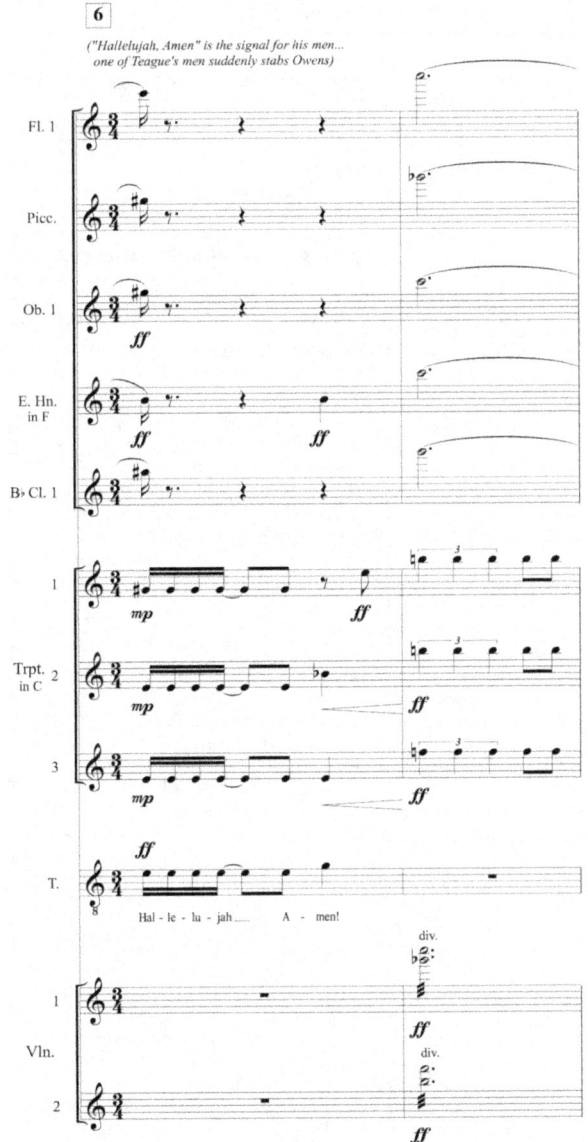

Figure 8-3. *Cold Mountain*; Act I, Scene 1, mm. 58–59.

several dissonant intervals in a rhythm that is comparatively slower than the strings while the latter have a descending tritone (D–Ab) that connects the music with Teague and the opera's opening. The two orchestral sections are

Figure 8-4. *Cold Mountain*; Act II, Scene 9, mm. 704.

unified by syncopated minor second intervals found in the contrabass and contrabassoon (Figure 8-5).

Figure 8-5. *Cold Mountain*; Act I, Scene 1, "counterpoint of textures" mm. 62-65.

At rehearsal number 7 (measure 71), the meter returns to the opening 4/4 and Teague repeats *Shady Grove*, in a faster tempo with more rhythmic manipulation that destroys the original four bar phrasing. Owens's part provides counterpoint as he begs his son to stay hidden before both the music and the character die. Teague continues with the final line of the folk song in an augmented rhythm to momentarily release the musical tension.

Owens's son enters to save his father and delivers rhythmically notated dialog accompanied by the full orchestra. Of particular interest are the chords found in measure 85 in the trumpets and expanded in the woodwinds. As seen previously, Higdon frequently scores major or minor chords for trumpets (and occasionally trombones); however, the chord quality here is augmented, highly atypical yet appropriate for the disturbing stage action. The son is captured and restrained as the music increases in intensity through faster augmented chords, descending tritone intervals in the trombones, frequent guiro strokes, increased dynamics, and a notated accelerando. The interlude peaks in measure 93 with the introduction of the thundertube to produce an ominous mood.

The characters withdraw from the stage at rehearsal ten (measure 106) leaving the orchestra to conclude the opening scene with the returning minor second intervals from Figure 8–5. Beginning in measure 109, one of Higdon's compositional traits emerges in the homorhythmic woodwinds. The flute, piccolo, and bass clarinet sound major chords while the oboe, English horn, and Bb clarinet produce minor chords. This bitonal dissonance is complemented by trills and tritones in the brass. Throughout *Cold Mountain*, scenes are connected by brief orchestral interludes that prevent disruption to the dramatic flow; however, this particular interlude is unique because it continues to heighten the drama even after the characters' exit and Scene 2 begins abruptly at rehearsal 11 (measure 115).

Act I, Scene 2, "What was his name?"

Scene 2 contrasts the previous material in almost every conceivable way. A meter change to 3/4 and a greatly reduced tempo facilitates the new setting of a Confederate hospital in Raleigh, North Carolina. The orchestration is immediately reduced and in fact, the only music in the first measure of the scene is the vibraphone's open fifths. This interval not only foreshadows the music of Inman but also reflects the similar feelings of emptiness shared by the injured Confederate soldiers portrayed by an all-male chorus.

The chorus enters in measure 116 doubled by the muted, *pianissimo* violas and celli to complement the voices. As mentioned previously, one of

Higdon's objectives in the opera was text comprehension and as such, the texture for the all-male choruses is primarily homorhythmic. Frequent meter changes also enhance textual clarity by accommodating the natural accents of the English language. After the men sing the initial phrase, trumpets one and two present open fifths to introduce the instrumentation and intervals that will be associated with Inman.

The text of the chorus is poignant: the soldiers wonder about a recently deceased comrade followed by the questioning of their own futures. They list particular cities and battles, ask when the war will end, and grieve the soldier that has been "buried and forgotten."[32] Because Scheer and Higdon are both Americans, it is tempting to interpret such scenes as a political commentary on the U.S.'s War on Terror, now in its second decade. Additional scenes in the opera may be viewed as anti-war in the physical devastation of the land, the death of soldiers who had little, if any, personal interest in the political agenda, and the destruction of homes and lives. The composer is not against such interpretations but they remain entirely dependent on the listener and such thoughts were never considered by Higdon during composition.[33] She and Scheer chose *Cold Mountain* because of the love story and for the composer, the familiarity of the characters. The possibility of such political undertones ringing familiar with contemporary audiences remains a tribute to the timelessness of Frazier's work.

The consonant harmony of the chorus is non-functional and consists primarily of major chords with a sprinkling of second intervals characteristic of Higdon. While the trumpets continue the parallel fifths associated with the protagonist, Inman silently looks through the fallen soldier's belongings. Curiously, when he makes his initial entrance prior to rehearsal 13 (measure 137), the trumpets and strings are replaced by the clarinets and principal bassoon. These instruments also double the chorus but the change in timbre provides a contrasting orchestration to the repeated text. Inman provides a countermelody to the homorhythmic chorus and his text suggests his feelings mirror those of the Confederate soldiers.

The chorus ceases prior to rehearsal 14 (measure 164) followed by an instrumental transition that has two alternating musical ideas: open fifth intervals in the trumpets later joined by the woodwinds and slower major and minor chords in the violas and celli. The transition concludes with a meter change to 3/4 to designate the subsequent recitative.

A dialog begins in rehearsal 15 (measure 176) between Inman and a Blindman (a minor character who doubles in the role of Stobrod). As mentioned in the previous chapter, Higdon avoids traditional recitatives that present large amounts of text in a narrow melodic range; however, dialog exists in this opera, of course, to progress the drama. This is one such example and through a conversation with the Blindman, the audience learns of Inman's injuries and shattered emotional state. The melodic contour contains meticulously notated rhythms in slower note values than customarily found in recitatives that reflect the leisurely lilt of the American Southern dialect.

The orchestration continues several of the elements from the previous interlude complemented by Higdon stylistic traits. When the Blindman sings Inman's name in the recitative's opening, he is accompanied only by the perfect fifth interval associated with Inman in the basses. The flutes subsequently enter with the fifth intervals from the preceding interlude joined by the clarinets and bassoons. As the passage progresses, the woodwinds are complemented by major chords in the second violins divided into threes, an orchestration characteristic of Higdon, that are interrupted by syncopated pizzicato pitches in the violas that return *marcato* in the subsequent aria. Also representative of Higdon's style are the orchestral soli found in the clarinet, viola, and oboe in small duets with Inman. The recitative concludes with Inman, because of what he has seen in the war, envious of the Blindman's disability. This prompts the Blindman to ask, "Come on, cite me one instance where you wish you were blind"[34] to introduce Inman's aria "The Metal Age Has Come."

A faster tempo and a meter change to 5/4 at rehearsal 18 (measure 224) mark the aria's opening complemented further by persistent rhythms in the percussion to suggest Inman's war memories. Rather than listing a single Civil War battle to answer the Blindman's question, Inman's text begins with several locations, "Malvern Hill. Sharpsburg. Petersburg"[35] that is followed by an excellent example of Higdon's text painting. With the words "dynamite thundered!,"[36] Inman's high pitches are marked fortissimo followed by an explosion of orchestral brass. The trombones, trumpets, and horns each present different major and minor chords in staggered entrances. Although such sonorities in the trumpets and trombones are typical of Higdon, the quickly swelling dynamics from mezzo forte to fortissimo are not and the disparity here is used to text paint this dramatic moment.

The subsequent phrase of Inman is one of particular musical interest. He sings of the goriness that followed the dynamite, "arms, shredded fingers, pieces of legs with boots still on them"[37] which almost certainly would have resulted in death. The orchestration of the syncopated violas paired again with the second violin chords is reminiscent of the preceding recitative when Inman relayed the death of a soldier to the Blindman; thus, the scene is unified through both the theme of death and the instrumentation.

At rehearsal 20 (measure 241), Inman announces in a fortissimo dotted rhythm that "the metal age has come. And the crust of bread, clenched in my fist was drenched in blood,"[38] are words that return later in the aria. Between these phrases, a solo trumpet is heard, not because the character is a soldier but because the brass instrument paints the metal referenced in the text. Inman is lost amidst an increasingly industrialized world and he is repulsed by the endless death and casualty resulting in the technological advancements of the so-called metal age. Beneath the trumpet, the trombones present modal mixture through alternating sustained F# major and minor chords while the strings consist of only the second violins and half of the first violin section. The violins present chords separate from the trombones to create Higdon's characteristic bitonality.

A return to a 5/4 meter at rehearsal 21 (measure 252) begins a new, contrasting section in the aria. The violas, celli, and bassoons present sixteenth note triplets comprised of alternating second intervals, a less prominent but still stylistic trait of Higdon. These faster rhythms provide urgency as Inman recalls the thousands of Union soldiers he encountered. The military reference is complemented by the third trumpet, clearly audible in the reduced instrumentation and while brief, is important for two reasons. First, the part consists of an ascending melodic fourth, an interval that remains a prominent Higdon compositional trait and secondly, the instrument is muted to reference the events are in the past. Although the moment is incredibly concise, the interval, rhythm, and instrumentation are also reminiscent of the taps bugle call, a sound that contemporary American audiences would associate with a military death. This is paired with Inman singing of the Union soldiers he faced to remind the listeners of the incredible danger. The military scene is further evoked through the scoring of the snare drum. This section builds in both dynamics and intensity while Inman, singing in the dramatically higher range, recalls the hours of gunfire text painted through the percussionists' whip and rim shot strikes in the snare. Accented, sforzando single eighth notes in the trumpets, horns, oboes, and clarinets enhance the effect.

At rehearsal 22 (measure 262), the mood changes considerably. Inman recalls his Commanding Officer reassuring the soldiers that upon the charge, their adversaries would "'fall like rain dripping down from the eves of a house.'"[39] To reference the death of countless men with a gentle simile may seem odd but perhaps necessary for the Confederate troops to disassociate from the killing. The orchestral accompaniment mirrors the text; the dynamics are decreased to varying levels of piano, the horns become tacet, and the trumpets present Higdon's stylistic sustained major and minor sonorities. Most significant, however, are the repeated pitches of the glockenspiel, performed with knitting needles, and the solo for the concertmaster presenting the same note an octave higher in different rhythms. Combined, these colors produce a tinkling sound to text paint the simile that is further complemented through a slowly descending line in the principal flute that mirrors the rain "dripping down."[40] When Inman concludes that his experience was neither "poetic" nor "as pure as a drop of water"[41] a descending contour in the harp and the glockenspiel continue the musical imagery.

As Inman recounts the sights and smells of the battlefield, the orchestration is comprised of primarily lower strings. Such instrumentation in Higdon often provides a lush and warm sound but here, the mood is ominous as the protagonist recalls being shot by a scared drummer boy, text painted similarly as the earlier gunshots. The aria nears its conclusion when Inman repeats and transposes the earlier phrase "the metal age has come.... With the crust of bread, clenched in my fist drenched with blood."[42] The accompaniment, however, is not duplicated until rehearsal 25 (measure 291) with a few minor additions in the viola, harp, and percussion.

As mentioned in the previous chapter, Black Cove Farm is set on stage left and Inman on stage right allowing the separate stories to unfold simultaneously. Ada enters at rehearsal 26 (measure 301) and is introduced to the audience by Inman when he explains to the Blindman that he would think of her after the battles. He wonders, "Ada Monroe ... what are you doing now?"[43] As he sings her name, warm, sustained chords are presented by the first stands of violins one, two, and violas, a scoring that is quintessentially Higdon, but also an orchestration that recurs consistently in the opera's flashbacks to project a happier, simpler time (Figure 8–6). Inman ponders if Ada is involved with the aristocratic hobbies she pursued prior to the war; however, her desperate circumstances are immediately apparent. Teague, accompanied by the slithering cabasa, appears at her farm and the two stories progress concurrently: Teague and Ada engage in conversation allowing the audience to learn of her father's death while Inman imagines her brushing her hair, drawing flowers, reading, and playing piano. Supported by the solo strings and harp, Inman's melody exudes a lyricism that indicates his tender feelings towards her. This second scene, although markedly different from the opening, is an excellent example of the realization of Higdon's goals for the opera: the text and diction are abundantly clear and the drama moves swiftly from a chorus to a recitative to an aria and finally, to a trio that provides much variety in texture and instrumentation.

Act I, Scene 3, "I don't like that man"

The third scene begins at rehearsal 31 (measure 352) with Ada at the grave of her late father. The transformation in dramatic focus is facilitated

Figure 8-6. *Cold Mountain*; Act I, Scene 2, mm. 310–312.

through a change in orchestration from brass to woodwinds, a defining characteristic of the music of Ada and Black Cove Farm. Additionally, string soli for the concertmaster and principal second violin, viola, and now cello create a seamless transition from the previous scene's first stand string soli.

Rehearsal 34 (measure 390) is a flashback to the initial meeting between

Ada and Inman that provides humor through her unimpressed reaction to him. This duet is of particular interest because of the similarities between this flashback and Inman's earlier daydream. Although far from her current reality, his images derive from their past experiences including this first contact. Higdon connects these episodes musically: the tempi are identical as is the orchestration of harp and soli for the first stands of both violin sections and viola.

Beginning at rehearsal 36 (measure 409), the crotales and triangle are struck with a knitting needle, a subtle foreshadowing of later duets between these characters where this sparkling timbre references the Orion constellation. Inman tells Ada she is the topic of conversation amongst the locals. She asks, "Like a novelty? A challenge?"[44] He says no and she instructs him to "supply the simile,"[45] the last word set syllabically with a short-short-long rhythmic motive (Figure 8–7) that returns in Scene 4. Inman compares Ada to "grabbing a chestnut burr"[46] which makes her laugh. She repeats the phrase melismatically, a style seldom found in *Cold Mountain*, thus making its use here important. As early as the Medieval writings of St. Augustine, melismas have been associated with profound bliss that transcends language[47] which is undoubtedly Higdon's intent here. As the flashback concludes, Ruby makes her stage entrance in preparation for the opening duet of the subsequent scene.

Figure 8–7. *Cold Mountain*; Act I, Scene 3, mm. 435–436.

Act I, Scene 4, "Who ya' talkin' to?"

Scene 4, beginning at rehearsal 38 (measure 443), requires no orchestral transition since it, too, occurs at Black Cove Farm; however, the new mood is immediately apparent in the faster tempo (quarter note=160–172) and orchestration. The solo strings are supplanted by the full sections using open strings when applicable which is significant for two reasons. First, open strings recall the fiddling technique of Appalachian folk traditions thus providing an indirect reference to Ruby's fiddling father. Secondly, this scoring, complemented by the cowbell, is indicative of Ruby's rural upbringing, a great contrast from Ada's urban education and experiences in Charleston.

As mentioned previously, Ruby's music reflects her energy emphasized through the sprightly tempo. In the scene's opening, Ruby overhears Ada speaking in the flashback and wonders about her mental stability. Ruby's lack of formal education is exposed when she asks Ada what a simile is, notated with a return of the short-short long rhythm (Figure 8–8). Not waiting for an answer, she quickly offers her assistance on the farm. Ruby assess the situation inadvertently using a simile which Ada points out through the aforementioned motive (Figure 8–9).

Figure 8–8. *Cold Mountain*; Act I, Scene 4, mm. 458–459.

Figure 8–9. *Cold Mountain*; Act I, Scene 4, mm. 486–487.

In measure 497, the illiterate Ruby verbalizes a list of chores, a recurring trend of this pragmatic character. The meter changes to a compound 12/8 with the rhythm comprised of moving eighth notes scored for the bass and celli doubled by woodwinds. Ruby's boundless energy is reflected through the staccato celli subsequently joined by the sandpaper blocks. A short-short-long rhythm, unrelated to the earlier "simile" motive, returns each time Ruby begins listing numerically (Figure 8–10). With her first list, Ruby describes the physical farming tasks that need to be completed; Ada thinks a man is necessary but Ruby responds, "Number two, every man worth hiring is off and gone."[48] Higdon text paints this phrase through the addition of a muted trumpet implying that the men have become soldiers and are away at war.

While Ruby is task-oriented, she is not a one dimensional character and expresses her condolences to Ada for the loss of her father with empathy, erroneously telling Ada her own father was killed in the war. In the orchestra, the rushing eighth notes are replaced by sustained string chords to complement the change in mood; however, Ruby is uncomfortable displaying feelings and the moment is short lived. She sings briefly of her childhood with notice-

Figure 8–10. *Cold Mountain*; Act I, Scene 4, mm. 497.

able resentment towards Stobrod and using the same short-short long motive from Figure 8–10, she lists his numerous shortcomings.

Throughout this scene, the characters demonstrate perfect contrasts to one another but discover they have "something in common"[49] with the loss of their mothers as children. Higdon text paints this unity by scoring their voices homorhythmically. This sentimental mood is subsequently replaced by the energetic tempo and percussion associated with Ruby's character. Ada, unsure when the war will end, likens the future to "a clock without any hands."[50] Using the rhythmic motive described above, Ruby asks if that is a simile which establishes her intelligence despite her lack of formal education.

The women's parts cease at measure 585 followed by an instrumental transition that returns the drama to Inman in the subsequent scene. The compound meter continues the earlier mood but Higdon varies the orchestration to complement the change in location. The moving eighth notes in the low strings are replaced by the trombones while newly added sextuplets are presented by the trumpets and vibraphone. The reintroduction of the brass foreshadows Inman's appearance.

Act I, Scene 5, "We once lived in a land of paradise"

The subsequent scene introduces Veasey, a preacher whose indiscretions have left a woman other than his fiancé with child. Although there is little admirable about this character, the Reverend provides humorous quips that lighten the tension of this tragic tale. Inman encounters Veasey about to murder his mistress and intervenes; the action, however is interrupted by the homeguard represented by an initially wordless male chorus singing softly in unison. The men are urgently looking for a particular person, whether or not this is Inman remains unclear, and their relentless determination reminds the audience of the grave danger facing the protagonist. Although this homeguard is not Teague's regiment, a descending, fortissimo portamento tritone is found consistently in the bass that connects the two locations and storylines.

Act I, Scene 6, "Sun's up. You'll eat later..."

Scene 6 begins with a seamless shift between locations: Ruby is chopping wood while Inman exits. The opening recitative between Ruby and Ada features unifying material from previous scenes sprinkled in the orchestra. Ruby calls, "Ada! Ada! Ada Monroe!" accompanied by soli for the first stand of violins, instrumentation reminiscent of Inman's initial mention of "Ada Monroe," as well as the flashback of their first meeting. These soli reference a simpler time and Ada's entrance here reveals she has momentarily returned to this former lifestyle by sleeping in and asking if breakfast is ready. The disappearance of the violin soli ushers the return to reality for both Ada and the listener. Ruby's response, "Sun's up. You'll eat later,"[51] is followed by her characteristic list of chores. The orchestration of Ruby's list is comparable to the corresponding sections from Scene 4 complemented by the short-short-long motive from Figure 8–10 for each numbered item.

Ruby's aria, recounting her troubled childhood and the root of her resentment towards Stobrod, begins at rehearsal 68 (measure 871) designated by a meter change to 3/4 and a slower tempo. Contrasting nearly all of her earlier music, the instrumentation is primarily comprised of four horns. At rehearsal 70 (measure 907), Ruby explains that in the evening, "For comfort, I counted every star in the sky"[52] to suggest that as an adult, she finds reassurance in counting and making lists. The orchestration here reflects a nocturnal, peaceful atmosphere through the violins' sustained major chords in a high range replaced subsequently by the lower strings, an orchestration far more typical of Higdon. The fairly short aria is followed by Ada showing Ruby Inman's letter stating that he is returning home. She tells Ruby that his name is "W.P. Inman"[53] (Figure 8-11) using the identical rhythms and text as the Blindman in Scene 2 (Figure 8-12).

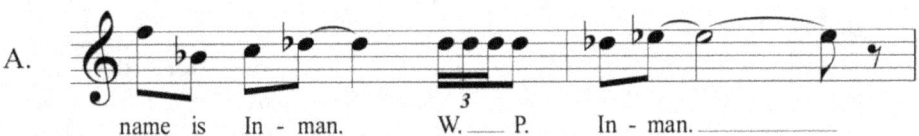

Figure 8-11. *Cold Mountain*; Act I, Scene 6, mm. 934–935.

Figure 8-12. *Cold Mountain*; Act I, Scene 2, mm. 177–178.

Rehearsal 77 (measure 1000) marks the beginning of the second flashback to Christmas, 1860 initiated by Inman's letter and accompanied by the string soli characteristic of the couple's happy memories. The thin string texture also includes sparse woodwinds but gradually increases to the entire ensemble. The text portrays the depth of feelings that have developed between the two main characters since their initial meeting but is far less light-hearted than the first flashback due to the looming threat of war. The sole example of text painting found in this duet begins at rehearsal 81 (measure 1046) with Ada and Inman singing in unison octaves "Why can't we just be here together?"[54] Throughout the latter portion of the duet, Ada repeats the text "Are we not all blossoms?"[55] several times which is noteworthy because of how rare text repetition occurs in this opera. Higdon explained her motivation:

> It's meant to evoke the fact that Ada is remembering her encounter with Inman, in kind of a dream like reverie. Practically speaking, it also allowed me to write two different types of

music overlapping: the sound of coming out of a flashback (memory) into the reality of the storm that engulfs Inman.[56]

Act I, Scene 8, "Look at me, I'm floating"

Scene 8 begins following rehearsal number 92 (measure 1205) with a clearing of the texture and a meter change. The narrative depicts Lila, a married woman, and her three sisters as Appalachian equivalents of the sailor-enticing Greek sirens[57] discovering the shipwrecked Inman and the Reverend Veasey. The orchestration utilizes bowed vibraphone, sustained low string chords, and harp to evoke a mythological association with the sirens. Lila projects the melody while the sisters present homorhythmic responses in closed harmony (Figure 8-13), music that reappears in the large ensemble number of Act II.

Before they discover Inman, Lila sings "Look at me, I'm floating.... Blown by the four winds..."[58] which is text painted at rehearsal 93 (measure 1221) through the scoring of fast rhythms in four woodwinds. All four women are clearly attracted to Inman but are interrupted by Lila's husband, Junior, who offers a drugged drink to Inman and Veasey that will incapacitate them so he can surrender them to the homeguard. After Inman partakes of the tainted offering, the stage direction reads, "Inman

Figure 8-13. *Cold Mountain*; Act I, Scene 8, mm. 1212-1213.

stands and is suddenly very unsteady on his feet. He is feeling the first effects of the drug that Junior poured in his cup,"[59] depicted musically through descending, string portamento figures.

Act I, Scene 9, "Listen"

At rehearsal 103 (measure 1332), the drama and music shift uncharacteristically abruptly to open scene 9 which features two of the most significant sections of the opera. Soft trills in the lower strings are joined by the wind players blowing air through their instruments without producing a pitch, one of the extended techniques mentioned earlier, to depict outdoor sounds. The synopsis presents a reversal of the social hierarchy: the formally uneducated Ruby is teaching the highly sophisticated Ada to interpret the natural environment. At first, Ada can hear only wind and birdsongs text painted by the aforementioned orchestration and complemented by a brief duet by the flute and piccolo. As Ruby instructs Ada, the orchestral texture thickens and definitive pitches replace the air in the woodwinds suggesting Ada's more focused listening.[60] At the close of the duet, the women hear something unexpected: Ruby's presumed dead father caught in their trap to catch a thief.

In the following recitative, Stobrod recounts his army desertion and serious pursuit of fiddling, the latter reflected through soli featuring open strings in the concertmaster and fifth intervals for the first stand of second violins. This musical nod to the Appalachian fiddle tradition will henceforth be associated with this character. When Stobrod insists that music has changed him, Ruby remains unconvinced while Ada wonders if people, and in particular, Inman, change. Stobrod explains that war transforms everyone, the subject of the ensuing quartet.

The re-entrance of Teague begins with his off stage singing of *Shady Grove* at rehearsal 116 (measure 1470) complemented by tritone intervals in the bass. With him is a recently orphaned boy, Birch, and the women distract them in conversation to protect Stobrod. An obvious friction exists between Ruby and Teague which Ada defuses by showing Teague the fence she built. The villain's recitative and subsequent aria are significant to understanding his character. Scheer clarified, "Whatever we feel about Teague, from his perspective, he's telling the truth [...] this is how he sees the world."[61] In the recitative, Teague explain that he is teaching Birch about "Nigger lovin' traitors and cowards hidin' out in these hills."[62] This demonstrates his us vs. them mentality, hence his belief in the importance of both physical and figurative fences (North vs. South, homeguard vs. deserters). While composing this scene, Higdon recalled that in her youth she, "watched people string barbed wire [...] they'll have these plier[s] and gloves and they pull it through a special kind of U-shaped nail and so that creates a visual [...] rhythm with those fence posts: it's a very square 2/4 sensation."[63] These childhood memories influenced the way she thought of the character; she commented, "That's Teague [...] he doesn't have a normal fence, his has like sharp things on it [...] he hurts people with it."[64] It is worth noting that the fence in the scene is not barbed wire, it was simply Higdon's imagery during composition. The cabasa reappears with Teague's entrance while the sliding string portamento figures continue to represent his slippery character.[65]

Teague's aria, "A Fence Is a Good Thing," begins at rehearsal 120 (measure 1537) with a 2/4 meter initially scored for pizzicato lower strings, cabasa, and vibraphone with the percussion subsequently expanded to the suspended cymbal and Chinese cymbal amongst others for the metallic sounds reflective of Higdon's barbed fence imagery. The aria closes with the timeless truths of war that serve as the foundation for the subsequent quartet: "Some wounds will never heal, some things you can't forget. Who you are the war reveals."[66]

An immense benefit opera has over other dramatic forms is the ability to present conflicting emotions and texts at the same time. Scheer explained, "We can have many people singing simultaneously, and the harmonies are telling the story, language is telling the story, the orchestra's telling the story, and it's this incredible window that opera can give to the soul."[67] Foglia also commented, "It's important because it [...] adapts it into another form. It is now no longer a book, it's no longer a narrative thing, but we're able to go inside everybody's heads."[68]

Rehearsal 122 (measure 1568) begins the quartet featuring Ada, Ruby, Stobrod, and Teague with the concluding text of Teague's aria, mentioned above, now representing a separate meaning for each character. Initially, the quartet is separated by ranges and genders: the women present one homorhythmic texture while the men sing different rhythms (Figure 8-14). Ada and Ruby begin with staggered entrances; Ada wonders if people (presumably Inman) change and Ruby questions if she can forgive her father. The reduced and soft orchestration of only the woodwinds doubling the voices and the third trumpet, trombones, and tuba leave the focus solely on the poignant text.

The drama increases beginning in measure 1581 through an accelerando followed by the joining of all four voices singing homorhythmically. The wind instrumentation is replaced by muted strings at rehearsal 123 (measure 1588) and the quartet ends a few measures later with a ritardando, a decrescendo, and rhythmic augmentation in the voices as the characters are left with their questions unanswered.

Eight. Cold Mountain: The Music 207

Figure 8-14. *Cold Mountain*; Act I, Scene 9, mm. 1577–1582.

The scene ends with Stobrod's thanks to his daughter for protecting him against the homeguard. He sings the phrase "Bless you Ruby"[69] set to a motive (Figure 8-15) that repeats in the subsequent measure. This motive is accompanied by an orchestration similar to the character's initial entrance: fifth intervals for the second violins and violas and a concertmaster solo featuring open strings. As a token of his gratitude, he vows to compose a song for her

Figure 8-15. *Cold Mountain*; Act I, Scene 9, mm. 1634–1635.

entitled "Bless you Ruby"[70] which is realized in Act II, Scene 4 and features the same motive.

Act I, Scene 10, "Come back to Cold Mountain"

The final scene in Act I opens at rehearsal 127 (measure 1638) with Inman tied to his fellow prisoners. A gun battle erupts between Federal troops and the homeguard leaving the vulnerable prisoners exposed and killed with the exception of Inman. Following this violent beginning, the Federal soldiers exit and the diminishing dynamic and thinner orchestral texture lead to a flashback. A brief solo for the second trumpet links the two passages that again is reminiscent of the taps bugle call, a fitting tribute to those just killed onstage. The prominence of string soli featured in earlier flashbacks return in the soli for the principal cello and concertmaster; combined with slower moving woodwinds in open fifths, the orchestration suggests a more innocent time in the lives of both the country and the characters. As Ada and Inman express their sadness at parting and reassure one another that they will be beside each other in spirit, the music soars to the characters' highest ranges marked fortissimo. It is important to note that a brief melisma, one of the very few in the entire opera, is found in Ada's part to express her overwhelming emotion.

In measure 1749, the mood and orchestration shift as the couple view Orion in the sky. Violins one and two present separate major chords initially in different rhythms while the percussionists play the crotales and the glockenspiel with knitting needles, a similar instrumentation used in subsequent mentions of the constellation in Act II, Scene 3 and the Epilogue. As the duet and the flashback come to a close, Inman returns to the heap of dead prisoners while Ada continues her pleas for him to return to Cold Mountain. The orchestration expands to the full ensemble growing in volume complemented by a dramatic molto ritardando to close the act.

There are several noteworthy elements in Act I's instrumental postlude. First and foremost, Higdon composed the music so that if the intermission is omitted, the orchestra can transition from the penultimate measure of Act I directly into Act II, Scene 1 (measure 18).[71] She explained:

> One of the reasons I decided to do that [was] in case someone made the decision they wanted to do a concert version of it and for some reason, they didn't want an intermission. I thought it might be kind of nice to have that option. It was something we talked about early on before I ever started writing so I kind of set that challenge up in my head.[72]

Secondly, beginning in rehearsal 140 (measure 1780), the trombones feature alternating sustained F# major and minor chords which also occurred in

Inman's first aria "The Metal Age Has Come." This suggests that Inman was in fact correct, and the metal age has arrived with disastrous consequences. Lastly, Act I concludes with the full ensemble simultaneously mixing an F# minor and major chord (amidst the sprinkling of other dissonances). This modal ambiguity leaves the music unresolved, a figurative harmonic cliffhanger. It is also worthy of mention that *Cold Mountain* opens with Teague singing unaccompanied on an F# and although the texture, dynamics, and context could not be more different, this brings the music of Act I full circle.

Act II

Act II begins with an instrumental introduction similar to Act I's conclusion which as just mentioned, may be omitted. Typical of Higdon, the returning material is not identical but varied, in this instance in the percussion. Additionally, the dramatic ritardando at the close of Act I is less extensive to facilitate the ensuing action.

Act II, Scene 1, "Is that all ya got?"

The opening scene of Act II was one of the most celebrated by the critics and begins with Lucinda, an escaped African American slave, searching for food in the belongings of the tied, dead prisoners. The scene begins at rehearsal 1 (measure 20) with a meter change to 5/4 and an orchestration featuring a basso ostinato between the bassoon and the contrabassoon (Figure 8–16). When Lucinda begins singing in measure 25, the bassoons repeat the opening material, identically in the contrabassoon but varied in the principal. With each repetition and variation of the opening bassoon duet, Higdon adds a new instrumental line, first in the Bb clarinet at rehearsal 2 (measure 30) followed by the flute in measure 38 (Figure 8–17).

Figure 8-16. *Cold Mountain*; Act II, Scene 1, mm. 21-23.

Figure 8-17. *Cold Mountain*; Act II, Scene 1, mm. 38–40.

At rehearsal 4 (measure 49) when Inman begins singing, he is still in chains while Lucinda holds his freedom in her hands, a complete reversal of the social hierarchy. Although their circumstances are starkly different, identical words capture their feelings at rehearsal six (measure 72) when they sing in unison octaves, "I am runnin', runnin' out of time. I am runnin' to another world, And I'm so tired."[73] Lucinda tells Inman she would kill every white person if she could, accompanied by the fortissimo, full ensemble to capture her rage. Conversely, Inman is so broken and void of feeling, his response is accompanied only by the sustained tremolo in the bass. He volunteers to be her first victim but taken aback by surprise, she changes the subject to Ada's picture.

A moment of great importance occurs at rehearsal ten (measure 102) when Lucinda explains to Inman that she will rely on the stars to lead her North, accompanied by the glockenspiel performed with knitting needles (or Magic Flute mallets). Similar orchestrations appear during mentions of stars or constellations numerous times in varied contexts throughout *Cold Mountain* allowing the recurring text painting to serve as a unifying element. In her final moments on stage, Lucinda finds the keys to unlock his chains, throws them to him, and exits quickly. As mentioned in the previous chapter, Inman has no direct contact with this character in Frazier's novel; however, Scheer's inventive reworking of Lucinda immediately re-immerses the audience into the drama following intermission while providing a sensitive and thoughtful voice to the marginalized.

Act II, Scene 2, "Interlude: Inman Walking" and Scene 3, "Orion"

The second scene is purely instrumental to accompany Inman walking under the changing moon to signify the passing of time. Scene 3, beginning at rehearsal 15 (measure 139), presents Inman and Ada in their respective locations gazing at Orion with nature sounds evoked by the winds blowing air through their instruments. Higdon musically connects this scene with the initial mention of the constellation in Act I, Scene 10 in two ways. First is the continued association of stars with the orchestration of glockenspiel and crotales, although neither have a lasting presence here and secondly, the tempo of the earlier scene returns. In the vocal writing, Higdon alternates the texture to demonstrate simultaneously the characters' emotional bond and geographical distance from one another, the former through homorhythmic writing and the latter by staggered entrances[74] (Figure 8–18).

Figure 8–18. *Cold Mountain*; Act II, Scene 3, mm. 142–146.

Act II, Scene 4, "Bless you, Ruby"

Scene 4 begins at rehearsal 19 (measure 177) with soli for the first stand of violins and either the principal second or Stobrod if the singer is able. The second violin part is comparatively simpler and features the open strings associated with this character. Stobrod opens the scene explaining that, as promised, he has composed a song entitled "Bless you, Ruby," using the same motive from Figure 8–15 (Figure 8–19). Throughout the passage, this returning motive is varied at each subsequent appearance.

Stobrod's song begins at rehearsal 20 (measure 187) with a sprightly tempo of quarter note=92. This entire passage represents Higdon's figurative tip of the hat to the Appalachian folk music tradition. While inspired by bluegrass, she also makes the music her own, first and foremost through the 5/4 meter. The folk elements present are as follows: an orchestration comprised only of strings, open string sounds, a fast tempo, portamento figures, and finally a pizzicato bass. Because the instrumental music increases in difficulty at the start of Stobrod's song, the singer no longer participates in the fiddling.

Stobrod is joined by his companion, Pangle, a baritone who doubles as

Figure 8-19. *Cold Mountain*; Act II, Scene 4, mm. 183-84.

Ada's father in Act I. Initially, Pangle interjects with an altered version of the "Bless You, Ruby" motive which illustrates Stobrod's description of Pangle as "kind of 'gentle' in the mind."[75] At the climax of the song, the duo perform in homorhythmic texture separated by consonant, parallel sixths intervals, an unusual choice for Higdon but reflective of the bluegrass style.

After Stobrod's aria, he joins in a recitative with Ada and Ruby that introduces Georgia Boy (Reid), a deserter scored for tenor. This is followed by an explanation of how music changed his life, complemented by another small violin solo of open fifths (optionally performed by the singer). Stobrod recounts his experience in Virginia fiddling for a dying girl accompanied by a slower harmonic rhythm and softer dynamics, a mood which is interrupted by a very brief, three measure instrumental interlude at rehearsal 25 (measure 251) that revisits several of the earlier folk characteristics: open fifth intervals, pizzicato bass, and portamento figures in the strings. The scene concludes with Ada warning Stobrod about Teague, a message that proves to be prophetic.

Act II, Scene 8, "I should be cryin' but I just feel numb"

Scene 8 features a quintet with five characters in four different locations: Stobrod and Pangle playing music near a campfire, Inman continuing his journey, Ada visiting her father's grave, and Ruby scouring a list of war casualties. The scene begins as a trio with Ada, Ruby, and Inman. As in the earlier "Orion" duet, the characters sing the same words in staggered entrances to depict their similar emotions but physical separation. The war has left each of them emotionally depleted as clearly demonstrated in their texts: "I should be cryin' but I just feel numb."[76] The focus is exclusively on the voices with the orchestration comprised only of the violins, pizzicato bass, and percussionists' pitch pipes, all performed at varying levels of piano. Most importantly is the alternating meters between 3/4 and 4/4 with an occasional 5/4. Higdon explained:

> You can tell the people are exhausted from four years of war and it's a little overwhelming. It's grief-filled [...] I created music that sounds like an American folk song but in fact isn't [...] it has a mournful quality but it has alternating meters of 5/4 and 4/4 and 3/4 so it's constantly a little uneven, a little uneasy.[77]

The trio closes at rehearsal 56 (measure 602) followed by another instrumental interlude comprised of strings and pitch pipes related, but slightly varied, to Act II, Scene 4 ("Bless you, Ruby") as an introduction to the entrances of Stobrod and Pangle in bar 611. These characters' imitative entrances are identical to those found earlier in Act II, Scene 4's measure 254 (Figure 8-20) but combined with new material presented by Ada, Inman, and Ruby. Such innovative reworking of earlier material remains an essential element of Higdon's style.

Figure 8-20. *Cold Mountain*; Act II, Scene 4, mm. 254-58.

Act II, Scene 10, "Our beautiful country"

Scene 10, beginning in rehearsal 66 (measure 725), was continually singled out by critics as one of the opera's most profound moments and features The Chorus of the Dead comprised of fallen soldiers. Numerous similarities exist between this number and Act I's Confederate Soldiers' Chorus including a nearly identical tempo, rich harmonies, and homorhythmic texture for textual clarity. The orchestration doubling the voices is also similar; the Act I chorus is accompanied by violas and celli later joined by clarinets, oboes, bassoons, and trumpets while Act II reverses the order: clarinets and bassoons[78] followed by the lower strings.

As the ghostly specters conclude their chorus, Ada and Ruby appear on stage in search of Stobrod, who has been shot along with Pangle by Teague's homeguard. They find Pangle's corpse and in the final phrases of the chorus, they spot the still breathing, but severely injured and unconscious Stobrod. Ruby quickly exits to gather medicinal herbs leaving Ada to perform one of the work's most moving arias.

Beginning at rehearsal 72 (measure 794), she sings of her pity for Stobrod for not realizing how wonderful his daughter is. This aria is in a three-part form with repeating elements and thus can be analyzed as such: 794–804 (A), 805–829 (A'), and 830–848 (A"). Each section features a meter change to 3/4 and a similar harmonic progression in the violas and celli, an orchestration characteristic of Higdon. These low, muted strings present lush major and minor chords with a harmonic rhythm of one beat (Figure 8–21). The second violins enter in measure 798 which brightens the sound to text paint Ada's description of Ruby's exemplary character. The vocal line of the A section concludes with an uncharacteristic, albeit rather brief, melisma to capture Ada's emotion. In measure 802, the meter changes to 3/4 which in the music of Higdon, indicates something new, in this case, a principal horn solo.

Figure 8–21. *Cold Mountain*; Act II, Scene 10, mm. 794–795.

This aria's form is comparable to Lucinda's opening of Act II in that each repetition includes a new contrapuntal line. A' begins with the previous section's chord progression in the low strings with Ada's opening melody reorchestrated as a solo for the second horn, later supplanted by the principal (Figure 8–22). The vocal line at rehearsal 73 (measure 805) is the newly composed line in A' and its pairing with the horns create a colorful effect that remains a distinctive element of this aria. The horns are subsequently replaced by major and minor chords for three solo first violins, a classic Higdon orchestration and harmony. The meter change in A' occurs at rehearsal 74 (measure 813) which coincides with the aria's climax clearly demonstrated through an expanded orchestration, the forte dynamic, Ada's soaring range, and a few brief melismas as well as a new instrument, a solo flute, paired with the soprano line. The A' section begins its conclusion at rehearsal 75 (measure 825) in a similar manner to its opening: the chord progression in the low strings with horn. The passage closes softly with voice, harp, and a return of the major and minor sonorities in the three violin soloists.

Figure 8–22. *Cold Mountain*; Act II, Scene 10, mm. 805–806.

A" begins at rehearsal 76 (measure 830) with the original chord progression in the muted violas and celli and a vocal line similar to the opening; however, a significant difference can be found in the 5/4 time signature. To accommodate this meter, the final note of each measure is extended from a quarter note to a half note that alters the phrasing. Such seemingly minor variations are typical of Higdon's style and essential in creating a newness to repeated material. Lastly, the orchestral postlude of the aria is particularly noteworthy. In measure 838, the second flute, doubled by the solo principal trumpet, repeats its material from the conclusion of A.' The trumpet foreshadows Inman's entrance in the subsequent scene which marks the first and only time, except for flashbacks, the couple are together in the opera.

Act II, Scene 11, "I'm lost" and Scene 12, "You just need to rest. We'll talk later"

In Scene 11, the couple finds each other accidentally followed by the lengthiest and most dramatic scene of the opera. Ada leads Inman to the temporary campsite arranged to nurse Stobrod and immediately before his first phrase, Inman's character is evoked through the trumpets' open fifth intervals in measure 950. He quickly falls asleep while Ada sings to him accompanied by a dream-like orchestration of vibraphones and harp.

When Inman awakes at rehearsal 88 (measure 998), the vibraphone gradually diminishes; the harp continues joined by sustained seventh and major/minor chords in the strings that provide a warmth indicative of the couple's feelings for one another. String soli were an essential component to the flashbacks in Act I and here, they likewise relate to an earlier time as they accompany Ada recounting her father's death.

The couple sings of their war experiences; Inman begins his description with the haunting line, "War chisels your soul with fear and bitterness … into something dark and strange."[79] Amidst the sparse orchestration is the solo trumpet associated with his military service while the strings alternate between F# major and minor chords, sonorities directly related to his war involvement. These harmonies were initially featured in Inman's aria, "The Metal Age Has Come" (Act I, Scene 2) and also in the brass at the end of Act I and opening of Act II; thus, their return here is significant in unifying the disparate scenes.

In measure 1065, Ada sings "Tell me everything"[80] which introduces the grand ensemble number "Tell Her." For this complex scene that features nearly all the secondary characters, Higdon first composed each character's melody based on their respective earlier passages before combining them masterfully. The order of the characters' entrance was a mutual decision between composer and librettist; Higdon specifically recalled that "Lucinda's melody would be such a wonderful way to start this chorus and then build all of the music on that melody."[81] An instrumental prelude begins at rehearsal 95 (measure 1066) with a bassoon duet and a few measures later, the changing meter stabilizes to 5/4. This meter and orchestration are nearly identical to Lucinda's aria from Act II, Scene 1 (measures 20–24). The woodwind duet repeats only once and as with the earlier corresponding passage, the material is varied through a countermelody here scored for the male chorus. The men, comprised of Veasey and the Chain Gang, present consonant third intervals in homorhythmic texture.

The texture thickens considerably in measure 1078 with the entrance of the three sisters (referred to here as Sirens) from Act I, Scene 8. The role of Lila, prominently featured in the earlier scene, is omitted for practical reasons. The composer explained that if a smaller company produced the opera, the role of Sara could be doubled by Lila which is why the latter is excluded from this ensemble number. The sisters' music maintains the previous characteristics of close harmony in homorhythmic texture. Sara enters in measure 1081 followed by a Soldiers' chorus with references to the death of Ballis which identifies them as the hospitalized Confederate soldiers from Act I, Scene 2. Comparable to their earlier scene, the orchestration is comprised of violas doubling the voices. Measure 1090 begins the climax of "Tell Her": the characters, minus Ada and Inman, sing at varying degrees of forte in homorhythmic texture accompanied by the full orchestra. The texture and syllabic setting place the emphasis on the poignant text as they sing:

> And the slaughter that went on and on.... Tell her.... Tell her everything. Tell her who we were, who we were.... Tell her everything. Tell her how the past is not the past, tell her everything ... but from now on all time's a blur ... a fog of memories, death and killing and sin.... If war is to ever end ... it is here that it must begin....[82]

While Higdon was writing this scene, she did not consciously compose the music as a protest against war but as she explained later, "I hadn't really thought about it but it's really an anti-war song [...] you want the war to stop, you want the death and killing to stop."[83]

Immediately at rehearsal 98 (measure 1104), the ensemble disperses, the tempo is reduced, and the instrumentation temporarily thinned to release the dramatic tension of "Tell Her." The lights fade on Ada and Inman implying their relationship is to be consummated resulting in a daughter in the Epilogue. The love scene is accompanied by the full ensemble featuring prominent Higdon traits of root position major and minor chords in a slow harmonic rhythm for the lower strings.

At rehearsal 101 (measure 1129), the opulent interlude merges into a greatly reduced texture as a transition for the subsequent stage action of Ruby nursing Stobrod. The music is of particular interest because it combines several earlier elements from Act II. First, the repeating chord progressions in the violas and celli are similar to that found in Ada's aria from Scene 10 ("I Feel So Sorry for You") (Figure 8–21) as is the identical tempo of quarter note=52. The reduced orchestration is also alike but varied here with an

English horn solo. Upon Ruby's entrance in measure 1134, she sings the same text as Stobrod in Scene 4 ("Bless You, Ruby") (Figure 8-20) and the preceding string progression is replaced by a concertmaster solo including several portamento figures, musical traits associated with her father. The first two phrases' pitches in each passage begin identically and although Ruby's line quickly strays from the original, the melodic contour remains comparable (Figure 8-23).

Figure 8-23. *Cold Mountain*; Act II, Scene 12, mm. 1134-37.

At rehearsal 103 (measure 1142), the mood is altered by a faster tempo when Inman discusses the future of Black Cove Farm with Ruby. Her response is accompanied by a further increase in tempo complemented by 32nd notes in the horns and syncopated violas to create the energy associated with her character. She tells him that she has many plans for the land while Inman explains he will surrender himself to the North and wait out the war in a POW camp. As Ada, Ruby, and Reid exit carrying Stobrod down Cold Mountain, Teague appears, his presence marked through the egg shaker in the orchestration and dissonant portamento string figures. Inman shoots a member of the homeguard sparking a violent gun battle at rehearsal 109 (measure 1192).

The ensuing combat is in a 3/8 meter and utilizes varying levels of forte with a tempo of dotted quarter note=72. The instrumentation initially consists of small punctuations from the woodwinds, harp, strings, and multiple percussion for various effects. In measure 1198, a striking dissonance is created through the two separate, harmonic tritones in the violins a minor second apart that continue in various guises through measure 1269. (Figure 8-24) Major or minor chords separated by second intervals are a Higdon stylistic trait; however, here she has reworked this concept for maximum dissonances to accompany the violence on stage. While the tempo gradually accelerates, the battle intensifies and two more of Teague's men are shot. By rehearsal 110 (measure 1219), the dotted quarter note has escalated to 92 and the dissonances in the violins are joined by descending melodic tritones in the woodwinds.

At rehearsal 112 (measure 1253), both Teague and Inman run out of bullets and the gun battle becomes hand-to-hand knife combat. The meter changes to 3/4 with the dotted half note= 60 accelerating further in two meas-

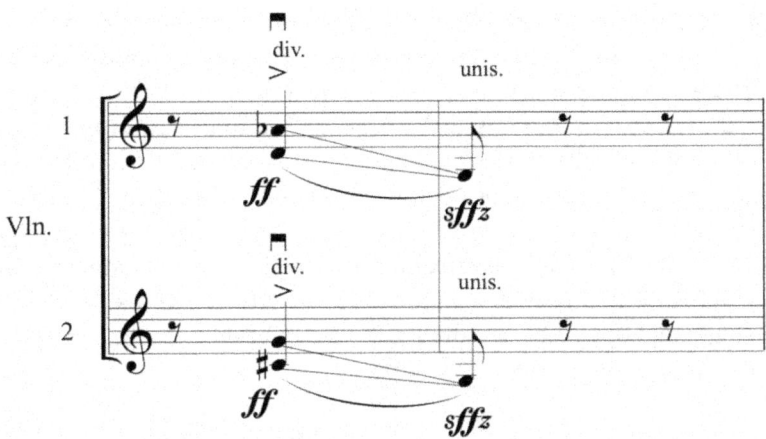

Figure 8–24. *Cold Mountain*; Act II, Scene 12, mm. 1198–99.

ure increments. The music remains highly dissonant and by rehearsal 113 (measure 1266), the tempo increases at each measure eventually reaching dotted half note=144.

The climax begins in measure 1272 scored for the full ensemble with loud dynamics and detailed musical instructions that incorporate aleatoric elements. While continuing the earlier tritone relationships in the woodwinds and strings, this passage also contains the most unconventional scoring in the entire opera. The two flute parts are each comprised of six notes separated by a tritone with the instructions to "play this pattern as fast as possible."[84] It would be nearly impossible for the musicians to play at an identical speed to produce parallel tritones of course, but undoubtedly at times, this will in fact occur. The subsequent solid black line for these parts indicate the continuation of this idea through measure 1280 (Figure 8–25).

The strings also contribute significantly to the dramatic and violent dissonance. The basses alternate descending portamento figures comprised of

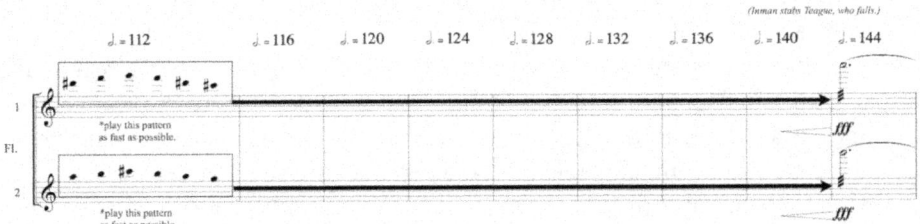

Figure 8–25. *Cold Mountain*; Act II, Scene 12, mm. 1272–1280.

tritones and major sevenths followed by a solid line that traces only a melodic contour with the instructions "bowed trem. through these 2 meas., but vary pitch wildly and independent of others."[85] The tremolo of the divisi celli consists of a perfect fifth and tritone transposed a minor second higher each measure to elevate the intensity. Finally, in measure 1274, the first violins alternate between two tritones in tremolo; Higdon notates in 1276 that the musicians should "continue trem. ... moving up through various pitches independently. (maintain tri-tone relationship.)."[86] These dissonant string lines (Figure 8–26), combined with loud punctuations from the brass and the ever-increasing tempo, peak in measure 1281, the height of the stage action when Inman stabs and kills Teague.

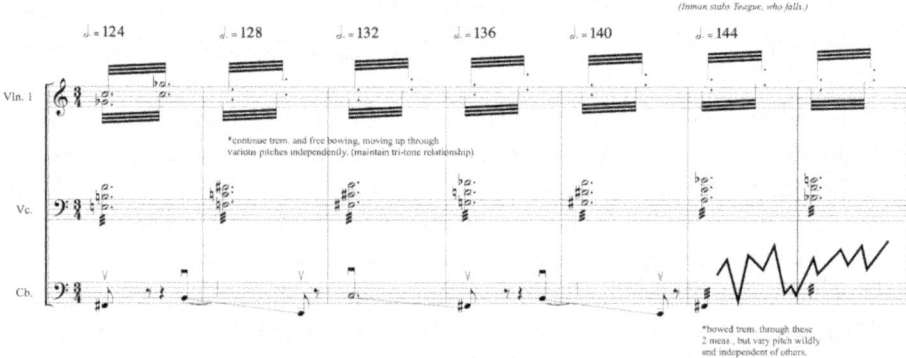

Figure 8–26. *Cold Mountain*; Act II, Scene 12, mm. 1275–1281.

Following the death of Teague, the only threat to Inman is Birch, the young orphaned boy under Teague's care. The orchestration and dynamics are greatly reduced while Inman convinces Birch to put down his rifle. As Inman bends down to retrieve the weapon, Birch shoots and mortally wounds Inman with a pistol. After the gunshot, Birch exclaims "Hallelujah, Amen,"[87] Teague's signal introduced in the opera's opening. The score designates this should be "shouted or spoken"[88] and includes a rhythm similar to Teague's from Act I.

Following the gunshot, the full orchestra enters fortississimo at rehearsal 116 (measure 1303) with a fast tempo that eventually increases to quarter note=104. The trumpets produce open fifth intervals, a sound exclusively associated with Inman while quintal harmonies are sounded in the celli and basses. To enhance the dissonance, the latter sustain a C, a tritone from the F# root of the ensemble. The simultaneous F# minor and major chords of the opening harmony are of great significance. Previously, these chords alternated and were initially introduced in Inman's first aria "The Metal Age Has Come" with recurrences in subsequent passages. The incorporation of these same harmonies at the character's death brings his music full circle (Figure 8–27).

Figure 8-27. *Cold Mountain*; Act II, Scene 12, m. 1303 Strings, Trombones, and Trumpets.

At rehearsal 117 (measure 1314), the orchestration gradually thins as Ada rushes to Inman. Her descending melody outlines a thirteenth interval and incorporates brief melismas indicative of her overwhelming emotion. Soli for the concertmaster and the principal viola accompany her final phrases that demonstrates Higdon's skillful chamber scoring. It is worthy of note that within this lament appears the phrase "Come back to me," an identical text also found repeatedly at the close of Act I.

When Inman dies at measure 1328, the full orchestra returns to express Ada's devastation. The transition to the Epilogue follows at rehearsal 119 (measure 1349) with another thinning of the texture and several string soli including the concertmaster, the first stand of celli, and the principal viola doubled by the third trumpet. With the exception of blowing through the instruments in the Epilogue, the trumpets, long associated with the character of Inman, are tacet for the remainder of the opera.

Act II, Scene 13, "Epilogue: 9 years later…"

Cold Mountain closes with an Epilogue that softens the heartbreaking demise of Inman. The setting is Black Cove Farm where Ruby is living with Stobrod and Reid, her husband and the father of her three children, along with Ada and her daughter with Inman. The scene begins at rehearsal 120 (measure 1357) with the glockenspiel marked to be performed by either Magic Flute mallets or knitting needles, a scoring previously associated with the Orion constellation. Orchestral soli are sprinkled amongst the principal viola and horn as well as the first stand of both violin sections. Ada's daughter calls to her mother and together they view Orion to the accompaniment of the crotales, glockenspiel, and the wind and brass instruments blowing through their instruments. The tempo is quarter note=52, recreating an orchestration and tempo identical to the Orion duet (Act II, Scene 3).

In the final moments of the opera, Ada is left alone onstage to view the constellation singing lines subtly connected to the end of Act I. In the pick-up to measure 1383 (Figure 8-28), the word "Orion" appears with the precise rhythm and nearly identical pitch content as that of Inman from Act I, Scene 10 in measure 1750 (Figures 8-29). Although the orchestral accompaniment differs between the sections, the focus on the violins remain similar. Additionally, Ada's rhythms in measure 1384 (Figure 8-28) echo Inman's identical text from the first Act's measure 1737 (Figure 8-30).

Higdon closes the opera with a light orchestration of lower strings and horns while Ada softly sings, "Oh, Inman." As her final phrase diminishes, pianissississimo fifth intervals are presented in the horns, an interval previously

Figure 8-28. *Cold Mountain*; Act II, Scene 13, mm. 1382–84.

Figure 8-29. *Cold Mountain*; Act I, Scene 10, m. 1750.

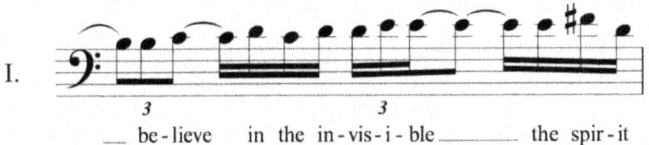

Figure 8-30. *Cold Mountain*; Act I, Scene 10, mm. 1737.

paired with the trumpet to reference Inman. Its appearance here with a different timbre signifies that the spirit of Inman, no longer a soldier, remains with the woman he loves (Figure 8-31). It is worth noting that the opera

Figure 8-31. *Cold Mountain*; Act II, Scene 13, mm. 1389–92.

closes in a similar fashion to its beginning: a single character accompanied by no, or sparse, instrumentation. The quiet end to this monumental opera leaves the listener reflective of the many emotions Higdon has evoked through her magnum opus: anger, resentment, forgiveness, passion, and most importantly, love.

Codetta

As clearly evidenced, the music of Higdon is wonderfully diverse and communicates extraordinarily well to audiences. Each of the preceding chapters examined a significant work in her overall output; however, this is just a mere sampling of her extensive and expanding oeuvre. She continues to work tirelessly and is in demand more now than ever with several projects in particular being noteworthy.

In February 2015, the song cycle *Civil Words* premiered at Carnegie Hall with internationally acclaimed baritone, Thomas Hampson. The work initially consisted of five songs with texts by various Civil War poets and excerpts from Lincoln's second inaugural speech. What is striking about this cycle is the large range of perspectives examined in the poetry which, through Higdon's music, gives a voice to both women and men, mothers and fathers, low-ranking soldiers and the commander-in-chief. The topic of the Civil War was dictated by the commission thus making any connection to *Cold Mountain* simply a remarkable coincidence. The cycle was so well received that Hampson requested a sixth song be added[1] and plans to record the work in 2018. In the fall of 2017, Higdon reworked *Civil Words* for soprano and a world premiere of this arrangement is planned with Marina De Ratmiroff, soprano, and Milton Laufer, piano at Western Carolina University, Cullowhee, North Carolina (USA) on an as-yet undecided date.

Since Santa Fe and Philadelphia, *Cold Mountain* was produced in 2017 by North Carolina Opera at Chapel Hill, North Carolina. Minnesota Opera is the next company to stage the work but in the interim, Higdon has been commissioned by Opera Philadelphia to compose her second opera. She is using an original libretto by Jerre Dye and the currently untitled work is scheduled to premiere in September 2020.

The composer has not abandoned orchestral music and continues to write large-scale works for a variety of international soloists and ensembles. Her previous concerti follow a steep musical tradition; however, in more recent years, her contributions to instruments featured less frequently is reminiscent of Paul Hindemith's legacy. In 2015, the *Viola Concerto* premiered at the Library of Congress in Washington, D.C. (USA), with Roberto Díaz, the president and CEO of the Curtis Institute of Music, and the Curtis Chamber Orchestra led by Robert Spano. The following year, Giancarlo Guerrero conducted a live recording of the work with the Nashville Symphony at Laura Turner Concert Hall in the Schermerhorn Symphony Center. The album, on the Naxos label, is the world premiere recording not only of the *Viola Concerto* but of Higdon's *Oboe Concerto* (2005) and also includes the four-movement work *All Things Majestic* (2011) for which the album is named. The *Viola Concerto* and the album received the prestigious Grammy awards for Best Contemporary Classical Composition and Best Classical Compendium, respectively. It is worth noting that nominees in the former category include fellow Atlanta School of Composer, Adam Schoenberg, and Higdon's former student, Zhou Tian.

Although Higdon focused exclusively on *Cold Mountain* for several years, this is certainly not the case for her second opera and in fact, 2018 features numerous significant compositions. First, her *Low Brass Concerto* will have its world premiere on February 1, 2018, with the Chicago Symphony Orchestra led by Riccardo Muti featuring the three CSO trombonists, Jay Friedman (principal), Michael Mulcahy, and Charlie Vernon (bass trombone) as well as principal tubist, Gene Pokorny. A co-commission of the CSO, the Philadelphia Orchestra, and the Baltimore Symphony Orchestra, the Concerto will receive its East Coast premiere in Philadelphia later the same month with conductor Cristian Măcelaru and members of Philadelphia's brass section. The BSO has scheduled their performance of the work for January 2019.[2]

In March 2018, the Pittsburgh Symphony Orchestra will host the world premiere of Higdon's *Tuba Concerto* with the ensemble's principal tubist, Craig Knox under the baton of her old friend and supporter, Spano. Finally, the *Harp Concerto* will premiere with Yolanda Kondonassis and the Rochester Philharmonic Orchestra conducted by Ward Stare in May 2018 with a recording planned for the subsequent season.[3]

The mark Higdon has made on contemporary American music is undeniable. She continues to be one of the most prolific and sought-after composers having collaborated with every significant contemporary musician and ensemble. Simultaneously, she is an incredibly approachable figure, perhaps due to her warm personality and trademark Reeboks, which makes art music less intimidating and more accessible to the average person.

For centuries, composers have struggled with defining American music and although Higdon has never offered a verbal solution, she herself is the answer. Her music communicates to diverse audiences and as a result, she has rightfully catapulted to phenomenal success and a place in the canon. Performances of her works are found from the high school gymnasium to the professional concert hall. There is no better representative of American music than Higdon whose works embody the spirit, vivacity, diversity, and warmth of her country. Indeed, she encompasses the American experience and notates the songs of its people with a unique vividness as she composes in color.

Fine

Chapter Notes

Chapter One

1. Mark Kanny, "Higdon Brings Energetic Works to the City," *Pittsburgh Tribune-Review*, October 30, 2005, LexisNexis Academic.
2. Cheryl Lawson and Jennifer Higdon, email messages to author, February 14–15, 2015.
3. Jennifer Higdon, interview by Kile Smith, "Composer Jennifer Higdon Tells Her Story: Part 2," *Philadelphia Music Makers*, WRTI 90.1, http://wrti.org/post/composer-jennifer-higdon-tells-her-story-part-2 (accessed November 5, 2016).
4. Jennifer Higdon, email messages to author, May 10–November 25, 2006.
5. David Patrick Stearns, "The Rock That Anchors a Classical Composer; the Beatles' 'Sgt. Pepper' Has Exerted a Major Influence on the Work of Jennifer Higdon," *Philadelphia Inquirer*, September 20, 2009, ProQuest Newsstand.
6. Doug Mason, "Prelude in Tennessee: Grammy Winning Composer Had Her Musical Beginnings in Blount County," *Knoxville News-Sentinel*, September 18, 2005, ProQuest Newsstand.
7. Karen Rile, "The Accidental Genius," *The Pennsylvania Gazette*, July/August 2005, http://www.upenn.edu/gazette/0705/feature01sidebar.html (accessed November 5, 2016).
8. Cheryl Lawson and Jennifer Higdon, email, February 14–15, 2015.
9. Rile, "The Accidental Genius."
10. Cheryl Lawson and Jennifer Higdon, email, February 14–15, 2015.
11. Jennifer Higdon interview by Paula Marantz Cohen, "Episode 37-Jennifer Higdon-Part 01," YouTube video, 14:59, posted by "Thedrexelinterview," June 15, 2011, https://www.youtube.com/watch?v=9rKLA_q4aJA (accessed November 5, 2016).
12. Jennifer Higdon interview by Matthew Harder, "Jennifer Higdon Webinar," YouTube video, 59:03, posted by "Wheeling Symphony," March 8, 2013, https://www.youtube.com/watch?v=1mYehn1FlEA (accessed November 5, 2016).
13. Brenda Rossow Phillips, "Jennifer Higdon: A Stylistic Analysis of Selected Flute and Orchestral Works," (DMA doc, Arizona State University, 2005), 3–4.
14. Michael Anthony, "Composing an Ode to the Oboe; Prolific Composer Jennifer Higdon Muses on Writing Her Latest Concerto, a Premiere by the St. Paul Chamber Orchestra," *Star Tribune* (Minneapolis, MN), September 4, 2005, ProQuest Newsstand.
15. Jennifer Higdon interview by Matthew Harder, "Jennifer Higdon Webinar."
16. Anthony, "Composing an Ode."
17. Higdon interview by Matthew Harder, "Jennifer Higdon Webinar."
18. Phillips, "Jennifer Higdon," 5–7.
19. Donald McKinney, "Jennifer Higdon," in *Women of Influence in Contemporary Music: Nine American Composers*, ed. Michael K. Slayton (Lanham, MD: Scarecrow, 2011), 155. Wallace DePue's son, Zachary, was a member of Time for Three, the trio for whom Higdon's *Concerto 4-3* was composed.
20. Phillips, "Jennifer Higdon," 6–7.
21. Cheryl Lawson and Jennifer Higdon, email, February 14–15, 2015.
22. Virginia Broffitt, "The Music of Jennifer Higdon: Perspectives on the Styles and Compositional Approaches in Selected Chamber Compositions" (DMA doc, University of Cincinnati, 2010), 11.
23. Jennifer Higdon interview by John Clare, "Composing Thoughts, Part 7," YouTube video, 4:35, posted by "John Clare," March 25, 2008, https://www.youtube.com/watch?v=txf_mYWUycU (accessed November 7, 2016).
24. McKinney, "Jennifer Higdon," in *Women of Influence*, 157.
25. Jennifer Higdon, *Biography*, http://www.

jenniferhigdon.com/biography.html (accessed November 7, 2016).

26. Rile, "The Accidental Genius."

27. Jennifer Higdon, interview by author, tape recording, Atlanta, Ga., September 19, 2006.

28. Broffitt, "The Music of Jennifer Higdon," 13.

29. Higdon, email, May 10–November 25, 2006.

30. Broffitt, "The Music of Jennifer Higdon," 13.

31. Lawson and Higdon, email, February 14–15, 2015.

32. *Ibid.*

33. Richard Dyer, "Composer Has Emotional Reach, Direct Appeal Jennifer Higdon Touches Many with Her Work," *The Boston Globe*, July 13, 2003, ProQuest Newsstand.

34. Jason Victor Serinus, "Interview: The Award-Winning Jennifer Higdon," *Secrets of Home Theater and High Fidelity*, June 2005, http://www.hometheaterhifi.com/volume_12_2/feature-interview-jennifer-higdon-6-2005.html.

35. Lawson and Higdon, email, February 14–15, 2015.

36. *Ibid.*

37. Phillips, "Jennifer Higdon," 10.

38. Higdon, email, May 10–November 25, 2006.

39. Lawson and Higdon, email, February 14–15, 2015.

40. Mason, "Prelude in Tennessee."

41. Lawson and Higdon, email, February 14–15, 2015.

42. *Ibid.*

43. Serinus, "Interview: The Award-Winning Jennifer Higdon."

44. Robert Spano, "Conference 2010: Atlanta School of Composers," YouTube video, 1:12:18, posted by "Leagueamer," July 1, 2010, https://www.youtube.com/watch?v=aWtZIuxILSc (accessed November 30, 2016).

45. *Ibid.*

46. Lawson and Higdon, email, February 14–15, 2015.

47. *Ibid.*

48. Kanny, "Higdon Brings Energetic Works."

49. Higdon, email, May 10–November 25, 2006.

50. Higdon interview by Paula Marantz Cohen, "Episode 37."

51. Higdon, interview by author, tape recording.

52. *Ibid.*

53. Jennifer Higdon interview by Hilary Hahn, "HIlary [Sic] Hahn Interviews Jennifer Higdon 2," YouTube video, 6:22, posted by "Hilaryhahnvideos," February 9, 2009, https://www.youtube.com/watch?v=AWGhLPEblR4 (accessed November 7, 2016).

54. Higdon interview by Matthew Harder, "Jennifer Higdon Webinar."

55. Higdon, interview by author, tape recording.

56. Higdon interview by Matthew Harder, "Jennifer Higdon Webinar."

57. Noteworthy among the latter was Maurice Ravel's *Daphnis Et Chloe*.

58. Pierre Ruhe, "Symphony Illuminates Soul of City," *Atlanta Journal-Constitution*, November 10, 2002, ProQuest Newsstand.

59. Higdon interview by Matthew Harder, "Jennifer Higdon Webinar."

60. *Ibid.*

61. Higdon, interview by author, tape recording.

62. *Ibid.*

63. *Ibid.*

64. Phillips, "Jennifer Higdon," 72.

65. David Patrick Stearns, "Jennifer Higdon Premieres Concerto 'On a Wire,'" *Philadelphia Inquirer*, June 8, 2010, ProQuest Newsstand.

66. Philip Gambone, *Travels in a Gay Nation: Portraits of LGBTQ Americans* (Madison: The University of Wisconsin Press, 2010), 167. http://site.ebrary.com/lib/hunter/reader.action?docID=10381815.

67. Nick Jones, Liner Notes, *Jennifer Higdon: City Scape/Concerto for Orchestra*, Robert Spano (cond.), Atlanta Symphony Orchestra, Telarc 80620, 2004, compact disc.

68. Higdon, interview by author, tape recording.

69. *Ibid.*

Chapter Two

1. Jennifer Higdon, *blue cathedral* (Philadelphia: Lawdon Press, 1999).

2. Andrew Druckenbrod, "Higdon Poured Grief into blue cathedral," *Pittsburgh Post-Gazette*, November 2, 2005, ProQuest Newsstand.

3. Higdon, *blue cathedral*.

4. Jennifer Higdon, Liner Notes, *Rainbow Body*, Robert Spano (cond.), Atlanta Symphony Orchestra, Telarc 80596, 2003, compact disc.

5. *Ibid.*

6. Jennifer Higdon, interview by author, tape recording, Atlanta, Ga., September 19, 2006.

7. *Ibid.*

8. *Ibid.*

9. Brenda Rossow Phillips, "Jennifer Higdon: A Stylistic Analysis of Selected Flute and Orchestral Works," (DMA doc, Arizona State University, 2005), 1.
10. Higdon, interview by author, tape recording.
11. Richard Dyer, "Composer Has Emotional Reach, Direct Appeal Jennifer Higdon Touches Many with Her Work," *The Boston Globe*, July 13, 2003, ProQuest Newsstand.
12. Higdon, *blue cathedral*.
13. *Ibid*.
14. Cheryl Lawson and Jennifer Higdon, email message to author, June 8, 2015.
15. *Ibid*.
16. Higdon, *blue cathedral*.
17. Higdon, Liner Notes, *Rainbow Body*.
18. Higdon, interview by author, tape recording.
19. *Ibid*.
20. Lawson and Higdon, email, June 8, 2015.
21. Higdon, interview by author, tape recording.
22. Higdon, Liner Notes, *Rainbow Body*.
23. Phillips, "Jennifer Higdon," 65.
24. Higdon, interview by author, tape recording.
25. Lawson and Higdon, email, June 8, 2015.
26. Higdon, interview by author, tape recording.
27. Lawson and Higdon, email, June 8, 2015.
28. Phillips, "Jennifer Higdon," 68.
29. Jennifer Higdon, email messages to author, May 10–November 25, 2006.
30. Higdon, interview by author, tape recording.
31. Janet K. Page, et al. "Oboe." *Grove Music Online. Oxford Music Online.* Oxford University Press, accessed March 10, 2015, http://0-www.oxfordmusiconline.com.wncln.wncln.org/subscriber/article/grove/music/40450.
32. Phillips, "Jennifer Higdon," 67.
33. Higdon, email, May 10–November 25, 2006.
34. Higdon, Liner Notes, *Rainbow Body*.
35. Higdon, *blue cathedral*.
36. Interpretations stem from the previously cited dissertation of Phillips and Druckenbrod, "Higdon Poured Grief."
37. Lawson and Higdon, email, June 8, 2015.
38. Higdon, interview by author, tape recording.
39. *Ibid*.
40. *Ibid*.
41. Higdon, *blue cathedral*.
42. Higdon, email, May 10–November 25, 2006.
43. Higdon, Liner Notes, *Rainbow Body*.
44. Higdon, interview by author, tape recording.
45. Lawson and Higdon, email, June 8, 2015.
46. Phillips, "Jennifer Higdon," 72.
47. *Ibid*.
48. Phillips, "Jennifer Higdon," 73.
49. *Ibid*.
50. Higdon, *blue cathedral*.
51. Phillips, "Jennifer Higdon," 73.
52. Higdon, interview by author, tape recording.
53. *Ibid*.
54. Phillips, "Jennifer Higdon," 74.
55. Higdon, Liner Notes, *Rainbow Body*.
56. Higdon, email, May 10–November 25, 2006.
57. *Ibid*.
58. Higdon, interview by author, tape recording.
59. Jennifer Higdon, Pittsburgh Symphony Orchestra, *Composer's Corner*, http://www.pittsburghsymphony.blogs.com/composers/2005/10/blue_cathedral_.html#more (accessed May 13, 2006).
60. Phillips, "Jennifer Higdon," 75.
61. Higdon, interview by author, tape recording.
62. Higdon, *Composer's Corner*.
63. Higdon, interview by author, tape recording.
64. *Ibid*.
65. *Ibid*.
66. Lawson and Higdon, email, June 8, 2015.
67. Druckenbrod, "Higdon Poured Grief."
68. Higdon, interview by author, tape recording.
69. David Patrick Stearns, "Curtis Orchestra Set for Prime Time," *Philadelphia Inquirer*, May 3, 2000, LexisNexis Academic.
70. Jeff Dunn, "Warhorseless," *San Francisco Classical Voice*, December 6, 2003, http://www.sfcv.org/arts_revs/starosasym_12_9_03.php (accessed January 13, 2016).
71. Bob Keyes, "New Year, New Magic from PSO; the First Tuesday Classical Series of 2005 Features a Guest Baton and an Ethereal Piece by an Acclaimed Female Composer," *Portland Press Herald* (Maine), January 30, 2005, LexisNexis Academic.
72. David Lindauer, "ASO'S 'Ode to Joy'-Musical, Masterful and Majestic," *The Capital* (Annapolis, MD), May 11, 2006, LexisNexis Academic.
73. Gilbert French, "Rainbow Body," *American Record Guide* Vol. 66, no. 5 (Sep/Oct 2003): 209–210, Academic Search Complete, EBSCOhost.

Chapter Three

1. Other compositions from these commissions included Aaron Jay Kernis's *Color Wheel*, Michael Daughtery's *Philadelphia Stories*, and Roberto Sierra's *Concierto Para Orquesta*, coincidentally a Spanish title for *Concerto for Orchestra*.
2. Higdon does not know which musician recommended her music. Jennifer Higdon, interview by author, tape recording, Atlanta, Ga., September 19, 2006.
3. Higdon, interview by author, tape recording.
4. *Ibid.*
5. Cheryl Lawson, email message to author, July 8, 2015.
6. Jennifer Higdon, "Publishing, Self-Publishing, and the Internet," from the Women's Philharmonic's "Composing a Career" Symposium, February 1, 2000, *NewMusicBox*, http://www.newmusicbox.org/article.nmbx?id=537 (accessed November 7, 2016).
7. Higdon, interview by author, tape recording.
8. *Ibid.*
9. *Ibid.*
10. Andrew Quint, "Speaking with Composer Jennifer Higdon," *Fanfare* Vol. 27, no. 5 (May/June 2005): 42–46, Arts Premium Collection.
11. Higdon, interview by author, tape recording.
12. *Ibid.*
13. *Ibid.*
14. "Jennifer Higdon's Concerto for Orchestra Highlights Premieres," *Sequenza 21*, June 3–10, 2002, http://www.sequenza21.com/060302.html (accessed November 8, 2016).
15. Nick Jones, Liner Notes, *City Scape/Concerto for Orchestra*, Jennifer Higdon (composer), Robert Spano (cond.), Atlanta Symphony Orchestra, Telarc 80620, 2004, compact disc.
16. Higdon, interview by author, tape recording.
17. *Ibid.*
18. Jennifer Higdon, email message to author, October 3, 2015.
19. Higdon, interview by author, tape recording.
20. Higdon, email, October 3, 2015.
21. Jennifer Higdon interview by Matthew Harder, "Jennifer Higdon Webinar," YouTube video, 59:03, posted by "Wheeling Symphony," March 8, 2013, https://www.youtube.com/watch?v=1mYehn1F1EA.
22. Lawson recalled this friend was a fellow flute student from college.—Lawson, email, July 8, 2015.
23. Higdon, interview by author, tape recording.
24. Jennifer Higdon, *Concerto for Orchestra* (Philadelphia: Lawdon Press, 2002).
25. Andrew Druckenbrod, "Composer Making Music History," *Pittsburgh Post-Gazette*, November 2, 2005, ProQuest Newsstand.
26. Higdon interview by Matthew Harder, "Jennifer Higdon Webinar."
27. Higdon, interview by author, tape recording.
28. *Ibid.*
29. Jennifer Higdon, program notes for *Concerto for Orchestra*, http://www.jenniferhigdon.com/pdf/program-notes/concerto-for-orchestra.pdf (accessed October 22, 2016).
30. Higdon, interview by author, tape recording.
31. *Ibid.*
32. The numbers in subscript refer to the beginning interval of each scale. OCT $_{0,1}$: C-C#-D#-E-F#-G-A-A#, OCT $_{1,2}$: C#-D-E-F-G-G#-A#-B, and OCT $_{2,3}$: C-D-D#-F-F#-G#-A-B
33. Donald McKinney, "Jennifer Higdon," in *Women of Influence in Contemporary Music: Nine American Composers*, ed. Michael K. Slayton (Lanham, MD: Scarecrow Press, 2011), 159.
34. Higdon, interview by author, tape recording.
35. She's referring to *Soliloquy*. Higdon, email, October 3, 2015.
36. Higdon, interview by author, tape recording.
37. *Ibid.*
38. *Ibid.*
39. Jones, Liner Notes, *City Scape/Concerto for Orchestra*.
40. Higdon, interview by author, tape recording.
41. *Ibid.*
42. *Ibid.*
43. Jones, Liner Notes, *City Scape/Concerto for Orchestra*.
44. Higdon, email, October 3, 2015.
45. Higdon, interview by author, tape recording.
46. *Ibid.*
47. *Ibid.*
48. *Ibid.*
49. This transposition recalls a similar occurrence found in measure ten that transposed the opening polyphonic material by a lowered minor second.
50. The use of inversion to vary significant sections appears fairly frequently in Higdon's

orchestral music as noted with the numerous inversions of the perfect fifth.

51. Higdon, interview by author, tape recording.
52. McKinney, "Jennifer Higdon," in *Women of Influence*, 160.
53. Higdon, interview by author, tape recording.
54. *Ibid.*
55. Higdon, email, October 3, 2015.
56. *Ibid.*
57. Higdon, interview by author, tape recording.
58. Pittsburgh Symphony Orchestra, "Jennifer Higdon Talks About Her Concerto for Orchestra," http://www.pittsburghsymphony.org/pghsymph.nsf/concert+listings/22DD934D488A89548525703500670D45?opendocument (accessed July 7, 2006).
59. Higdon, interview by author, tape recording.
60. Higdon interview by Matthew Harder, "Jennifer Higdon Webinar."
61. Bowed vibraphones are found starting at measure seven in *blue cathedral*.
62. Higdon, interview by author, tape recording.
63. *Ibid.*
64. *Ibid.*
65. Higdon, email, October 3, 2015.
66. Higdon, interview by author, tape recording.
67. *Ibid.*
68. Although the composer had not originally considered this option, she would consider it if an ensemble expressed interest.—Higdon, interview by author, tape recording and Lawson, email, July 8, 2015.
69. Higdon, interview by author, tape recording.
70. Higdon, program notes for *Concerto for Orchestra*.
71. Higdon, interview by author, tape recording.
72. *Ibid.*
73. Higdon, *Concerto for Orchestra*.
74. *Ibid.*
75. Higdon, interview by author, tape recording.
76. *Ibid.*
77. Higdon, *Concerto for Orchestra*.
78. "Battuto." *Grove Music Online. Oxford Music Online*. Oxford University Press, accessed March 13, 2015, http://0-www.oxfordmusiconline.com.wncln.wncln.org/subscriber/article/grove/music/02237.
79. This directive is comparable to the marking of the timpani in measure 66 of the fourth movement which reads, "Whichever Drum Is Convenient." Higdon, *Concerto for Orchestra*.
80. Jennifer Higdon, email messages to author, May 10–November 25, 2006.
81. David Patrick Stearns, "Whistling a Grammy Tune; with a Week Till the Awards, Heres [Sic] a Sampling of Nominees Who Have Already Captured the Sounds of Success. to Philadelphia Classical Composer Jennifer Higdon, It's an Honor—And a Career Boost—Just to Be Nominated," *Philadelphia Inquirer*, February 6, 2005, LexisNexis Academic.
82. Higdon, email, May 10–November 25, 2006.
83. Jeffrey Rossman, "An Evening of Baby-Boomer Composers," *Classical Voice of North Carolina*, http://www.cvnc.org/reviews/2006/012006/NCScrossing1.html (accessed January 12, 2016).
84. Perry Tannenbaum, "North Carolina Symphony: In Search of New Classics," *American Record Guide* Vol. 69, no. 3 (May 2006): 17–18, Academic Search Complete, EBSCOhost.
85. Andrew Clark, "BBC Symphony/Slatkin Barbican, London ANDREW CLARK THE CRITICS: [LONDON 1ST EDITION]," *Financial Times* (London, UK), April 8, 2004, ProQuest Newsstand.
86. Mark L. Lehman, "Higdon: Concerto for Orchestra; City Scape (Music)," *American Record Guide* Vol. 67, no. 4 (Jul/Aug 2004): 118, Academic Search Complete, EBSCOhost.
87. John von Rhein, "Jennifer Higdon; Concerto for Orchestra, City Scape: Atlanta Symphony Orchestra, Robert Spano, Conductor (Telarc): [Chicago Final Edition]," *Chicago Tribune*, July 25, 2004, ProQuest Newsstand.
88. Cheryl Lawson, email, July 8, 2015.
89. "World-Renowned Composer Higdon Visits Boston Crusaders' Rehearsal," *Drum Corps International*, August 17, 2006, http://dci271.dci.org/news/view.cfm?news_id=dafbea7b-e3f4-415a-9bb4-e232be3305dc (accessed November 8, 2016).

Chapter Four

1. Jennifer Higdon, *City Scape* (Philadelphia: Lawdon Press, 2002).
2. Nick Jones, Liner Notes, *City Scape/Concerto for Orchestra*, Jennifer Higdon (composer), Robert Spano (cond.), Atlanta Symphony Orchestra, Telarc 80620, 2004, compact disc.
3. Pierre Ruhe, "Symphony Illuminates Soul of City," *Atlanta Journal-Constitution*, November 10, 2002, ProQuest Newsstand.

4. Jennifer Higdon, "Episode 37—Jennifer Higdon—Part 01," YouTube video, 14:59, posted by "Thedrexelinterview," June 15, 2011, https://www.youtube.com/watch?v=9rKLA_q4aJA (accessed January 11, 2015).

5. Donald McKinney, "Jennifer Higdon," in *Women of Influence in Contemporary Music: Nine American Composers*, ed. Michael K. Slayton (Lanham, MD: Scarecrow Press, 2011), 152.

6. Ruhe, "Symphony Illuminates Soul of City."

7. *Ibid.*

8. Cheryl Lawson and Jennifer Higdon, email message to author, June 30, 2016.

9. Ruhe, "Symphony Illuminates Soul of City."

10. The omission of capital letters in the second movement is reminiscent of the composer's earlier tone poem *blue cathedral*.

11. Jennifer Higdon, quoted in Pierre Ruhe, "Symphony Illuminates Soul of City."

12. Jennifer Higdon, program notes, *City Scape*, http://www.jenniferhigdon.com/pdf/program-notes/City-Scape.pdf (accessed January 15, 2016).

13. Ruhe, "Symphony Illuminates Soul of City."

14. Jennifer Higdon in Nick Jones, Liner Notes, *City Scape/Concerto for Orchestra*.

15. Higdon, program notes, *City Scape*.

16. Mark Gresham, "Sounds Like Home," *Creative Loafing*, November 13, 2002, http://www.clatl.com/home/article/13009858/sounds-like-home (accessed November 8, 2016).

17. Jones, Liner Notes, *City Scape/Concerto for Orchestra*.

18. Ruhe, "Symphony Illuminates Soul of City."

19. Jennifer Higdon, interview by author, tape recording, Atlanta, Ga., September 19, 2006.

20. *Ibid.*

21. Ruhe, "Symphony Illuminates Soul of City."

22. Lawson and Higdon, email, June 30, 2016. Examples of works that utilize nature themes include *Autumn Reflection, an Exaltation of Larks, Mountain Songs, Sky Quartet,* and *Wissahickon PoeTrees.*

23. Ruhe, "Symphony Illuminates Soul of City."

24. Gresham, "Sounds Like Home."

25. *Ibid.*

26. John Jascoll, "Orchestra, Chorus Join in a Nautical Extravaganza," *Sunday News* (Lancaster, PA), March 30, 2008, ProQuest Newsstand.

27. Higdon in Nick Jones, Liner Notes, *City Scape/Concerto for Orchestra*.

28. Nicolette Norris, "LSO Sets Sail with a Choral Symphony," *Intelligencer Journal* (Lancaster, PA), March 28, 2008, ProQuest Newsstand.

29. James Blades, et al. "Gong." *Grove Music Online. Oxford Music Online*. Oxford University Press, accessed July 15, 2015, http://0-www.oxfordmusiconline.com.wncln.wncln.org/subscriber/article/grove/music/42877.

30. Lawson and Higdon, email, June 30, 2016.

31. Andrew Quint, "Speaking with Composer Jennifer Higdon," *Fanfare* 27, no. 5 (May/June 2005): 42–46, Arts Premium Collection.

32. *Sul Tasto* refers to playing near or above the fingerboard of a string instrument.

33. This orchestration can be found in measure 134 of the final movement.

34. Ruhe, "Symphony Illuminates Soul of City."

35. Jones, Liner Notes, *City Scape/Concerto for Orchestra.*

36. Higdon in Nick Jones, Liner Notes, *City Scape/Concerto for Orchestra.*

37. Lawson and Higdon, email, June 30, 2016.

38. All subsequent appearances of the Rondo theme are somewhat varied.

39. Lawson and Higdon, email, June 30, 2016.

40. *Ibid.*

41. *Ibid.*

42. Robert Battey, "From NSO, the Energy of a 'City,'" *The Washington Post,* May 18, 2007, ProQuest Newsstand.

43. David Patrick Stearns, "Jennifer Higdon's Exterior/Interior *City Scape,*" November 2002, Andante Corporation.

44. Battey, "From NSO, the Energy of a 'City.'"

45. Pierre Ruhe, "Spano Tailors Brahms Requiem," *The Atlanta Journal-Constitution,* November 3, 2007, ProQuest Newsstand.

Chapter Five

1. "About Time for Three," *Time for Three,* http://www.tf3.com/ (accessed April 25, 2016).

2. DePue left the group to dedicate his time exclusively to the Indianapolis Symphony Orchestra where he serves as concertmaster. He was replaced by violinist, Nikki Chooi who subsequently became concertmaster of the Metropolitan Opera Orchestra and was replaced by Charles Yang.—"Time for Three Is Excited to Announce a New Adventure!" *Time for Three,* http://www.tf3.com/ (accessed August 22, 2016)

and http://www.tf3.com/aabout (accessed December 14, 2016).

3. Andrew Druckenbrod, "Classical Musicians Break from the Mold," *Pittsburgh Post-Gazette*, Dec. 3, 2008, ProQuest Newsstand.

4. Jennifer Higdon, email message to author, September 19, 2016.

5. Jennifer Higdon, "Jennifer Higdon 'Being Creative in Philadelphia,'" YouTube Video, 3:38, posted by "Happyidiot90049," June 4, 2008, https://www.youtube.com/watch?v=c25lmEHOzZw (accessed April 25, 2016).

6. Jennifer Higdon, Liner Notes, *Take 6*, Miguel Harth-Bedoya (cond.), Fort Worth Symphony Orchestra, 2012, compact disc.

7. Mark Kanny, "Composer's Voice Suits Eclectic Philadelphia String Trio," *Pittsburgh Tribune-Review*, December 4, 2008, ProQuest Newsstand.

8. Higdon, email, September 19, 2016.

9. Kanny, "Composer's Voice Suits Eclectic Philadelphia String Trio."

10. Although the invention of notational symbols is rarely necessary in her orchestral works, similar creations are present in earlier compositions, notably *Rapid.Fire* for unaccompanied flute.—Higdon, email, September 19, 2016.

11. Higdon, email, September 19, 2016.

12. Jennifer Higdon, compact disc provided to author, August 24, 2016.

13. Jennifer Higdon interview by Michael Christie, "Higdon and Rachmaninoff," YouTube Video, 6:36, posted by "The Phoenix Symphony," March 4, 2009, https://www.youtube.com/watch?v=R2DPLW4v8WM (accessed April 25, 2016).

14. Jennifer Higdon, program notes for *Concerto 4-3*, http://www.jenniferhigdon.com/pdf/program-notes/Concerto-4-3.pdf (accessed April 21, 2016).

15. David Patrick Stearns, "A 'What's This' Kind of Concert: Higdons [Sic] New Genre-Bender Is Not for Listening Comfort," *Philadelphia Inquirer*, January 6, 2008, ProQuest Newsstand.

16. *Ibid.*

17. Higdon, program notes for *Concerto 4-3*.

18. Higdon, email, September 19, 2016.

19. Stearns, "A 'What's This' Kind of Concert."

20. Jennifer Higdon, *Concerto 4-3* (Philadelphia: Lawdon Press, 2007).

21. *Ibid.*

22. Higdon, email, September 19, 2016.

23. Higdon, program notes for *Concerto 4-3*.

24. Higdon, *Concerto 4-3*.

25. *Ibid.*

26. *Ibid.*
27. *Ibid.*
28. *Ibid.*
29. *Ibid.*

30. Such a designation is incredibly uncommon for Higdon; the only other occurrence appears in *Concerto for Orchestra*'s second movement.

31. Higdon, *Concerto 4-3*.

32. *Ibid.*

33. Druckenbrod, "Classical Musicians Break from the Mold."

34. Higdon, program notes for *Concerto 4-3*.

35. Stearns, "A 'What's This' Kind of Concert."

36. Kanny, "Composer's Voice Suits Eclectic Philadelphia String Trio."

37. Alexander Silbiger. "Chaconne." *Grove Music Online. Oxford Music Online.* Oxford University Press, accessed September 2, 2016, http://www.oxfordmusiconline.com.proxy195.nclive.org/subscriber/article/grove/music/05354.

38. Higdon, email, September 19, 2016.

39. Higdon, *Concerto 4-3*.

40. Higdon, program notes for *Concerto 4-3*.

41. Jennifer Higdon, email message to author, October 10, 2016.

42. Higdon, *Concerto 4-3*.

43. Higdon, email, September 19, 2016.

44. Higdon, *Concerto 4-3*.

45. Higdon, email, September 19, 2016.

46. Higdon, *Concerto 4-3*.

47. The year of *City Scape* is incorrect in this review; the work dates from 2002.

48. Lewis Whittington, "Orchestra Plays Higdon 'Concerto 4-3,'" *Broad Street Review,* January 13, 2008, http://www.broadstreetreview.com/music/Orchestra_plays_Higdon_Concerto_43 (accessed Sept. 13, 2016).

49. Joseph Dalton, "Three Weeks at Saratoga: From Argerich to Time for Three," *American Record Guide* Vol. 71, no. 6 (Nov. 2008): 9–12, Academic Search Complete, EBSCO host.

50. Andrew Druckenbrod, "Trio, PSO, Slatkin Make Beautiful Music," *Pittsburgh Post-Gazette*, Dec. 6, 2008, ProQuest Newsstand.

51. *Ibid.*

52. John von Rhein, "Higdon's Premiere a Blowout at Ravinia," *Chicago Tribune*, July 27, 2009, ProQuest Newsstand.

53. Lindsay Christians, "Terrific Time for Three Tears Up Capitol Theatre," *The Capital Times* (Madison, WI), March 5, 2011, ProQuest Newsstand.

54. Jeff Dunn, "The Newer Music Cure," *American Record Guide* Vol. 77, no. 6 (Nov/Dec 2014): 23–25, Academic Search Complete, EBSCO host.

55. Marin Alsop, "Time for Three-BSO Webumentary Series," YouTube Video, 3:03, posted by "Baltimoresymphonyorchestra," January 16, 2013, https://www.youtube.com/watch?v=W0Jp_V0sw5k (accessed January 15, 2015).
56. Anne Midgette, "Baltimore Symphony Orchestra Makes Itself at Home at Carnegie Festival: The Baltimore Symphony Orchestra Performs at Carnegie Hall's Creative Spring for Music Festival," *The Washington Post*, May 9, 2013, ProQuest Newsstand.
57. Tim Smith, "Alsop, BSO Deliver Diverse, Propulsive Program: Concert Review," *The Baltimore Sun*, May 4, 2013, ProQuest Newsstand.
58. Higdon, email, September 19, 2016.
59. Higdon's *Loco* also appears on the album.
60. *Take 6*, Miguel Harth-Bedoya (cond.), Fort Worth Symphony Orchestra, 2012, compact disc.

Chapter Six

1. Emily Cary, "Hilary Hahn, Philly Orchestra Reunite," *The Examiner* (Washington, D.C.), May 1, 2013, ProQuest Newsstand.
2. Jennifer Higdon, program notes for *Violin Concerto*, http://www.jenniferhigdon.com/pdf/program-notes/Violin-Concerto.pdf (accessed January 26, 2016).
3. Jennifer Higdon, "Hilary Hahn Interview Jennifer Higdon 1," YouTube Video, 6:43, posted by "Hilaryhahnvideos," February 9, 2009, https://www.youtube.com/watch?v=YRHR6NyVRAA (accessed January 27, 2016).
4. James Reel, "Every Composer's Dream," *Strings* Vol. 23, no.10 (May 2009): 34–37, ProQuest Central.
5. Ibid.
6. Ibid.
7. Higdon, "Hilary Hahn Interview Jennifer Higdon 1."
8. Max Brenton Harkey Williams, "Jennifer Higdon's *Violin Concerto: The* Genesis of a Twenty-First Century Work" (DM diss, Florida State University, 2010), 38.
9. Reel, "Every Composer's Dream."
10. James Reel, "STRINGS ATTACHED," *Strings* Vol. 23, no. 6 (Jan. 2009): 49–53, ProQuest Central.
11. David Patrick Stearns, "The Pulitzers: Top Honors for Daily News, Phila. Composer Curtis' Jennifer Higdon Took the Prize for 'Violin Concerto,'" *Philadelphia Inquirer*, April 13, 2010, ProQuest Newsstand.
12. Reel, "Every Composer's Dream."
13. Hilary Hahn, "Higdon & Tchaikovsky Concertos," YouTube Video, 9:44, posted by "Hilaryhahnvideos," Sept. 12, 2010, https://www.youtube.com/watch?v=GiO1oSKGTxY (Accessed January 26, 2016).
14. Williams, "Jennifer Higdon's *Violin Concerto: The* Genesis of a Twenty-First Century Work," 47.
15. Jennifer Higdon, email message to author, June 28, 2010.
16. Robert Raines, *Composition in the Digital World: Conversations with 21st Century American Composers* (New York: Oxford University Press, 2015), 122, books.google.com/books?id=wp_4BQAAQBAJ&dq=Cold+Mountain+Jennifer+Higdon&source=gbs_navlinks_s (accessed November 9, 2016).
17. Williams, "Jennifer Higdon's *Violin Concerto: The* Genesis of a Twenty-First Century Work," 38.
18. Jennifer Higdon, *Violin Concerto* (Philadelphia: Lawdon Press, 2008).
19. Cheryl Lawson, email message to author, June 8, 2015.
20. Harkey Williams, "Jennifer Higdon's *Violin Concerto*," 47.
21. Milena Pajaro-van de Stadt, "Onetime Teacher, Student Find Success as Composer, Violinist," YouTube Video, 6:51, posted by "PBS Newshour," October 8, 2010, https://www.youtube.com/watch?v=IuZEc9H6lgA (accessed January 26, 2016).
22. Hilary Hahn, "Rain, Rain," *Postcards from the Road*, http://hilaryhahn.com/2008/09/rain-rain/ (accessed March 16, 2016).
23. Benjamin Beilman, interview by Susan Lewis, "The Philadelphia Orchestra in Concert on WRTI: Benjamin Beilman, Higdon & Debussy, May 10, 1 pm," WRTI 90.1, http://wrti.org/post/philadelphia-orchestra-concert-wrti-benjamin-beilman-higdon-debussy-may-10-1-pm (accessed April 26, 2017).
24. Hilary Hahn, "Origins of This Album," Liner Notes, *Hilary Hahn Plays Higdon & Tchaikovsky Violin Concertos*, Vasily Petrenko (cond.), Royal Liverpool Philharmonic Orchestra, Deutsche Grammophon, B0014698–02, 2010, compact disc.
25. Higdon, program notes for *Violin Concerto*.
26. Ibid.
27. Harkey Williams, "Jennifer Higdon's *Violin Concerto*," 77.
28. Hahn, "Hilary Hahn Interview Jennifer Higdon 1."
29. Ibid.
30. Higdon, *Violin Concerto*.
31. Ibid.

32. *Ibid.*
33. This phrase originated with Higdon.
34. Raines, *Composition in the Digital World: Conversations with 21st Century American Composers*, 122.
35. Higdon, *Violin Concerto*.
36. Benjamin Beilman, interview by Susan Lewis, "The Philadelphia Orchestra in Concert on WRTI: Benjamin Beilman, Higdon & Debussy, May 10, 1pm."
37. Cheryl Lawson, email message to author, May 7, 2015.
38. Higdon, program notes for *Violin Concerto*.
39. Higdon, "Hilary Hahn Interview Jennifer Higdon 1."
40. Reel, "Every Composer's Dream."
41. Higdon, "Higdon & Tchaikovsky Concertos."
42. Tom Huizenga, "Jennifer Higdon Wins Music Pulitzer," npr.org, April 12, 2010, http://www.npr.org/templates/story/story.php?storyId=125872042 (accessed March 3, 2016).
43. Higdon, program notes for *Violin Concerto*.
44. Higdon, *Violin Concerto*.
45. *Ibid.* The listing of Mena of the Philadelphia premiere is not in the score, this information came from a press release available from: https://www.curtis.edu/resources/uploads/embeds/file/About%20Curtis/Press-Media%20Room/Curtis%20Symphony%20Orchestra%20Feb%2014%20&%2015%20Juanjo%20Mena%20and%20Hilary%20Hahn.pdf (accessed April 21, 2016).
46. Mary Ellyn Hutton, "Violin Concerto," *American Record Guide* Vol. 72, no. 3 (May 2009): 23–24, Academic Search Complete EBSCOhost.
47. Tim Smith, "Alsop Rock-Solid, Hahn Shows Bravura in Violin Concerto," *The Baltimore Sun*, June 6, 2009, ProQuest Newsstand.
48. Hilary Finch, "RLPO/Petrenko: First Night Concert," *The Times*, June 1, 2009, ProQuest Newsstand.
49. David Fanning, "Bewitching Blend to Tickle the Ear," *Daily Telegraph* (London), June 1, 2009, ProQuest Newsstand.
50. Jennifer Higdon, "Everyone Has to Find Their Own Voice," *Strad* 123 no. 1466 (June 2012): 34, Academic Search Complete, EBSCOhost.
51. Hahn, "Origins of This Album."
52. Lawrence Hansen, "Guide to Records—Higdon & Tchaikovsky: Violin Concertos," *American Record Guide* Vol. 74, no. 1 (Jan. 2011): 140–141, Academic Search Complete, EBSCOhost.
53. Geoff Brown, "Hilary Hahn Higdon/Tchaikovsky: Classical," *The Times* (London UK), Jan. 7, 2011, ProQuest Newsstand.
54. Anne Midgette, "Classical Music," *The Washington Post*, Dec. 19, 2010, ProQuest Newsstand.
55. Allan Kozinn, "Sound That's Lush and Slow, Speedy and Precise," *New York Times*, February 17, 2011, ProQuest Newsstand.
56. Seymour Topping with Sig Gissler, "History of the Pulitzer Prizes," The Pulitzer Prizes, http://www.pulitzer.org/page/history-pulitzer-prizes (accessed March 13, 2016).
57. Seymour Topping with Sig Gissler, "Administration of the Prizes," The Pulitzer Prizes, http://www.pulitzer.org/page/administration-prizes (accessed March 13, 2016).
58. "*Violin Concerto*, by Jennifer Higdon (Lawdon Press)," The Pulitzer Prizes, http://www.pulitzer.org/winners/jennifer-higdon (accessed March 13, 2016).
59. *Ibid.*
60. *Ibid.*
61. David Ng and Carolyn Kellogg, "THE PULITZERS; Awards Spur Shock and Aw, Shucks," *Los Angeles Times*, April 13, 2010, ProQuest Newsstand.
62. Huizenga, "Jennifer Higdon Wins Music Pulitzer."
63. David Patrick Stearns, "Higdon's New Concerto a Triumph, Times 6," *Philadelphia Inquirer*, June 8, 2010, ProQuest Newsstand.
64. The unnamed work refers to *Shine*, a 1995 co-commission by ASCAP and the Oregon Symphony; the late conductor's last name was spelled DePreist.
65. "ASCAP Composer Jennifer Higdon Wins 2010 Pulitzer Prize in Music for 'Violin Concerto,'" *Playback Magazine*, April 12, 2010, http://www.ascap.com/playback/2010/04/action/jenniferhigdon.aspx (accessed January 25, 2016).
66. Huizenga, "Jennifer Higdon Wins Music Pulitzer."
67. NewMusicBox Staff, "Jennifer Higdon Awarded 2010 Pulitzer Prize in Music," *NewMusicBox*, April 12, 2010, http://www.newmusicbox.org/articles/Jennifer-Higdon-Awarded-2010-Pulitzer-Prize-in-Music/ (accessed January 25, 2016).
68. Raines, *Composition in the Digital World: Conversations with 21st Century American Composers*, 122.
69. Jennifer Higdon, "Jennifer Higdon, by Hilary Hahn, for 'In 27 Pieces,'" YouTube Video, 16:56, posted by "Hilaryhahnvideos," January 31, 2012, https://www.youtube.com/watch?v=pu7PewnFGxo (accesses April 14, 2016).

70. Reel, "Every Composer's Dream."
71. "Concerts—Saturday, 28 February 2015," *Benjamin Beilman, Violinist,* http://benjaminbeilman.instantencore.com/web/events.aspx?date=2%2F28%2F2015 (accessed March 14, 2016).
72. "Concerts—Sunday, 12 July 2015," *Benjamin Beilman, Violinist,* http://benjaminbeilman.instantencore.com/web/events.aspx?date=7%2f12%2f2015 (accessed March 14, 2016).
73. "Barnett & Company Masterworks Series," *Chattanooga Symphony & Opera,* http://chattanoogasymphony.org/event/tchaikovskys-6th/ (accessed March 14, 2016).
74. Holly Mulcahy, "Concerto in Cocktail Form," *Neo Classical,* February 11, 2015, http://www.insidethearts.com/neoclassical/2015/02/concerto-in-cocktail-form/ (accessed March 14, 2016).
75. Calendar," Caroline Chin, Violin, http://www.carolineevachin.com/calendar.html (accessed Dec. 20, 2016).

Chapter Seven

1. Jennifer Higdon, interview by Marc A. Scorca, "Jennifer Higdon on Creating Cold Mountain," *OPERA America,* Sept. 29, 2015, https://medium.com/@OPERAAmerica/jennifer-higdon-on-creating-cold-mountain-ae1054a6623d (accessed November 10, 2016).
2. Cheryl Lawson and Jennifer Higdon, email message to author, December 12, 2015.
3. *Ibid.*
4. Charles MacKay, "Santa Fe Opera 2014 Press Conference," YouTube video, 47:11, posted by "The Santa Fe Opera," May 14, 2014, https://www.youtube.com/watch?v=gstRqu_I_qQ (accessed February 4, 2015).
5. Nathan Gunn, "Santa Fe Opera 2014 Press Conference," YouTube video, 47:11, posted by "The Santa Fe Opera," May 14, 2014, https://www.youtube.com/watch?v=gstRqu_I_qQ (accessed February 4, 2015).
6. MacKay, "Santa Fe Opera 2014 Press Conference."
7. David Patrick Stearns, "Opera's Gunn to Promote American Works in Philadelphia," *McClatchy-Tribune Business News,* Sept. 12, 2012, ProQuest Newsstand.
8. David Patrick Stearns, "Gunn Recital Bodes Well for Higdon Opera," *Philadelphia Inquirer,* April 24, 2013, ProQuest Newsstand.
9. Lawson and Higdon, email, December 12, 2015.
10. *Ibid.*
11. Rodney Punt, "Jennifer Higdon's Cold Mountain Has World Premiere at Santa Fe Opera," *San Francisco Classical Voice,* August 4, 2015, https://www.sfcv.org/reviews/-quot-None-quot-/Jennifer-Higdon-s-Cold-Mountain-Has-World-Premiere-at-Santa-Fe-Opera (accessed November 10, 2016).
12. David Patrick Stearns, "For OCP, a Brisk Pace and a Bold Repertoire," *Philadelphia Inquirer,* August 14, 2011, ProQuest Newsstand.
13. "In Memoriam," Santa Fe Opera 2015 Season Program Booklet, *Cold Mountain,* Santa Fe Opera, Santa Fe, New Mexico, 2015.
14. Jennifer Higdon, *Cold Mountain* (Philadelphia: Lawdon Press, 2012).
15. Bent Pen Music, Inc., "Moby-Dick (2010)," http://jakeheggie.com/moby-dick-2010/ (accessed November 9, 2015).
16. Lawson and Higdon, email, December 12, 2015.
17. Jonathan Richards, "Mountain Do: Stage Director Leonard Foglia," *Santa Fe New Mexican,* July 31, 2015, http://www.santafenewmexican.com/pasatiempo/opera/mountain-do-stage-director-leonard-foglia/article_be8cc5ea-c586-515e-9860-16097fb28ada.html (accessed November 10, 2016).
18. Jeffrey Brown, "Civil War Tragedy 'Cold Mountain' Inspires Opera," pbs.org, http://www.pbs.org/newshour/bb/civil-war-tragedy-cold-mountain-inspires-opera/ (accessed November 13, 2015).
19. Cheryl Lawson and Jennifer Higdon, email message to author, July 16, 2016.
20. Jennifer Higdon, interview by Susan Lewis, "Jennifer Higdon's Opera 'Cold Mountain,' and Its East Coast Premiere," WRTI 90.1, http://wrti.org/post/jennifer-higdons-opera-cold-mountain-and-its-east-coast-premiere (accessed November 10, 2016).
21. Lawson and Higdon, email, December 12, 2015.
22. Gregory Sullivan Isaacs, "Miguel Harth-Bedoya Brings Jennifer Higdon's Music to Life in 'Cold Mountain,'" *Star-Telegram* (Fort Worth, TX), August 5, 2015, http://www.star-telegram.com/entertainment/arts-culture/article30037590.html (accessed November 10, 2016).
23. Jennifer Higdon, interview by Jim Cotter, "Jennifer Higdon on Cold Mountain," WRTI 90.1, http://wrti.org/post/jennifer-higdon-cold-mountain (accessed November 10, 2016).
24. Paul Ingles, "'Cold Mountain' Takes Civil War Odyssey to the Opera Stage," *National Public Radio,* http://www.npr.org/sections/deceptivecadence/2015/08/05/429370329/cold-mountain-takes-civil-war-odyssey-to-the-opera-stage (accessed August 5, 2015).

25. Charles Frazier, "Works & Process at the Guggenheim: Santa Fe Opera: Cold Mountain with Jennifer Higdon," YouTube video, 1:09:23, posted by "Works & Process at the Guggenheim," April 7, 2015, https://www.youtube.com/watch?v=6ObRKcZhuSs (accessed December 10, 2015).
26. Ibid.
27. Charles Frazier, interview by Michael Edward Miller, "Celebration of Southern Literature: What Charles Frazier Thinks of 'Cold Mountain' Opera," WUTC, http://wutc.org/post/celebration-southern-literature-what-charles-frazier-thinks-cold-mountain-opera (accessed November 10, 2016).
28. Higdon, "Santa Fe Opera 2014 Press Conference."
29. Higdon, interview by Jim Cotter, "Jennifer Higdon on Cold Mountain."
30. Lawson and Higdon, email, December 12, 2015.
31. Higdon, "Works & Process at the Guggenheim: Santa Fe Opera: Cold Mountain with Jennifer Higdon."
32. Jackie Jadrnak, "Popular Culture Leaps to High Culture," *Albuquerque Journal*, June 12, 2015, http://www.abqjournal.com/597617/entertainment/popular-culture-leaps-to-high-culture.html (accessed November 10, 2016).
33. Burdette had planned to use his own instrument in the premiere but because Brill's set was an abstract, layered design, it was considered too dangerous to risk tripping and possibly damaging his instrument so another was brought in.—Lawson and Higdon, email, December 12, 2015.
34. Stearns, "For OCP, a Brisk Pace and a Bold Repertoire."
35. Bill Kohlhaase, "Scaling New Heights: Cold Mountain Composer Jennifer Higdon," *Santa Fe New Mexican*, July 31, 2015, http://www.santafenewmexican.com/pasatiempo/opera/scaling-new-heights-cold-mountain-composer-jennifer-higdon/article_61bd37ae-e184-52bd-afce-977c216bf365.html (accessed November 10, 2016).
36. Lawson and Higdon, email, December 12, 2015.
37. Ingles, "'Cold Mountain' Takes Civil War Odyssey to the Opera Stage."
38. Maren Larsen, "Accented Arias: Jennifer Higdon on Opera, *Star Wars*, and Adapting *Cold Mountain* for the Stage," *The Smart Set,* March 10, 2016, http://thesmartset.com/accented-arias/ (accessed April 8, 2016).
39. Peter Crimmins, "'Cold Mountain' Finds Fresh Voice with Opera Philadelphia," *news works.com*, February 3, 2016, http://www.newsworks.org/index.php/local/item/90702-cold-mountain-finds-voice-with-opera-philadelphia (accessed February 5, 2016).
40. Charles Frazier, "The 'Cold Mountain' Opera" from *RadioTimes*, Marty Moss-Coane, host, *WHYY Public Media*, February 2, 2016, http://whyy.org/cms/radiotimes/2016/02/02/34685/ (accessed February 3, 2016).
41. Gene Scheer, "Ascending Cold Mountain," Santa Fe Opera 2015 Season Program Booklet, *Cold Mountain*, Santa Fe Opera, Santa Fe, New Mexico, 2015.
42. Philip Kennicott, "Mountain Time," *Opera News*, June 2015, Vol. 79, no. 12, http://www.operanews.com/Opera_News_Magazine/2015/6/Features/Mountain_Time.html (accessed November 10, 2016).
43. Steve Kemple, "Modern Composition," *Library Journal*, 139, no. 20 (2014): 1, Academic Search Complete, EBSCO host.
44. "COLD MOUNTAIN Preview | Opera Philadelphia," YouTube video, 4:14, posted by "Opera Philadelphia," February 17, 2015, https://www.youtube.com/watch?v=lGLUISHZL00 (accessed December 10, 2015).
45. Higdon, interview by Marc A. Scorca, "Jennifer Higdon on Creating Cold Mountain."
46. Lawson and Higdon, email, July 16, 2016.
47. Lawson and Higdon, email, December 12, 2015.
48. Ibid.
49. Lawson and Higdon, email, July 16, 2016.
50. Kennicott, "Mountain Time."
51. David Patrick Stearns, "Jennifer Higdon's 'Cold Mountain [Sic] Turns the Epic Novel into Opera," *TCA Regional News*, April 5, 2015, ProQuest Newsstand.
52. Higdon, interview by Marc A. Scorca, "Jennifer Higdon on Creating Cold Mountain."
53. Lawson and Higdon, email, December 12, 2015.
54. Jennifer Higdon interview by Hilary Hahn, "Jennifer Higdon, by Hilary Hahn, for 'In 27 Pieces,'" YouTube video, 16:56, posted by "Hilaryhahnvideos," January 31, 2012, https://www.youtube.com/watch?v=pu7PewnFGxo (accessed January 7, 2016).
55. Philip Kennicott, "Mountain Time."
56. Ibid.
57. Larsen, "Accented Arias: Jennifer Higdon on Opera, *Star Wars*, and Adapting *Cold Mountain* for the Stage."
58. Higdon, interview by Jim Cotter, "Jennifer Higdon on Cold Mountain."
59. Arlene and Larry Dunn, "5 Questions to Jennifer Higdon (Composer)," *I Care If You Lis-*

ten, http://www.icareifyoulisten.com/2015/03/5-questions-jennifer-higdon-composer/ (accessed November 9, 2015).

60. Higdon, interview by Jim Cotter, "Jennifer Higdon on Cold Mountain."

61. Higdon, interview by Marc A. Scorca, "Jennifer Higdon on Creating Cold Mountain."

62. Jennifer Higdon, "Jennifer Higdon—On Composing Music," YouTube video, 3:14, posted by "UALRTV," March 11, 2013, https://www.youtube.com/watch?v=C5dpEIXpPT4 (accessed January 24, 2015).

63. Kohlhaase, "Scaling New Heights: Cold Mountain Composer Jennifer Higdon."

64. Lawson and Higdon, email, December 12, 2015.

65. Jennifer Higdon, "Cabrillo Festival of Contemporary Music-Meet the Composers 2014," YouTube video, 1:05:51, posted by "CTV Santa Cruz County," September 8, 2014, https://www.youtube.com/watch?v=GyJbRbnA_54 (accessed January 26, 2015).

66. Higdon interview by Hilary Hahn, "Jennifer Higdon, by Hilary Hahn, for 'In 27 Pieces.'"

67. Lawson and Higdon, email, December 12, 2015.

68. Cheryl Lawson, email message to author, July 8, 2015.

69. Lawson and Higdon, email, December 12, 2015.

70. Ibid.

71. Heidi Waleson, "Creating Cold Mountain: Student Singers Help to Shape a Major Modern Opera," *Overtones*, Spring 2014, http://www.curtis.edu/about-curtis/press-media-room/overtones-1/past-issues/ (accessed February 19, 2015).

72. Lawson and Higdon, email, December 12, 2015.

73. Ibid.

74. Charles Frazier, "COLD MOUNTAIN Preview | Opera Philadelphia."

75. Charles Frazier interview by Jennifer Lynn, "One Book, One Philadelphia Kickoff Event Featuring Charles Frazier, Jennifer Higdon, and Performances from Opera Philadelphia and the Curtis Institute of Music," *Free Library Podcast*, http://tunein.com/topic/?topicId=103433870&utm_source=tiEmbed&utm_medium=referral&utm_content=t103433870 (accessed February 10, 2016).

76. Lawson and Higdon, email, December 12, 2015.

77. Waleson, "Creating Cold Mountain: Student Singers Help to Shape a Major Modern Opera."

78. Ibid.

79. Stearns, "Jennifer Higdon's 'Cold Mountain [Sic] Turns the Epic Novel into Opera."

80. Waleson, "Creating Cold Mountain: Student Singers Help to Shape a Major Modern Opera."

81. The Orion duet was the scene moved to occur earlier in Act II. Lawson and Higdon, email, December 12, 2015.

82. Higdon, interview by Marc A. Scorca, "Jennifer Higdon on Creating Cold Mountain."

83. Jennifer Higdon, "Jennifer Higdon's Cold Mountain," WFMT 98.7, May 9, 2015, http://blogs.wfmt.com/relevanttones/2015/05/09/jennifer-higdons-cold-mountain/ (accessed November 10, 2016).

84. Stearns, "Jennifer Higdon's 'Cold Mountain [Sic] Turns the Epic Novel into Opera."

85. Tom Rescigno, "Biography," http://eriemills.com/ (accessed December 14, 2015).

86. Lawson and Higdon, email, December 12, 2015.

87. Jackie Jadrnak, "New Mexico History Museum Shows Cased Photographs and Other Civil War Artifacts," *Albuquerque Journal*, April 24, 2015, https://www.abqjournal.com/574272/new-mexico-history-museum-shows-cased-photographs-and-other-civil-war-artifacts.html (accessed November 10, 2016).

88. Jennifer Higdon, email message to author, August 9, 2016.

89. David Patrick Stearns, "New Operas Highlight a Longstanding Divide," *Philadelphia Inquirer*, August 23, 2015, http://www.philly.com/philly/columnists/david_patrick_stearns/20150823_New_operas_highlight_a_longstanding_divide.html (accessed November 10, 2016).

90. T.R. Reid, "Santa Fe Opera Breathes New Life into Epic Civil War Tale 'Cold Mountain,'" *The Washington Post*, August 16, 2015, http://www.washingtonpost.com/entertainment/music/santa-fe-opera-breathes-new-life-into-epic-civil-war-tale-cold-mountain/2015/08/16/c21ce65e-444c-11e5-8ab4-c73967a143d3_story.html (accessed November 10, 2016).

91. James M. Keller, "Cold Mountain Opera Review: Long-Lost Love Among the Ruins," *Santa Fe New Mexican*, August 2, 2015, http://www.santafenewmexican.com/news/local_news/cold-mountain-opera-review-long-lost-love-among-the-ruins/article_0a701696-2671-5d57-bb71-121d8e05864b.html (accessed November 10, 2016).

92. Ray Mark Rinaldi, "Santa Fe Opera Ascends with Jennifer Higdon's 'Cold Mountain,'" *Denver Post*, August 4, 2015, http://www.denverpost.com/entertainment/ci_28582823/santa-fe-

opera-ascends-jennifer-higdons-cold-mountain?source=infinite (accessed November 10, 2016).

93. *Ibid.*

94. David Patrick Stearns, "Review: Higdon's New Opera, Cold Mountain, at Santa Fe," Phillywww, August 3, 2015, http://www.philly.com/philly/entertainment/20150803_Review__Higdon_s_new_opera__Cold_Mountain__at_Santa_Fe.html (accessed November 10, 2016).

95. Keller, "Cold Mountain Opera Review: Long-Lost Love Among the Ruins."

96. Rinaldi, "Santa Fe Opera Ascends with Jennifer Higdon's 'Cold Mountain.'"

97. David Patrick Stearns, "What 'Cold Mountain' Gets Right," *TCA Regional News*, August 9, 2015, ProQuest Newsstand.

98. Terry Ponick, "Higdon's 'Cold Mountain' Scores Big Time for Santa Fe Opera," *Communities Digital News*, August 9, 2015, http://www.commdiginews.com/entertainment/higdons-cold-mountain-scores-big-time-for-santa-fe-opera-46415/ (accessed November 11, 2016).

99. T.R. Reid, "Santa Fe Opera Breathes New Life into Epic Civil War Tale 'Cold Mountain.'"

100. Punt, "Jennifer Higdon's Cold Mountain Has World Premiere at Santa Fe Opera."

101. Stearns, "What 'Cold Mountain' Gets Right."

102. William Burnett, "World Premiere Review: All-Star Cast and Crew, Ardent Audience Ovation for Higdon's 'Cold Mountain'–Santa Fe Opera, August 1, 2015," Opera Warhorses, http://www.operawarhorses.com/2015/08/03/world-premiere-review-all-star-cast-and-crew-ardent-audience-ovation-for-higdons-cold-mountain-santa-fe-opera-august-1-2015/ (accessed August 3, 2015).

103. Greg Hettmansberger, "Sampling Perennial Desert Blooms, Part II," *Madison Magazine*, August 20, 2015, http://www.channel3000.com/madison-magazine/arts-culture/Sampling-Perennial-Desert-Blooms-Part-II/34822898 (accessed November 11, 2016).

104. Ponick, "Higdon's 'Cold Mountain' Scores Big Time for Santa Fe Opera."

105. Punt, "Jennifer Higdon's Cold Mountain Has World Premiere at Santa Fe Opera."

106. Lawson and Higdon, email, July 16, 2016.

107. Lawson and Higdon, email, December 12, 2015.

108. Higdon, interview by Susan Lewis, "Jennifer Higdon's Opera 'Cold Mountain,' and Its East Coast Premiere."

109. Lewis Whittington, "Higdon: Cold Mountain Opera Philadelphia," *American Record Guide* Vol. 79, no. 3 (May/June 2016): 39–40, Academic Search Complete, EBSCO host.

110. David Shengold, "Cold Mountain," *Opera News*, February 7, 2016, 2015, Vol. 80, no. 8, http://www.operanews.com/Opera_News_Magazine/2016/2/Reviews/PHILADELPHIA__Cold_Mountain.html (accessed November 11, 2016).

111. *Ibid.*

112. Peter Dobrin, "'Cold Mountain' Stirring, If Not Inspired," *Philadelphia Inquirer*, February 7, 2016, ProQuest Newsstand.

113. Philip Kennicott, "CORIGLIANO the Ghosts of Versailles. HIGDON Cold Mountain," *Gramophone,* http://www.gramophone.co.uk/review/corigliano-the-ghosts-of-versailles-higdon-cold-mountain (accessed May 24, 2016).

114. "Jennifer Higdon-Cold Mountain," PENTATONE, http://www.pentatonemusic.com/jennifer-higdon-cold-mountain-santa-fe-opera-orchestra (accessed May 6, 2016).

115. David Patrick Stearns, "Civil War Epic Deserves the Love: Opera Has Its Mainstream Hit—'Cold Mountain' Delivers on Nearly Every Level," *Philadelphia Inquirer*, August 9, 2015, ProQuest Newsstand.

116. T.R. Reid, "Santa Fe Opera Breathes New Life into Epic Civil War Tale 'Cold Mountain.'"

117. Naomi Lewin, "Contemporary Opera: Pleasing Both Connoisseurs and the Masses?" *Conducting Business,* August 31, 2015, http://www.wqxr.org/#!/story/contemporary-opera-pleasing-both-connoisseurs-and-masses/ (accessed November 11, 2016).

Chapter Eight

1. Jennifer Higdon, *Cold Mountain* (Philadelphia: Lawdon Press, 2012).

2. Jennifer Higdon, email message to author, August 9, 2016.

3. Higdon, *Cold Mountain*.

4. Cheryl Lawson and Jennifer Higdon, email message to author, December 12, 2015.

5. Jennifer Higdon, interview by Adam Pangburn, "Creative Team and Cast," *Cold Mountain—Opera Philadelphia*, Lily Kass and Michael Bolton, eds., Drexel University, Blackboard Online (accessed May 9, 2016).

6. Maren Larsen, "Accented Arias: Jennifer Higdon on Opera, *Star Wars*, and Adapting *Cold Mountain for the* Stage," *The Smart Set*, March 10, 2016, http://thesmartset.com/accented-arias/ (accessed April 8, 2016).

7. Bill Kohlhaase, "Scaling New Heights: Cold Mountain Composer Jennifer Higdon," *Santa Fe New Mexican*, July 31, 2015, http://www.santafenewmexican.com/pasatiempo/opera/scaling-new-heights-cold-mountain-composer-jennifer-higdon/article_61bd37ae-e184-52bd-afce-977c216bf365.html (accessed November 11, 2016).

8. Charles Frazier interview by Jennifer Lynn, "One Book, One Philadelphia Kickoff Event Featuring Charles Frazier, Jennifer Higdon, and Performances from Opera Philadelphia and the Curtis Institute of Music," *Free Library Podcast*, http://tunein.com/topic/?topicId=103433870&utm_source=tiEmbed&utm_medium=referral&utm_content=t103433870 (accessed February 10, 2016).

9. Larsen, "Accented Arias: Jennifer Higdon on Opera, *Star Wars*, and Adapting *Cold Mountain for the* Stage."

10. Jennifer Higdon interview by Phil Oliver, "Jennifer Higdon Writes an Opera," *The Musicalist Podcast*, http://themusicalist.net/jennifer-higdon/ (accessed May 31, 2016).

11. Higdon, email, August 9, 2016.

12. Higdon, *Cold Mountain*.

13. Jennifer Higdon, interview by Jim Cotter, "Jennifer Higdon on Cold Mountain," WRTI 90.1, http://wrti.org/post/jennifer-higdon-cold-mountain (accessed November 10, 2016).

14. Jennifer Higdon, "COLD MOUNTAIN Preview | Opera Philadelphia," YouTube video, 4:14, posted by "Opera Philadelphia," February 17, 2015, https://www.youtube.com/watch?v=lGLUISHZL00 (accessed December 10, 2015).

15. Philip Kennicott, "Mountain Time," *Opera News*, June 2015, Vol. 79, no. 12, http://www.operanfews.com/Opera_News_Magazine/2015/6/Features/Mountain_Time.html (accessed November 10, 2016).

16. Jennifer Higdon interview by Jennifer Lynn, "One Book, One Philadelphia Kickoff Event Featuring Charles Frazier, Jennifer Higdon, and Performances from Opera Philadelphia and the Curtis Institute of Music."

17. Cheryl Lawson and Jennifer Higdon, email message to author, August 27, 2016.

18. Jennifer Higdon, "Santa Fe Opera 2014 Press Conference," YouTube video, 47:11, posted by "The Santa Fe Opera," May 14, 2014, https://www.youtube.com/watch?v=gstRqu_I_qQ (accessed February 4, 2015).

19. Jay Hunter Morris, "Jennifer Higdon's Cold Mountain," WFMT 98.7, May 9, 2015, http://blogs.wfmt.com/relevanttones/2015/05/09/jennifer-higdons-cold-mountain/ (accessed November 10, 2016).

20. Lawson and Higdon, email, December 12, 2015.

21. Jennifer Higdon, interview by Susan Lewis, "Jennifer Higdon's Opera 'Cold Mountain,' and Its East Coast Premiere," WRTI 90.1, http://wrti.org/post/jennifer-higdons-opera-cold-mountain-and-its-east-coast-premiere (accessed November 10, 2016); Higdon and Lawson, email, August 27, 2016.

22. Lawson and Higdon, email, December 12, 2015.

23. Higdon, interview by Susan Lewis, "Jennifer Higdon's Opera 'Cold Mountain,' and Its East Coast Premiere."

24. Lawson and Higdon, email, December 12, 2015.

25. Bill Kohlhaase, "Scaling New Heights: Cold Mountain Composer Jennifer Higdon."

26. Higdon, interview by Susan Lewis, "Jennifer Higdon's Opera 'Cold Mountain,' and Its East Coast Premiere."

27. Higdon interview by Jennifer Lynn, "One Book, One Philadelphia Kickoff Event Featuring Charles Frazier, Jennifer Higdon, and Performances from Opera Philadelphia and the Curtis Institute of Music."; Higdon and Lawson, email, August 27, 2016.

28. Higdon interview by Phil Oliver, "Jennifer Higdon Writes an Opera."

29. Gene Scheer and Jennifer Higdon, *Cold Mountain* (Philadelphia: Lawdon Press, 2012).

30. *Ibid.*
31. *Ibid.*
32. *Ibid.*
33. Higdon, email, August 9, 2016.
34. Gene Scheer and Jennifer Higdon, *Cold Mountain*.
35. *Ibid.*
36. *Ibid.*
37. *Ibid.*
38. *Ibid.*
39. *Ibid.*
40. *Ibid.*
41. *Ibid.*
42. *Ibid.*
43. *Ibid.*
44. *Ibid.*
45. *Ibid.*
46. *Ibid.*
47. Richard L. Crocker. "Melisma." *Grove Music Online. Oxford Music Online.* Oxford University Press, accessed June 4, 2016, http://0-www.oxfordmusiconline.wncln.wncln.org/subscriber/article/grove/music/18332.

48. Gene Scheer and Jennifer Higdon, *Cold Mountain*.
49. *Ibid.*
50. *Ibid.*
51. *Ibid.*

52. *Ibid.*
53. *Ibid.*
54. *Ibid.*
55. *Ibid.*
56. Higdon, email, August 9, 2016.
57. The opening of the score refers to the three sisters as 3 Sisters/Sirens and their return in Act II's ensemble number "Tell Her" lists them simply as Sirens.
58. Gene Scheer and Jennifer Higdon, *Cold Mountain*.
59. *Ibid.*
60. Maria Murphy, "Musical Analysis What Do You Hear?" *Cold Mountain—Opera Philadelphia*, Lily Kass and Michael Bolton, eds., Drexel University, Blackboard Online (accessed May 9, 2016).
61. Gene Scheer, "Works & Process at the Guggenheim: Santa Fe Opera: Cold Mountain with Jennifer Higdon," YouTube video, 1:09:23, posted by "Works & Process at the Guggenheim," April 7, 2015, https://www.youtube.com/watch?v=6ObRKcZhuSs (accessed December 10, 2015).
62. Gene Scheer and Jennifer Higdon, *Cold Mountain*.
63. Higdon and Lawson, email, August 27, 2016.
64. Jennifer Higdon, "Works & Process at the Guggenheim: Santa Fe Opera: Cold Mountain with Jennifer Higdon."
65. Jennifer Higdon, "The 'Cold Mountain' Opera" from *RadioTimes*, Marty Moss-Coane, host, *WHYY Public Media*, February 2, 2016, http://whyy.org/cms/radiotimes/2016/02/02/34685/ (accessed February 3, 2016).
66. Gene Scheer and Jennifer Higdon, *Cold Mountain*.
67. Scheer, "Works & Process at the Guggenheim: Santa Fe Opera: Cold Mountain with Jennifer Higdon."
68. Leonard Foglia, "Works & Process at the Guggenheim: Santa Fe Opera: Cold Mountain with Jennifer Higdon."
69. Gene Scheer and Jennifer Higdon, *Cold Mountain*.
70. *Ibid.*
71. Higdon, email, August 9, 2016.
72. Higdon interview by Phil Oliver, "Jennifer Higdon Writes an Opera."
73. Gene Scheer and Jennifer Higdon, *Cold Mountain*.
74. Lily Kass, "Musical Analysis: Orion … Orion," *Cold Mountain—Opera Philadelphia*, Lily Kass and Michael Bolton, eds., Drexel University, Blackboard Online (accessed May 9, 2016).
75. Gene Scheer and Jennifer Higdon, *Cold Mountain*.
76. *Ibid.*
77. Jennifer Higdon, "Jennifer Higdon's Cold Mountain."
78. The trumpet is unnecessary in Act II, its function in Act I introduced Inman.
79. Gene Scheer and Jennifer Higdon, *Cold Mountain*.
80. *Ibid.*
81. Higdon, email, August 9, 2016.
82. Gene Scheer and Jennifer Higdon, *Cold Mountain*.
83. Higdon, "The 'Cold Mountain' Opera."
84. Higdon, *Cold Mountain*.
85. This is comparable to the instructions in Higdon's *Violin Concerto* (Figure 6–2). Similar notation was found here and also in *Concerto 4–3*; Higdon, *Cold Mountain*.
86. Higdon, *Cold Mountain*.
87. Gene Scheer and Jennifer Higdon, *Cold Mountain*.
88. Higdon, *Cold Mountain*.

Codetta

1. At the time of this writing (January 2018), the text and the new song has not yet been composed.
2. Cheryl Lawson, e-mail message to author, January 25, 2018.
3. *Ibid.*

Bibliography

Anthony, Michael. "Composing an Ode to the Oboe; Prolific Composer Jennifer Higdon Muses on Writing Her Latest Concerto, a Premiere by the St. Paul Chamber Orchestra." *Star Tribune* (Minneapolis, MN). September 4, 2005. ProQuest Newsstand.

"ASCAP Composer Jennifer Higdon Wins 2010 Pulitzer Prize in Music for 'Violin Concerto.'" *Playback Magazine*, April 12, 2010. Accessed January 25, 2016. http://www.ascap.com/playback/2010/04/action/jenniferhigdon.aspx.

Battey, Robert. "From NSO, the Energy of a 'City.'" *The Washington Post*. May 18, 2007. ProQuest Newsstand.

"Battuto." *Grove Music Online. Oxford Music Online*. Oxford University Press. http://0-www.oxfordmusiconline.com.wncln.wncln.org/subscriber/article/grove/music/02337.

Blades, James, et al. "Gong." *Grove Music Online. Oxford Music Online*. Oxford University Press. http:// 0-www.oxfordmusiconline.com.wncln.wncln.org/subscriber/article/grove/music/42877.

Broffitt, Virginia. "The Music of Jennifer Higdon: Perspectives on the Styles and Compositional Approaches in Selected Chamber Compositions." DMA document, University of Cincinnati, 2010.

Brown, Geoff. "Hilary Hahn Higdon/Tchaikovsky: Classical." *The Times* (London, UK). Jan. 7, 2011. ProQuest Newsstand.

Brown, Jeffrey. "Civil War Tragedy 'Cold Mountain' Inspires Opera." *Pbs.Org*, August 5, 2015. Accessed November 13, 2015. http://www.pbs.org/newshour/bb/civil-war-tragedy-cold-mountain-inspires-opera/.

Burnett, William. "World Premiere Review: All-Star Cast and Crew, Ardent Audience Ovation for Higdon's 'Cold Mountain'—Santa Fe Opera, August 1, 2015." *Opera Warhorses*, August 3, 2015. Accessed August 3, 2015. http://www.operawarhorses.com/2015/08/03/world-premiere-review-all-star-cast-and-crew-ardent-audience-ovation-for-higdons-cold-mountain-santa-fe-opera-august-1–2015/.

"Cabrillo Festival of Contemporary Music-Meet the Composers 2014." YouTube video, 1:05:51. Posted by "CTV Santa Cruz County," September 8, 2014. https://www.youtube.com/watch?v=GyJbRbnA_54.

Cary, Emily. "Hilary Hahn, Philly Orchestra Reunite." *The Examiner* (Washington, D.C.). May 1, 2013. ProQuest Newsstand.

Christians, Lindsay. "Terrific Time for Three Tears Up Capitol Theatre." *The Capital Times* (Madison, WI). March 5, 2011. ProQuest Newsstand.

Clark, Andrew. "BBC Symphony/Slatkin Barbican, London ANDREW CLARK THE CRITICS: [LONDON 1st EDITION]." *Financial Times* (London, UK). April 8, 2004. ProQuest Newsstand.

"COLD MOUNTAIN Preview | Opera Philadelphia." YouTube video, 4:14. Posted by "Opera Philadelphia," February 17, 2015. https://www.youtube.com/watch?v=lGLUISHZL00.

"Composing Thoughts, Part7." YouTube video, 4:35. Posted by "John Clare," March 25, 2008. https://www.youtube.com/watch?v=txf_mYWUycU.

"Conference 2010: Atlanta School of Composers." YouTube video, 1:12:18. Posted by "Leagueamer," July 1, 2010. https://www.youtube.com/watch?v=aWtZIuxILSc.

Cotter, Jim. "Jennifer Higdon on Cold Mountain." *WRTI 90.1*. November 16, 2012. http://wrti.org/post/jennifer-higdon-cold-mountain.

Crimmins, Peter. "'Cold Mountain' Finds Fresh Voice with Opera Philadelphia." *news works.com*, February 3, 2016. Accessed February 5, 2016. http://www.newsworks.org/index.php/local/item/90702-cold-mountain-finds-voice-with-opera-philadelphia.

Crocker. Richard L. "Melisma." *Grove Music Online. Oxford Music Online*. Oxford University Press. http://www.oxfordmusiconline.com.proxy195.nclive.org/subscriber/article/grove/music/18332.

Dalton, Joseph. "Three Weeks at Saratoga: From Argerich to Time for Three." *American Record Guide* 71, no. 6 (Nov. 2008): 9–12. Academic Search Complete, EBSCOhost.

Dobrin, Peter. "'Cold Mountain' Stirring, If Not Inspired." *Philadelphia Inquirer*. February 7, 2016. ProQuest Newsstand.

Druckenbrod, Andrew. "Classical Musicians Break from the Mold." *Pittsburgh Post-Gazette*. Dec. 3, 2008. ProQuest Newsstand.

———. "Composer Making Music History." *Pittsburgh Post-Gazette*. November 2, 2005. ProQuest Newsstand.

———. "Higdon Poured Grief into blue cathedral." *Pittsburgh Post-Gazette*. November 2, 2005. ProQuest Newsstand.

———. "Trio, PSO, Slatkin Make Beautiful Music." *Pittsburgh Post-Gazette*. Dec. 6, 2008. ProQuest Newsstand.

Dunn, Arlene, and Larry Dunn. "5 Questions to Jennifer Higdon (Composer)." *I Care If You Listen*, March 3, 2015. Accessed November 9, 2015. http://www.icareifyoulisten.com/2015/03/5-questions-jennifer-higdon-composer/.

Dunn, Jeff. "The Newer Music Cure." *American Record Guide* Vol. 77, no. 6 (Nov/Dec 2014): 23–25. Academic Search Complete, EBSCO host.

———. "Warhorseless." *San Francisco Classical Voice*, December 6, 2003. Accessed January 13, 2016. http://www.sfcv.org/arts_revs/starosasym_12_9_03.php.

Dyer, Richard. "Composer Has Emotional Reach, Direct Appeal Jennifer Higdon Touches Many with Her Work." *The Boston Globe*. July 13, 2003. ProQuest Newsstand.

"Episode 37-Jennifer Higdon- Part 01." YouTube video, 14:59. Posted by "Thedrexelinterview," June 15, 2011. https://www.youtube.com/watch?v=9rKLA_q4aJA.

Fanning, David. "Bewitching Blend to Tickle the Ear." *Daily Telegraph* (London). June 1, 2009. ProQuest Newsstand.

Finch, Hilary. "RLPO/Petrenko: First Night Concert." *The Times*. June 1, 2009. ProQuest Newsstand.

French, Gilbert. "Rainbow Body." *American Record Guide* Vol. 66, no. 5 (Sep/Oct 2003): 209–210. Academic Search Complete, EBSCOhost.

Gambone, Philip. *Travels in a Gay Nation: Portraits of LGBTQ Americans*. Madison: The University of Wisconsin Press, 2010. http://site.ebrary.com/lib/hunter/reader.action?docID=10381815.

Gresham, Mark. "Sounds Like Home." *Creative Loafing*, November 13, 2002. Accessed November 8, 2016. http://www.clatl.com/home/article/13009858/sounds-like-home.

Hahn, Hilary. "Origins of This Album," Liner Notes to *Hilary Hahn Plays Higdon & Tchaikovsky Violin Concertos*. Vasily Petrenko (cond.), Royal Liverpool Philharmonic Orchestra. Deutsche Grammophon B0014698–02. CD. 2010.

Hansen, Lawrence. "Guide to Records—Higdon & Tchaikovsky: Violin Concertos." *American Record Guide* Vol. 74, no. 1 (Jan/Feb 2011): 140–141. Academic Search Complete, EBSCOhost.

Hettmansberger, Greg. "Sampling Perennial Desert Blooms, Part II." *Madison Magazine*, August 20, 2015. Accessed November 11, 2016. http://www.channel3000.com/madison-magazine/arts-and-culture/sampling-perennial-desert-blooms-part-ii/158224250.

Higdon, Jennifer. *blue cathedral*. Philadelphia: Lawdon Press, 1999.

———. *City Scape*. Philadelphia: Lawdon Press, 2002.

———. *Cold Mountain*. Philadelphia: Lawdon Press, 2012.

———. *Concerto for Orchestra*. Philadelphia: Lawdon Press, 2002.

———. *Concerto 4–3*. Philadelphia: Lawdon Press, 2007.

———. "Everyone Has to Find Their Own Voice." *Strad* 123 no. 1466 (June 2012): 34. Academic Search Complete, EBSCOhost.

———. Liner Notes to *Rainbow Body*. Robert

Spano (cond.), Atlanta Symphony Orchestra. Telarc 80596. CD. 2004.

———. Liner Notes to *Take 6*. Miguel Harth-Bedoya (cond.), Fort Worth Symphony Orchestra. CD. 2012.

———. Program notes for *City Scape*. Accessed January 15, 2016. http://www.jenniferhigdon.com/pdf/program-notes/City-Scape.pdf.

———. Program notes for *Concerto for Orchestra*. Accessed October 22, 2016. http://www.jenniferhigdon.com/pdf/program-notes/concerto-for-orchestra.pdf.

———. Program notes for *Concerto 4–3*. Accessed April 21, 2016. http://www.jenniferhigdon.com/pdf/program-notes/Concerto-4-3.pdf.

———. Program notes for *Violin Concerto*. Accessed January 26, 2016. http://www.jenniferhigdon.com/pdf/program-notes/Violin-Concerto.pdf.

———. "Publishing, Self-Publishing, and the Internet." From the Women's Philharmonic's "Composing a Career" Symposium. *NewMusicBox*, February 1, 2000. Accessed November 7, 2016. http://www.newmusicbox.org/article.nmbx?id=537.

———. *Violin Concerto*. Philadelphia: Lawdon Press, 2008.

"Higdon and Rachmaninoff." YouTube Video, 6:36. Posted by "The Phoenix Symphony," March 4, 2009. https://www.youtube.com/watch?v=R2DPLW4v8WM.

"Higdon & Tchaikovsky Concertos." YouTube Video, 9:44. Posted by "Hilaryhahnvideos," Sept. 12, 2010. https://www.youtube.com/watch?v=GiO1oSKGTxY.

"Hilary Hahn Interview Jennifer Higdon 1." YouTube Video, 6:43. Posted by "Hilaryhahnvideos," February 9, 2009. https://www.youtube.com/watch?v=YRHR6NyVRAA.

"HIlary [Sic] Hahn Interviews Jennifer Higdon 2." YouTube video, 6:22. Posted by "Hilaryhahnvideos," February 9, 2009. https://www.youtube.com/watch?v=AWGhLPEblR4.'

Huizenga, Tom. "Jennifer Higdon Wins Music Pulitzer." *Npr.Org*. April 12, 2010. http://www.npr.org/templates/story/story.php?storyId=125872042.

Hutton, Mary Ellyn. "Violin Concerto." *American Record Guide* Vol. 72, no. 3 (May 2009): 23-24. Academic Search Complete, EBSCOhost.

"In Memoriam." Santa Fe Opera 2015 Season Program Booklet. Santa Fe Opera: Santa Fe, New Mexico, 2015.

Ingles, Paul. "'Cold Mountain' Takes Civil War Odyssey to the Opera Stage." *National Public Radio*, August 5, 2015. Accessed August 5, 2015. http://www.npr.org/sections/deceptivecadence/2015/08/05/429370329/cold-mountain-takes-civil-war-odyssey-to-the-opera-stage.

Isaacs, Gregory Sullivan. "Miguel Harth-Bedoya Brings Jennifer Higdon's Music to Life in 'Cold Mountain.'" *Star-Telegram* (Fort Worth, TX), August 5, 2015. Accessed November 10, 2016. http://www.star-telegram.com/entertainment/arts-culture/article30037590.html.

Jadrnak, Jackie. "New Mexico History Museum Shows Cased Photographs and Other Civil War Artifacts." *Albuquerque Journal*, April 24, 2015. Accessed November 10, 2016. https://www.abqjournal.com/574272/new-mexico-history-museum-shows-cased-photographs-and-other-civil-war-artifacts.html.

———. "Popular Culture Leaps to High Culture." *Albuquerque Journal*, June 12, 2015. Accessed November 10, 2016. http://www.abqjournal.com/597617/entertainment/popular-culture-leaps-to-high-culture.html.

Jascoll, John. "Orchestra, Chorus Join in a Nautical Extravaganza." *Sunday News* (Lancaster, PA). March 30, 2008. ProQuest Newsstand.

"Jennifer Higdon 'Being Creative in Philadelphia.'" YouTube Video, 3:38. Posted by "Happyidiot90049," June 4, 2008. https://www.youtube.com/watch?v=c25lmEHOzZw.

"Jennifer Higdon, by Hilary Hahn, for 'In 27 Pieces.'" YouTube Video, 16:56. Posted by "Hilaryhahnvideos," January 31, 2012. https://www.youtube.com/watch?v=pu7PewnFGxo.

"Jennifer Higdon—On Composing Music." YouTube video, 3:14. Posted by "UALRTV," March 11, 2013. https://www.youtube.com/watch?v=C5dpEIXpPT4.

"Jennifer Higdon Webinar." YouTube video, 59:03. Posted by "Wheeling Symphony," March 8, 2013. https://www.youtube.com/watch?v=1mYehn1F1EA.

"Jennifer Higdon's Cold Mountain." *WFMT 98.7*, May 9, 2015. Accessed November 10, 2016. http://blogs.wfmt.com/relevanttones/2015/05/09/jennifer-higdons-cold-mountain/.

"Jennifer Higdon's Concerto for Orchestra Highlights Premieres." *Sequenza 21*, June 3–10, 2002. Accessed November 8, 2016. http://www.sequenza21.com/060302.html.

Jones, Nick. Liner Notes to *Jennifer Higdon: City Scape/Concerto for Orchestra*. Robert Spano (cond.), Atlanta Symphony Orchestra. Telarc 80620. CD. 2004.

Kanny, Mark. "Composer's Voice Suits Eclectic Philadelphia String Trio." *Pittsburgh Tribune-Review*. December 4, 2008. ProQuest Newsstand.

———. "Higdon Brings Energetic Works to the City." *Pittsburgh Tribune-Review*. October 30, 2005. LexisNexis Academic.

Kass, Lily. "Musical Analysis: Orion ... Orion." *Cold Mountain—Opera Philadelphia*. Eds. Lily Kass and Michael Bolton. Accessed May 9, 2016. Drexel University, Blackboard Online.

Keller, James M. "Cold Mountain Opera Review: Long-Lost Love Among the Ruins." *Santa Fe New Mexican*, August 2, 2015. Accessed November 10, 2016. http://www.santafenewmexican.com/news/local_news/cold-mountain-opera-review-long-love-among-the-ruins/article_0a701696-2671-5d57-bb71-121d8e05864b.html.

Kemple, Steve. "Modern Composition." *Library Journal*, 139, no. 20 (2014): 1. Academic Search Complete, EBSCO host.

Kennicott, Philip. "CORIGLIANO the Ghosts of Versailles. HIGDON Cold Mountain." *Gramophone*. Accessed May 24, 2016. http://www.gramophone.co.uk/review/corigliano-the-ghosts-of-versailles-higdon-cold-mountain.

———. "Mountain Time." *Opera News* Vol. 79, no. 12, June 2015. Accessed November 10, 2016. http://www.operanews.com/Opera_News_Magazine/2015/6/Features/Mountain_Time.html.

Keyes, Bob. "New Year, New Magic from PSO; the First Tuesday Classical Series of 2005 Features a Guest Baton and an Ethereal Piece by an Acclaimed Female Composer." *Portland Press Herald* (Maine). January 30, 2005. LexisNexis Academic.

Kohlhaase, Bill. "Scaling New Heights: Cold Mountain Composer Jennifer Higdon." *Santa Fe New Mexican*, July 31, 2015. Accessed November 10, 2016. http://www.santafenewmexican.com/pasatiempo/opera/scaling-new-heights-cold-mountain-composer-jennifer-higdon/article_61bd37ae-e184-52bd-afce-977c216bf365.html.

Kozinn, Allan. "Sound That's Lush and Slow, Speedy and Precise." *New York Times*. February 17, 2011. ProQuest Newsstand.

Larsen, Maren. "Accented Arias: Jennifer Higdon on Opera, *Star Wars*, and Adapting *Cold Mountain for the Stage*." *The Smart Set*, March 10, 2016. Accessed April 8, 2016. http://thesmartset.com/accented-arias/.

Lehman, Mark L. "Higdon: Concerto for Orchestra; City Scape (Music)." *American Record Guide* Vol. 67, no. 4 (July 2004): 118. Academic Search Complete, EBSCOhost.

Lewin, Naomi. "Contemporary Opera: Pleasing Both Connoisseurs and the Masses?" *Conducting Business*, August 31, 2015. Accessed November 11, 2016. http://www.wqxr.org/#!/story/contemporary-opera-pleasing-both-connoisseurs-and-masses/.

Lewis, Susan. "Jennifer Higdon's Opera 'Cold Mountain,' and Its East Coast Premiere." *WRTI 90.1*. February 15, 2016. http://wrti.org/post/jennifer-higdons-opera-cold-mountain-and-its-east-coast-premiere.

———. "The Philadelphia Orchestra in Concert on WRTI: Benjamin Beilman, Higdon & Debussy, May 10, 1pm." *WRTI 90.1*. May 8, 2015. http://wrti.org/post/philadelphia-orchestra-concert-wrti-benjamin-beilman-higdon-debussy-may-10-1-pm.

Lindauer, David. "ASO'S 'Ode to Joy'-Musical, Masterful and Majestic." *The Capital* (Annapolis, MD). May 11, 2006. LexisNexis Academic.

Lynn, Jennifer. "One Book, One Philadelphia Kickoff Event Featuring Charles Frazier, Jennifer Higdon, and Performances from Opera Philadelphia and the Curtis Institute of Music." *Free Library Podcast*. Accessed February 10, 2016. http://tunein.com/topic/?topicId=103433870&utm_source=tiEmbed&utm_medium=referral&utm_content=t103433870.

Mason, Doug. "Prelude in Tennessee: Grammy Winning Composer Had Her Musical Beginnings in Blount County." *Knoxville News-Sentinel*. September 18, 2005. ProQuest Newsstand.

McKinney, Donald. "Jennifer Higdon." In *Women of Influence in Contemporary Music: Nine American Composers*, edited by Michael K. Slayton, 155. Lanham, MD: Scarecrow, 2011.

Midgette, Anne. "Baltimore Symphony Orchestra Makes Itself at Home at Carnegie Festival: The Baltimore Symphony Orchestra Performs at Carnegie Hall's Creative Spring for Music Festival." *The Washington Post*. May 9, 2013. ProQuest Newsstand.

———. "Classical Music." *The Washington Post*. Dec. 19, 2010. ProQuest Newsstand.

Miller, Michael Edward. "Celebration of Southern Literature: What Charles Frazier Thinks of 'Cold Mountain' Opera." *WUTC*, April 15, 2015. Accessed November 10, 2016. http://wutc.org/post/celebration-southern-literature-what-charles-frazier-thinks-cold-mountain-opera.

Moss-Coane, Marty. "The 'Cold Mountain' Opera." *WHYY Public Media*. February 2, 2016. Accessed February 3, 2016. http://whyy.org/cms/radiotimes/2016/02/02/34685/.

Murphy, Maria. "Musical Analysis What Do You Hear?" *Cold Mountain—Opera Philadelphia*. Eds. Lily Kass and Michael Bolton. Accessed May 9, 2016. Drexel University, Blackboard Online.

NewMusicBox Staff. "Jennifer Higdon Awarded 2010 Pulitzer Prize in Music." *NewMusicBox*, April 12, 2010. Accessed January 25, 2016. http://www.newmusicbox.org/articles/Jennifer-Higdon-Awarded-2010-Pulitzer-Prize-in-Music/.

Ng, David, and Carolyn Kellogg. "THE PULITZERS; Awards Spur Shock and Aw, Shucks." *Los Angeles Times*. April 13, 2010. ProQuest Newsstand.

Norris, Nicolette. "LSO Sets Sail with a Choral Symphony." *Intelligencer Journal* (Lancaster, PA). March 28, 2008. ProQuest Newsstand.

"Onetime Teacher, Student Find Success as Composer, Violinist." YouTube Video, 6:51. Posted by "PBS Newshour," October 8, 2010. https://www.youtube.com/watch?v=IuZEc9H6lgA.

Page, Janet K., et al. "Oboe." *Grove Music Online*. *Oxford Music Online*. Oxford University Press. http://0 www.oxfordmusiconline.com.wncln.wncln.org/subscriber/article/grove/music/40450.

Pangburn, Adam. "Creative Team and Cast." *Cold Mountain—Opera Philadelphia*. Eds. Lily Kass and Michael Bolton. Accessed May 9, 2016. Drexel University, Blackboard Online.

Phillips, Brenda Rossow. "Jennifer Higdon: A Stylistic Analysis of Selected Flute and Orchestral Works." DMA document, Arizona State University, 2005.

Pittsburgh Symphony Orchestra. "Jennifer Higdon Talks About Her Concerto for Orchestra." Accessed July 7, 2006. http://www.pittsburghsymphony.org/pghsymph.nsf/concert+listings/22DD934D488A89548525703500670D45?opendocument.

Ponick, Terry. "Higdon's 'Cold Mountain' Scores Big Time for Santa Fe Opera." *Communities Digital News*, August 9, 2015. Accessed November 11, 2016. http://www.commdiginews.com/entertainment/higdons-cold-mountain-scores-big-time-for-santa-fe-opera-46415/.

Punt, Rodney. "Jennifer Higdon's Cold Mountain Has World Premiere at Santa Fe Opera." *San Francisco Classical Voice*, August 4, 2015. Accessed November 10, 2016. https://www.sfcv.org/reviews/quot-None-quot-/Jennifer-Higdon-s-Cold-Mountain-Has-World-Premiere-at-Santa-Fe-Opera.

Quint, Andrew. "Speaking with Composer Jennifer Higdon." *Fanfare* Vol. 27, no. 5 (May/June 2005): 42–46. Arts Premium Collection.

Raines, Robert. *Composition in the Digital World: Conversations with 21st Century American Composers*. New York: Oxford University Press, 2015. Accessed November 9, 2016. http://books.google.com/books?id=wp_4BQAAQBAJ&dq=Cold+Mountain+Jennifer+Higdon&source=gbs_navlinks_s.

Reel, James. "Every Composer's Dream." *Strings* Vol. 23, no.10 (May 2009): 34–37. ProQuest Central.

———. "STRINGS ATTACHED." *Strings* Vol. 23, no. 6 (Jan. 2009): 49–53. ProQuest Central.

Reid, T.R. "Santa Fe Opera Breathes New Life into Epic Civil War Tale 'Cold Mountain.'" *The Washington Post*, August 16, 2015. Accessed November 10, 2016. https://www.washingtonpost.com/entertainment/music/santa-fe-opera-breathes-new-life-into-epic-civil-war-tale-cold-mountain/

2015/08/16/c21ce65e-444c-11e5-8ab4-c73967a143d3_story.html.

Rhein, John von. "Higdon's Premiere a Blowout at Ravinia." *Chicago Tribune*. July 27, 2009. ProQuest Newsstand.

———. "Jennifer Higdon; Concerto for Orchestra, City Scape: Atlanta Symphony Orchestra, Robert Spano, Conductor (Telarc): [Chicago Final Edition]." *Chicago Tribune*. July 25, 2004. ProQuest Newsstand.

Richards, Jonathan. "Mountain Do: Stage Director Leonard Foglia." *Santa Fe New Mexican*, July 31, 2015. Accessed November 10, 2016. http://www.santafenewmexican.com/pasatiempo/opera/mountain-do-stage-director-leonard-foglia/article_be8cc5ea-c586-515e-9860-16097fb28ada.html.

Rile, Karen. "The Accidental Genius." *The Pennsylvania Gazette*. July/August 2005, http://www.upenn.edu/gazette/0705/feature01sidebar.html.

Rinaldi, Ray Mark. "Santa Fe Opera Ascends with Jennifer Higdon's 'Cold Mountain.'" *Denver Post*, August 4, 2015. Accessed November 10, 2016. http://www.denverpost.com/entertainment/ci_28582823/santa-fe-opera-ascends-jennifer-higdons-cold-mountain/.

Rossman, Jeffrey. "An Evening of Baby-Boomer Composers." *Classical Voice of North Carolina*. Accessed January 12, 2016. http://www.cvnc.org/reviews/2006/012006/NCScrossing1.html.

Ruhe, Pierre. "Spano Tailors Brahms Requiem." *The Atlanta Journal-Constitution*. November 3, 2007. ProQuest Newsstand.

———. "Symphony Illuminates Soul of City." *Atlanta Journal-Constitution*. November 10, 2002. ProQuest Newsstand.

"Santa Fe Opera 2014 Press Conference." YouTube video, 47:11. Posted by "The Santa Fe Opera," May 14, 2014. https://www.youtube.com/watch?v=gstRqu_I_qQ.

Scheer, Gene. "Ascending Cold Mountain." Santa Fe Opera 2015 Season Program Booklet. Santa Fe Opera: Santa Fe, New Mexico, 2015.

Scorca, Marc A. "Jennifer Higdon on Creating Cold Mountain." *OPERA America*, Sept. 29, 2015. Accessed November 10, 2016. https://medium.com/@OPERAAmerica/jennifer-higdon-on-creating-cold-mountain-ae1054a6623d.

Serinus, Jason Victor. "Interview: The Award-Winning Jennifer Higdon." *Secrets of Home Theater and High Fidelity*. June 2005. http://www.hometheaterhifi.com/volume_12_2/feature-interview-jennifer-higdon-6-2005.html.

Shengold, David. "Cold Mountain." *Opera News* Vol. 80, no. 8. February 7, 2016. Accessed November 11, 2016. http://www.operanews.com/Opera_News_Magazine/2016/2/Reviews/PHILADELPHIA_Cold_Mountain.html.

Silbiger, Alexander. "Chaconne." *Grove Music Online*. Oxford Music Online. Oxford University Press. http://www.oxfordmusiconline.com.proxy195.nclive.org/subscriber/article/grove/music/05354.

Smith, Kile. "Composer Jennifer Higdon Tells Her Story: Part 2." *WRTI 90.1*. March 24, 2015. http://wrti.org/post/composer-jennifer-higdon-tells-her-story-part-2.

Smith, Tim. "Alsop, BSO Deliver Diverse, Propulsive Program: Concert Review." *The Baltimore Sun*. May 4, 2013. ProQuest Newsstand.

———. "Alsop Rock-Solid, Hahn Shows Bravura in Violin Concerto." *The Baltimore Sun*. June 6, 2009. ProQuest Newsstand.

Stearns, David Patrick. "Civil War Epic Deserves the Love: Opera Has Its Mainstream Hit—'Cold Mountain' Delivers on Nearly Every Level." *Philadelphia Inquirer*. August 9, 2015. ProQuest Newsstand.

———. "Curtis Orchestra Set for Prime Time." *Philadelphia Inquirer*. May 3, 2000. Lexis-Nexis Academic.

———. "For OCP, a Brisk Pace and a Bold Repertoire." *Philadelphia Inquirer*. August 14, 2011. ProQuest Newsstand.

———. "Gunn Recital Bodes Well for Higdon Opera." *Philadelphia Inquirer*. April 24, 2013. ProQuest Newsstand.

———. "Higdon's New Concerto a Triumph, Times 6." *Philadelphia Inquirer*. June 8, 2010. ProQuest Newsstand.

———. "Jennifer Higdon Premieres Concerto 'On a Wire.'" *Philadelphia Inquirer*. June 8, 2010. ProQuest Newsstand.

———. "Jennifer Higdon's 'Cold Mountain [Sic] Turns the Epic Novel into Opera." *TCA Regional News*. April 5, 2015. ProQuest Newsstand.

———. "Jennifer Higdon's Exterior/Interior City Scape." November 2002. Andante Corporation.

———. "New Operas Highlight a Longstanding Divide." *Philadelphia Inquirer.* August 23, 2015. Accessed November 10, 2016. http://www.philly.com/philly/columnists/david_patrick_stearns/20150823_New_operas_highlight_a_longstanding_divide.html.

———. "Opera's Gunn to Promote American Works in Philadelphia." *McClatchy-Tribune Business News.* Sept. 12, 2012. ProQuest Newsstand.

———. "The Pulitzers: Top Honors for Daily News, Phila. Composer Curtis' Jennifer Higdon Took the Prize for 'Violin Concerto.'" *Philadelphia Inquirer.* April 13, 2010. ProQuest Newsstand.

———. "Review: Higdon's New Opera, Cold Mountain, at Santa Fe." *philly.com*, August 3, 2015. Accessed November 10, 2016. http://www.philly.com/philly/entertainment/20150803_Review__Higdon_s_new_opera_Cold_Mountain__at_Santa_Fe.html.

———. "The Rock That Anchors a Classical Composer; the Beatles' 'Sgt. Pepper' Has Exerted a Major Influence on the Work of Jennifer Higdon." *Philadelphia Inquirer.* September 20, 2009. ProQuest Newsstand.

———. "What 'Cold Mountain' Gets Right." *TCA Regional News.* August 9, 2015. ProQuest Newsstand.

———. "A 'What's This' Kind of Concert: Higdons [Sic] New Genre-Bender Is Not for Listening Comfort." *Philadelphia Inquirer.* January 6, 2008. ProQuest Newsstand.

———. "Whistling a Grammy Tune; with a Week Till the Awards, Heres [Sic] a Sampling of Nominees Who Have Already Captured the Sounds of Success. To Philadelphia Classical Composer Jennifer Higdon, It's an Honor—and a Career Boost—Just to Be Nominated." *Philadelphia Inquirer.* February 6, 2005. LexisNexis Academic.

Take 6. Miguel Harth-Bedoya (cond.), Fort Worth Symphony Orchestra. CD. 2012.

Tannenbaum, Perry. "North Carolina Symphony: In Search of New Classics." *American Record Guide* Vol. 69, no. 3 (May 2006): 17–18. Academic Search Complete, EBSCOhost.

"Time for Three-BSO Webumentary Series." YouTube Video, 3:03. Posted by "Baltimore symphonyorchestra," January 16, 2013. https://www.youtube.com/watch?v=W0Jp_V0sw5k.

Waleson, Heidi. "Creating Cold Mountain: Student Singers Help to Shape a Major Modern Opera." *Overtones*, Spring 2014. Accessed February 19, 2015. http://www.curtis.edu/about-curtis/press-media-room/overtones-1/past-issues/.

Whittington, Lewis. "Higdon: *Cold Mountain* Opera Philadelphia." *American Record Guide* Vol. 79, no. 3 (May/June 2016): 39–40. Academic Search Complete, EBSCOhost.

———. "Orchestra Plays Higdon 'Concerto 4–3.'" *Broad Street Review,* January 13, 2008. Accessed September 13, 2016. http://www.broadstreetreview.com/music/Orchestra_plays_Higdon_Concerto_43.

Williams, Max Brenton Harkey. "Jennifer Higdon's *Violin Concerto*: The Genesis of a Twenty First Century Work." DM dissertation, Florida State University, 2010.

"World-Renowned Composer Higdon Visits Boston Crusaders' Rehearsal." *Drum Corps International,* August 17, 2006. Accessed November 8, 2016. http://dci271.dci.org/news/view.cfm?news_id=dafbea7b-e3f4-415a-9bb4-e232be3305dc.

"Works & Process at the Guggenheim: Santa Fe Opera: Cold Mountain with Jennifer Higdon." YouTube video, 1:09:23. Posted by "Works & Process at the Guggenheim," April 7, 2015. https://www.youtube.com/watch?v=6ObRKcZhuSs.

Index

Academy of Music 182, 184
Adamo, Mark 13
Adams, John 174
Adès, Thomas 169
All Things Majestic 226
Alsop, Marin 12–13, 131–132, 163
American Anthem 168
American Symphony Orchestra League 43, 78
An American Tragedy 168
Andante Cantabile 12
Annapolis Symphony Orchestra 37
Atlanta School of Composers 13, 226
Atlanta Symphony Orchestra 13, 22, 26, 37, 43, 78, 80–81, 98, 105–106, 168

Bach, Johann Sebastian 107
The Baltimore Symphony Orchestra 13, 105, 132, 135, 163, 226
Barber, Samuel 37
Bartók, Béla 40, 46, 78–79
BBC Scottish Symphony Orchestra 105
BBC Symphony Orchestra 43, 78
The Beatles 8, 14, 107
Beilman, Benjamin 135, 145, 166
Bentley, Judith 9
Bernstein, Leonard 78
blue cathedral 13, 15, 17, 20–22, 24–39, 41, 43, 64, 77, 79–81
bluegrass 8, 107–109, 111–112, 115, 131–132, 185–186, 211–212
The Bonesetter's Daughter 174
Boston Crusaders 79
Bowling Green Philharmonia 167
Bowling Green State University 9–10, 12–13, 107, 167
Brahms, Johannes 77
Bravo! Vail Valley Music Festival 166
Brill, Robert 170, 180, 183
Britten, Benjamin 134, 174
Brown, Emily Freeman 167
Burdette, Kevin 169, 172
Burns, Ken 168

Cabrillo Festival of Contemporary Music 13, 131

Cage, John 8, 90
California Chamber Orchestra 79
Capitol Theatre (Wheeling, WV) 130
Carnegie Hall 132
Chattanooga Symphony 166
Chicago Symphony 132, 226
Chin, Caroline 167
City Scape 16–17, 22, 43, 78, 80–106, 131
Civil Words 225
Cleveland Institute of Music 43
Cold Mountain (novel) 170–173, 179, 185–186, 210
Cold Mountain (opera) 8, 11, 16, 114, 128, 168–226
Concerto for Orchestra 11, 16–17, 21–22, 38–81, 94
Concerto 4–3 8, 17, 22, 107–132, 134–135, 140, 147, 171, 185
Copland, Aaron 9, 37
Corigliano, John 13, 43
counterpoint of textures 20, 33–34, 142, 152, 191–192
country 8, 14
The Curtis Chamber Orchestra 135, 226
The Curtis Institute of Music 10, 12–13, 20, 24–25, 30, 41, 49, 53, 107–109, 133–136, 164–166, 170, 176–177, 226
Curtis Opera Theatre 176
The Curtis Symphony Orchestra 24, 28, 49, 135–136, 163
Crumb, George 8, 11, 16, 64, 90

Dallas Opera 170
Dallas Symphony Orchestra 43
Dan, Kayoko 166
DePreist, James 11, 165
DePue, Wallace 9, 107
DePue, Zachary 107–108, 120, 131–132, 135
De Ratmiroff, Marina 225
Devan, David 176
Diaz, Roberto 135, 226
Dooryard Bloom 169
Dye, Jerre 225

251

Index

Echo Dash 166
Eliasen, Mikael 176–178
Eminem 14
Eschenbach, Christoph 107, 130

Fauré, Gabriel 106
Fisher, Kimberly 49
A Flowering Tree 174
Foglia, Leonard 170, 175–177, 180, 206
Fons, Emily 169, 181–182
Fort Worth Symphony Orchestra 132, 170
Frazier, Charles 170–173, 176–79, 185–186, 194, 210
Frazier, Katherine 176–177
Friedman, Jay 226

Gandolfi, Michael 13
Gier, Delta David 165
Gilmore Variation 12
Glass, Philip 10
Golijov, Osvaldo 13
Gould, Morton 165
Grammys 14, 78, 165–166, 183, 226
Greenholtz, Naha 166
Guerrero, Giancarlo 226
Gulf Coast Symphony 79
Gunn, Nathan 168–169, 176–177, 181–182, 186

Hahn, Hilary 14, 133–138, 145, 147, 150, 155–156, 163–164, 166
Hampson, Thomas 225
Harp Concerto 226
Harrison, Lou 90
Harth-Bedoya, Miguel 132, 170, 179, 181
Hear My Voice 12
Heggie, Jake 168, 170, 174
Heinz Hall (Pittsburgh, PA) 130
Ein Heldenleben 43
Higdon, Andrew Blue 7–8, 24–28, 30, 35–37, 172
Higdon, Jennifer: *All Things Majestic* 226; *Andante Cantabile* 12; *blue cathedral* 13, 15, 17, 20–22, 24–28, 41, 43, 64, 77, 79–81; *City Scape* 16–17, 22, 43, 78, 80–106, 131; *Civil Words* 225; *Cold Mountain* (opera) 8, 11, 16, 114, 128, 168–226; *Concerto for Orchestra* 11, 16–17, 21, 22, 38–81, 94; *Concerto 4-3* 8, 17, 22, 107–132, 134–135, 140, 147, 171, 185; *Dooryard Bloom* 169; *Echo Dash* 166; *Gilmore Variation* 12; *Harp Concerto* 226; *Hear My Voice* 12; *Low Brass Concerto* 226; *Night Creatures* 9; *Oboe Concerto* 109, 135, 226; *On a Wire* 135; *Percussion Concerto* 14, 135, 165; *Piano Concerto* 15, 109, 135; *rapid.fire* 11; *Rhythm Stand* 12; *Shine* 11, 39; *The Singing Rooms* 135; *Soprano Saxophone Concerto* 135; *Tuba Concerto* 226; *Viola Concerto* 135, 226; *Violin Concerto* 14–15, 17, 22, 120, 133–167; *Voices* 10
Higdon, Key 13
Higgins, Richard G. 169–170

Hindemith, Paul 226
Houston Symphony Orchestra 43, 105

In 27 Pieces: The Hilary Hahn Encores 166
Indianapolis Symphony Orchestra 132, 135, 163

jazz 131
The Juilliard School 10

Keller, Lisa 176–178
Kendall, Nicolas 107, 110, 131
Khaner, Jeffrey 39
Kimmel Center 42–43, 130
Knox, Craig 226
Kodály, Zoltán 40
Kondonassis, Yolanda 226

Laufer, Milton 225
Lawdon Press 12, 26, 108, 135, 179
Lawson, Cheryl 9, 12–13, 26, 39, 41, 169–170, 174, 176–177
League of American Orchestras 168
Leonard, Isabel 169, 171, 176, 181, 186
Lerdahl, Fred 165
Liebermann, Lowell 106
Liuzzi, Don 42, 64
Loeb, David 10
Low Brass Concerto 226
Lutosławski, Witold 40

Macelaru, Christian 226
MacKay, Charles 168–169, 176–177
McCarthy, Elaine J. 170, 180
Meckavich, Joseph 177
Melbourne Symphony Orchestra 105
Mena, Juanjo 163
Metropolitan Opera 178
Meyer, Edgar 134
Meyer, Ranaan 107, 120, 131
Mills, Erie 178
Minghella, Anthony 172
Minnesota Opera 169, 225
Miramax 172
Moby Dick 168, 170, 174
Morris, Jay Hunter 169, 176–177, 181, 187
Mozart, Wolfgang Amadeus 41, 174–175
Mulcahy, Holly 166
Mulcahy, Michael 226
Muti, Riccardo 226

Nashville Symphony 79, 226
Nason, Brian 182–183
National Symphony Orchestra 43, 105–106
Naxos 226
Neale, Alasdair 167
Night Creatures 9
North Carolina Opera 169, 225

Oberlin Conservatory of Music 43
Oboe Concerto 109, 135, 226

On a Wire 135
Opera Philadelphia 169, 176, 180, 182–183, 225
Opera Theatre of St. Louis 178
Oregon Symphony 11
Ott, Jarred 177–178, 182–183
Oundjian, Peter 163
Owen, Chuck 165

Pajaro-van de Stadt, Milena 135
Parameswaran, Vinay 176
Pentatone 183
Percussion Concerto 14, 135, 165
Petrenko, Vasily 163–164
Philadelphia Chamber Music Society 10
Philadelphia Orchestra 11, 23, 30, 39–43, 49, 51, 56, 107, 110, 130–131, 166, 226
Phillips, Brenda Rossow 30, 34–36
Phoenix Symphony 132
Piano Concerto 15, 109, 135
Picker, Tobias 168
Pittsburgh Symphony Orchestra 43, 63, 110, 130, 226
Pokorny, Gene 226
Portland Symphony Orchestra 165
Prokofiev, Sergei 164
Puccini, Giacomo 174
Pulitzer Prize 14, 120, 133, 164–167

Quad City Symphony Orchestra (Davenport, IA) 166

Rainbow Body 26–27, 37
rap 14
rapid.fire 11
Ravinia Festival 131
Reise, Jay 10
Rhythm Stand 12
Richard, Fran 165
Rochester Philharmonic Orchestra 226
rock 10, 14, 107, 131
Rockwell, John 165
Rorem, Ned 10
Rosen, Jesse 168
Royal Liverpool Philharmonic Orchestra 163–164
Runnicles, Donald 168

St. Augustine 199
Santa Fe Opera Company (SFO) 168–170, 175–179, 182–183, 225
Saratoga Performing Arts Center 131
Sawallisch, Wolfgang 43, 64–65
Scheer, Gene 168, 170–177, 180, 189, 194, 205–206, 210

Schneider, Maria 165
Schoenberg, Adam 13, 226
Schoenberg, Arnold 41, 134, 137, 143
Schwantner, Joseph 165
Sessions, Roger 40
Sewell, Andrew 131
Shine 11, 39
Shleswig-Holstein Festival 132
Shrude, Marilyn 9
The Singing Rooms 135
Slatkin, Leonard 130–131
Smith, André Raphel 130
Sollberger, Harvey 9
Soprano Saxophone Concerto 135
Spano, Robert 9–10, 13, 24, 27, 37, 43, 78, 80, 166, 168, 226
Stare, Ward 226
Sterrenberg, Rachel 177
Strauss, Richard 43
Stravinksy, Igor 41, 46, 174
Sydney Symphony 132

Take 6 132
Tchaikovsky, Pyotr 164
Telarc 37, 43, 78
The Tempest 169
Theofanidis, Christopher 13, 37
Tian, Zhou 226
Time for Three 107, 109, 131–132, 135
Toronto Symphony Orchestra 135, 163
Toscanini, Cia 165
Tower, Joan 40
Tuba Concerto 226

University of Michigan 10
University of Pennsylvania 10–11, 64

Venzago, Mario 163
Verizon Hall 130
Vernon, Charlie 226
Vinci, Jan 9
Viola Concerto 135, 226
Violin Concerto 14–15, 17, 22, 120, 133–167
Voices 10

Wallace, Stewart 174
Western Carolina University 225
Wheeling Symphony Orchestra 110, 130
Wichita Symphony 132
Wisconsin Chamber Orchestra 131
Wolfe, Julia 165
Woodhams, Richard 30
Woods, Simon 39
Woolbright, Brad 176

www.ingramcontent.com/pod-product-compliance
Lightning Source LLC
Chambersburg PA
CBHW061346300426
44116CB00011B/2007